The Sociopragmatics of Attitude Datives in Levantine Arabic

*For every refugee and every child in a war zone,
May you find a home!*

THE SOCIOPRAGMATICS OF ATTITUDE DATIVES IN LEVANTINE ARABIC

Youssef A. Haddad

EDINBURGH
University Press

Edinburgh University Press is one of the leading university presses in the UK. We publish academic books and journals in our selected subject areas across the humanities and social sciences, combining cutting-edge scholarship with high editorial and production values to produce academic works of lasting importance. For more information visit our website: edinburghuniversitypress.com

© Youssef Haddad, 2018
Edinburgh University Press Ltd
The Tun – Holyrood Road, 12(2f) Jackson's Entry, Edinburgh EH8 8PJ

Typeset in Ehrhardt MT by
Servis Filmsetting Ltd, Stockport, Cheshire

A CIP record for this book is available from the British Library

ISBN 978 1 4744 3407 2 (hardback)
ISBN 978 1 4744 3408 9 (webready PDF)
ISBN 978 1 4744 3409 6 (epub)
ISBN 978 1 4744 5228 1 (paperback)

The right of Youssef Haddad to be identified as the author of this work has been asserted in accordance with the Copyright, Designs and Patents Act 1988, and the Copyright and Related Rights Regulations 2003 (SI No. 2498).

Contents

Preface vii
Abbreviations and Other Notes ix

1 Introduction 1
  1 Putting things in perspective 1
  2 Attitude dative constructions: an overview 3
    2.1 Topic/affectee-oriented ADs 4
    2.2 Speaker-oriented ADs 8
    2.3 Hearer-oriented ADs 10
    2.4 Subject-oriented ADs 12
  3 Purpose and significance 14
  4 Data sources 16
  5 A roadmap 21

2 Attitude Datives in Social Context – The Analytic Tools 23
  1 Introduction 23
  2 ADCs and context 28
    2.1 The sociocultural context 29
    2.2 The situational context 29
    2.3 The co-textual context 31
    2.4 ADs in context 32
  3 ADs and evaluation 33
  4 ADCs and the stancetaking stage model 37
    4.1 Theory of stance 37
    4.2 The stage model 39
    4.3 ADCs in the stancetaking stage model 44
  5 Putting it all together 46
  6 Conclusion 51

3 Speaker-Oriented Attitude Datives in Social Context   53
   1   Introduction   53
   2   SP-ADCs as directives   57
        2.1   SP-AD directives and hierarchical authority   58
        2.2   SP-AD directives and reciprocal authority   78
        2.3   SP-AD directives and knowledge authority   83
   3   SP-ADCs as representatives   85
       3.1 SP-AD representatives as second-person complaints   87
       3.2 SP-AD representatives as third-person complaints   91
   4   Conclusion   96

4 Hearer-Oriented Attitude Datives in Social Context   98
   1   Introduction   98
   2   HR-ADs, attention grabbing, and hearer engagement   100
   3   HR-ADCs as commissives: recognizing the hearer as an authority   102
   4   HR-ADCs as representatives   109
        4.1   HR-AD representatives as first-person bragging   109
        4.2   HR-AD representatives as third-person praise and criticism   113
   5   Conclusion   129

5 Subject-Oriented Attitude Datives in Social Context   131
   1   Introduction   131
   2   SUBJ-ADCs as representatives   133
        2.1   SUBJ-AD representatives about insignificant events   133
        2.2   SUBJ-ADCs about surprising events   140
   3   SUBJ-ADCs as directives   144
        3.1   SUBJ-AD directives as requests   144
        3.2   SUBJ-ADCs as suggestions   148
        3.3   SUBJ-ADCs as challenges   153
   4   Conclusion   155

6 Final Remarks   156

Bibliography   158
Index   167

Preface

I first came across the topic of non-core arguments in 2010 when I attended a talk on personal datives in Southern American English at the Arizona Linguistics Circle 4 in Tucson. A personal dative is an optional pronoun that is coreferential with the subject in a sentence: for example, *me* in *I wanna hear me a sad song* (from Toby Keith's country song 'Get My Drink On'). I realized then, somewhat to my own surprise, that personal datives also exist in my native variety of Lebanese Arabic. Given my background in syntax, I immediately began to wonder: how are personal datives licensed in a position where reflexive pronouns are expected? I went on to analyze the syntax of personal datives, as well as other types of non-core arguments that are licensed in Lebanese Arabic, and before long I found myself delving into the pragmatic functions of these datives and the attitudinal contributions they make to utterances. That was when I started to refer to them as 'attitude datives'.

For my syntactic and pragmatic analyses, I initially relied on constructed examples, elicited examples, and attested data that I collected during fieldwork. Four points became clear in the process. First, attitude datives are not unique to Lebanese Arabic, and are in fact a regional feature of Levantine Arabic (that is, Jordanian, Lebanese, Palestinian, and Syrian Arabic) in general. They are also licensed in most, if not all, other Arabic dialects; however, cross-dialectal variations become more apparent once one moves outside the Levant.

Second, the pragmatic contributions of attitude datives depend crucially on who is saying what to whom, where, when, and to what end. This means that syntactic and semantic accounts of these datives may successfully answer questions about their distribution and overarching meanings, but may not capture the wide range of meanings and functions that they can bring to an interaction. Instead, we need an analysis that goes beyond the sentence level, examining the social functions of a sizeable corpus of attitude datives as they are employed in situated utterances. I quickly realized that elicited examples and a small number of attested data in limited settings just would not do the trick.

Third, at least in Levantine Arabic, these datives are notoriously inconspicuous. In fact, I had hardly noticed their existence prior to the talk in Arizona. Language users are very sensitive to their effect, and yet they are hardly aware that they are a feature of their own speech. When I point out to native speakers that they have just used one of these optional datives, they are often surprised and entertained. Importantly, when I continue to ask about the intended meaning of the dative, or why the speaker had used it, she or he is usually unable to provide a clear answer. In this respect, these datives stand in stark contrast with other pragmatic phenomena that speakers are able to explain metapragmatically. For example, native speakers of Lebanese Arabic are often able to explain quite adequately why they add a curse word to an utterance, or why they occasionally swear in English or French instead of in Arabic. Attitude datives prove to be more difficult to tap into metapragmatically.

Fourth, these datives are not easy to translate into other languages. For example, they are often ignored in movie subtitles and in translations of literary works that use colloquial Arabic. This may be the case either because they pass unnoticed, or because the translator is not able to find an equivalent in the target language.

These four points led me to conduct a study on attitude datives in their social contexts, focusing primarily on Levantine Arabic. The last two points are especially relevant to the topic of teaching an Arabic dialect as a foreign language. Native instructors of a Levantine variety of Arabic intuitively know how, where, when, and with whom to use attitude datives, but they may struggle to teach them, or about them, effectively. A systematic analysis of the social functions of these datives may make this task easier.

This work would not have been possible without the support of my institution, the University of Florida. I am especially thankful for the two Humanities Scholarship Enhancement Fund awards I received in the summers of 2012 and 2014, and for a sabbatical leave in 2016–17. I am also grateful to Sara Court, Hamed Al-Jaraadaat, Virginia LoCastro, and Iman Al-Ramadan for reading earlier versions of this book and for all their input. I thank Aida Bamia, two anonymous reviewers, and the audience at the 31st Annual Symposium on Arabic Linguistics in Oklahoma for valuable feedback. I am grateful to Wendy Lee for copy-editing the book. Laura Williamson, Richard Strachan, Joannah Duncan, Rebecca Mackenzie and the rest of the Edinburgh University Press team were also wonderful; I thank them for their promptness and professionalism.

Finally, I owe a lot to my family and friends for being so loving and supportive throughout the whole process. I thank God for seeing me through it all. 'Thy rod and thy staff, they comfort me' – they always have.

Abbreviations and Other Notes

Abbreviations of Arabic varieties

JOR	Jordanian Arabic
LEB	Lebanese Arabic
PAL	Palestinian Arabic
SYR	Syrian Arabic

Other abbreviations and symbols

1SG	first person singular
ACC	accusative
D	dative
INTER	interjection
NEG	negation
POSS	possessive marker
PROG	progressive
Q	question
VOC	vocative
.	final intonation
,	continuing intonation
?	rising/question intonation
!	exclamatory intonation
(.)	short pause
...	ellipsis
((laugh))	researcher comments
\<stretch of talk\>	words or phrases that may not be properly identified

Some remarks about the gloss and translation as used in this book

- All linguistic data are presented in International Phonetic Alphabet (IPA) characters. Data from Facebook are additionally included as snapshots of the original posts, all of which were available for public viewing at the time of research. Most data from TV shows, movies, and plays are also available as audiovisual files on a companion website https://edinburghuniversitypress.com/haddad.
- Pronouns: Levantine Arabic – and Arabic in general – does not have neutral versus feminine/masculine pronouns or agreement. For the sake of clarity, however, when a pronoun or agreement morphology is linked to a neutral entity, I gloss it as 'it.'
- Prepositions: The same Levantine Arabic preposition may have different English meanings in different contexts, and vice versa (different Levantine Arabic prepositions in different contexts may translate into the same English preposition). The gloss tries to capture the English meaning. For example, the Lebanese Arabic preposition ʕa- in ʕa-l-tʕa:wle 'on-the-table' is glossed as 'on,' while ʕa in ʕa-l-madrase 'on-the-school' is glossed as 'to.'
- Verb agreement: Arabic, including Levantine Arabic, is a subject pro-drop language with rich verbal agreement. In the examples, if the subject is present, verbs are glossed only as verbs: for example, *na:dya ʔakalit* 'Nadia ate.' If the subject is dropped and context is not enough to determine who the subject is, the gloss includes agreement in the form of subject/nominative pronouns: for example, *ʔakalit* 'she.ate.'
- The English translation of the Levantine Arabic examples tries to provide a general sense of their truth conditions without trying to capture their pragmatic nuances. Discussion of relevant pragmatic contribution is provided in the text.

Remark on feature films, plays, series, and talk shows

All of the audiovisual materials from films, plays, and so on that I use for this study, including materials obtained from my personal collection, were accessible on Youtube at the time of research. Most materials were made publicly available on Youtube by the production companies or TV stations that originally produced them. In order to facilitate access to the data and provide the reader with a feel as to how the attitude dative constructions I examine sound in context, I have prepared trimmed 5- to 50-second videos of most examples. These are available on a companion website https://edinburghuniversitypress.com/haddad.

A video may start 1 or more seconds before the actual example and may continue 1 or more seconds beyond it.

1

Introduction

1 Putting things in perspective

One of the most powerful scenes that I have ever experienced in an American movie is from the 1996 adaptation of John Grisham's 1989 novel, *A Time to Kill*. Jake Brigance, a white lawyer played by Matthew McConaughey, is giving his closing argument during the trial of Carl Lee Hailey (Samuel Jackson), an African American man whose ten-year-old daughter had been raped by two white supremacists in 1980s Canton, Mississippi. Hailey, driven by the thought that the rapists may not be convicted, had shot the two men dead and was now on trial for their murder, with Brigance as his lawyer.

In his closing argument, Brigance starts addressing the all-white jury by saying, 'Now I wanna tell you a story. I'm gonna ask y'all to close your eyes while I tell you this story. I want you to listen to me. I want you to listen to yourselves.' He goes on to describe the rape of a ten-year-old girl, in reference to what happened to Hailey's daughter: 'This is a story about a little girl walking home from the grocery store one sunny afternoon,' he says. 'I want you to picture this little girl. Suddenly a truck races up. Two men jump out and grab her.' He goes on to describe in ruthless detail what happened to the little girl. Choked up, he wraps up with: 'Now imagine she's white.' He wins the case, and Carl Lee Hailey is found not guilty.

This last directive, *Now imagine she's white*, instructs the jury to look at the tragic incident from a different perspective. It instructs the jury, the rest of the people in the courthouse, and even the viewers of the movie to attend to the tragic story in a special way, through a specific filter. In Verhagen's (2005; 2010: 9–10) terms, the directive functions as a perspectivizer via which the lawyer and the jurors engage in cognitive coordination in an attempt by the former to influence the latter's 'thoughts, attitudes, or even immediate behavior.' The perspectivizer renders the rape story a perspectivized thought. A perspectivized thought is not only informative but also argumentative (see Verhagen 2010).

A perspectivizer like the one just described does not occur in a vacuum. To be effective in its intended function – namely, influencing the hearer's thoughts and actions – it needs to be informed by elements of the context. These include the type of activity the speaker and hearers are involved in, the identities of the speaker and hearers, and the sociocultural background, including underlying values, beliefs, and norms. This is so even if the expression means to challenge some or all of these elements. Brigance and the jurors in the above scene are involved in the closing argument of a trial for murder. Brigance is a white man addressing a group of white people, and as such he invokes a shared in-group membership. The expression may have been perceived differently and served a different function if the lawyer were an African American man addressing a white jury. In addition, this perspectivizer makes sense only in the sociocultural context that is invoked in the movie, where an African American person may not receive a fair trial in the southern United States, a sentiment expressed by Brigance himself.

Fortunately, most of our daily interactions do not address issues that are nearly as intense or as tragic as the one just described. Still, no matter how trivial the topic of interaction may be, social actors often employ perspectivizers in order to influence other social actors' thoughts and actions. And while the perspectivizer in the above movie scene is rather explicit and presents an alternate reality, not all perspectivizers need to be characterized in the same way. In fact, they are often quite subtle, taking the form of pragmatic markers (for example, *well* and *you know* in English) that do not contribute to or alter the reality of the at-issue content of utterances. These markers do, however, make a pragmatic contribution that may be textual (organizational) or interpersonal (relational, attitudinal) (Halliday 1970; Brinton 1996; Culpeper and Haugh 2014).

This study is concerned with optional pronouns that serve as interpersonal pragmatic markers in four Levantine Arabic dialects: Syrian, Lebanese, Jordanian, and Palestinian (listed in order of emphasis). These pronouns take the form of dative clitics. I refer to them as attitude datives (ADs), and to the utterances that they are embedded in as attitude dative constructions (ADCs). Like other interpersonal pragmatic markers, ADs serve two broad functions: first, an attitudinal function whereby a speaker uses an AD to express a stance toward the at-issue content or the main message of her[1] utterance and toward any underlying values and beliefs, and/or, second, a relational function, in which case an AD is used to manage (affirm, maintain, challenge, and so on) relationships between the interlocutors (see Brinton 1996: Chapter 2 and Beeching 2016: Chapter 1, as well as work cited there). This study will focus on the sociopragmatics of ADs, or their use 'in human communication as determined by the conditions of society' (Mey 2001: 6). Four types of AD are licensed in Levantine Arabic; Section 2 of this chapter provides an overview of these datives. Section 3 highlights the purpose and significance of the study. Section 4 lists the data sources, states some of their characteristics, and discusses the motivations behind the choices. Section 5 provides a brief roadmap of the rest of the study.

2 Attitude dative constructions: an overview

When speakers express a thought via a simple sentence, their utterance typically consists of a predicate and its participants. For example, the English sentence *Michelle built a treehouse for her sons* describes a building event and relates it to three participants, also known as arguments. These are Michelle, the treehouse she built, and her sons. These participants are core arguments in the sense that they contribute to the truth conditions of the utterance; as such, they are important components of its meaning. The utterance is considered true if there is a building event, Michelle is its agent, a treehouse is its theme (that is, the participant that underwent a change of state), and the sons are the beneficiaries and recipients. Any change to these arguments alters the truth conditions of the utterance. For example, if the agent is Fiona instead of Michelle, the result is a different utterance with different truth conditions.

In addition to core arguments, languages may license non-core arguments. These are optional pronominal elements that may be added to utterances without altering their main content. English, French, Hebrew, and Hungarian are only a few examples of such languages, as (1) through (4) illustrate. The boldface pronouns in these examples are non-core arguments. A speaker may use these pronominal elements in order to express an attitude toward the at-issue content of her utterance by presenting it from a specific perspective. For example, by using the non-core argument *him*, the speaker in (1) assumes that 'the action expressed has or would have a positive effect on the subject' (Horn 2008:181) and she invites the hearer to view it from the same perspective. Structurally, non-core arguments are usually dative clitics or weak pronouns. In terms of register, they normally occur in informal interaction.

1. English
   He's gonna buy **him** a pick-up for his son.
   Adapted from Horn (2013: 164 (23a))

2. French
   Je **te**   **me**   vais **te**   **me**   vous   lui
   I **you.D** **me.D** go   **you.D** **me.D** you.all.D him.D
   faire passer un   sale   quart d'heure ...
   make pass   a   dirty quarter-hour ...
   'I'm gonna make him spend a lousy quarter-hour ...'
   Adapted from Jouitteau and Rezac (2007: 98; (9))

3. Hebrew
   hem   kol ha-zman   mitxatnim **li** .
   they all the-time marry   **me.D** .
   'They are getting married on me all the time (and it bothers me).'
   Adapted from Borer and Grodzinsky (1986: 179; (9a))

4. Hungarian
Ez   meg   mi-t   csinál   itt   **nek-em** ?
this and   what-ACC   does   here   **D-1SG** ?
'And what (the hell) is this one doing here?'
Adapted from Rákosi (2008: 413; (2))

Arabic also licenses non-core arguments or what I call attitude datives (ADs). These are mentioned briefly in Brustad (2000: 359–61) and Holes (2016: 435–7). ADs in Arabic share similar structural, semantic, and pragmatic characteristics with non-core arguments in other languages. That is to say, they are optional clitics (more specifically, they are pronominal enclitics that attach to the end of a verbal element), they do not alter the truth conditions of utterances, and they serve pragmatic, attitudinal and/or relational functions.

The first extensive analysis of these datives is Al-Zahre and Boneh's (2010) article on coreferential dative constructions (or constructions with subject-oriented ADs) in Syrian Arabic, followed a few years later by Al-Zahre and Boneh (2016). Other publications on the topic include Haddad (2013, 2014, 2016, to appear) on Lebanese Arabic. Speakers of Levantine Arabic make use of four types of AD. I present an overview of these four types in the next subsections. For each type, I provide examples from the four dialects collectively referred to as Levantine Arabic, and I highlight the overarching meaning contribution of each type.

2.1 Topic/affectee-oriented ADs

Speakers may use an AD to designate its referent as a topic (the one we are talking about) and/or as an affectee (someone that has been affected positively or negatively by an action or a behavior). ADs that are used for this purpose are topic/affectee-oriented ADs (or TOP/AFF-ADs). The ADs in boldface in (5) through (8) belong to this category.[2] By using a TOP/AFF-AD, the speakers in these examples characterize the AD referent as a topic and as an individual who has been negatively affected by the at-issue content of the utterance. In (5), (6), and (8), the speakers invite the hearers to view the AD referents in the same way, while intending to invoke the hearers' empathy. In (7), there is no hearer since the speaker is soliloquizing. Note that example (8) also contains a subject-oriented AD in italics; this type of AD will be discussed in Section 2.4.[3]

5. Context: Abu Draa is a farrier who works for Abu l-Nar. He explains to his boss how his sisters, all now married and with families to take care of, argue every day about whose turn it is to take care of his sick mother. He also complains how he is caught in the middle of it all with no solution in sight.
ʔalla: waki:l-ak   mʔadˤi:n-**li:**   yya:ha: kil   yo:m
God   sponsor-your   they.spend-**me.D** it   every   day
ʕala: ʔinti   lyo:m   do:r-ek   w-ʔinti   lyo:m   do:r-ek
on   you   today   turn-your   and-you   today   turn-your

'Believe me, they argue [**me**] every day about whose turn it is (to take care of our mother).'
From *ba:b l-ha:ra* 'the neighborhood gate' – Season 1 – Episode 12 – 00:30:20 – SYR

6. Context: Three murders have taken place in a rich household. The victim of the third murder is a butler called Jalil, who has worked for the family for thirty years. Jalil's boss addresses the detective, Mr. Kammun, expressing how devastated she is.
  monsieur   kammu:n   ʃu: ʕam-bisˤi:r   fi:-na: ?
  Mr.   Kammun   what PROG-happen   to-us ?
  . . .
  ʔatalu:-**lna:**   ʒali:l !   ma: le:ʔu: yiʔitlu: ʔilla: ʒali:l ?
  they.kill-**us.D** Jalil !   NEG   they.consider kill   except   Jalil ?
  'Mr. Kummun, what is happening to us? They killed [**us**] Jalil! Why would they even consider killing Jalil?'
From *Meryana* – Episode 10 – 00:00:45 – LEB

7. Context: A woman sees her husband standing in front of a mirror, getting dressed up and wearing cologne. She becomes concerned that he might be seeing another woman. She soliloquizes:
  we:n   ra:yeh   ha-l-zalame   w-bizabbitˤ-**li:**
  where going   this-the-man   and-dressing.up-**me.D**
  b-ha:l-o ?   ya: hasert-i: !
  with-self-him ? VOC   heartbreak-my !
  'Where is this man going and getting [**me**] dressed up? Poor me!'
From *nahafa:t ʕaylitna:* 'our family anecdotes' – *mawʕed ɣara:mi:* 'a love date' – 00:02:15 – JOR

8. Context: A woman complains about how irresponsible her brother is.
  bada:l   ma: huwwa   ʔa:ʕed   yitsakkaʕ   w-yiʕʃaʔ . . .
  instead   that   he   keep.on   wasting.time   and-have.affairs . . .
  yla:ʔi:-*lo*   ʃaɣle   ʔaw   ʕamle   ytˤalleʕ   min-ha:
  let.him.find-*him.D* job   or   work   earn   from-it
  masˤru:f-o .   ʃa:tˤer yiktib-**li:**   ha-l-ʃe:ka:t   min ɣe:r
  pocket.money-his . smart   he.write-**me.D** these-the-checks without
  rasˤi:d,   w-ʔana: lli: ʔasadded   ʃe:ka:t-o .
  funds,   and-I   who   pay   checks-his .
  'Instead of wasting all his time getting involved in love affairs, he should find *[him]* a job or something to do to earn his pocket money. He is only good at writing [**me**] checks without funds, and I am the one who ends up paying off his checks.'
From *l-mi:ra:θ* 'the inheritance,' a novel by Sahar Khalifeh (1997: 70) – PAL

Note that the utterance in (6) contains one AD linked to the first instance of the verb 'to kill.' Alternatively, the utterance could contain an AD linked to the second verb only, to both, or to neither, with no change in meaning. Pragmatically, the first instance of the verb 'to kill' plus the AD depicts the speaker and her family as victims because of the loss they have endured. The second instance focuses solely on the murdered butler as the victim.

Other TOP/AFF-ADs are possessively construed ADs. Like the ADs in (5) through (8), these depict their referent as a topic, affectee, and/or object of empathy. In addition, the referent is also interpreted as a possessor of an argument, which could be the subject, an object, or an object of preposition. The utterances in (9) through (12) are examples from the four different varieties of Levantine Arabic. In (9), in addition to portraying the father as an affectee, the AD marks him as the possessor of the argument 'head.' In (10), the AD maintains its referent as a topic and refers to him as the possessor of 'brothers.' In (11), the speaker uses an AD to characterize herself as an affectee and as the possessor of 'face.' In (12), the mother uses an AD to characterize her son as an affectee (in her view, cutting his pants into shorts must make him happy) and as the possessor of the pair of jeans. Structures like these are normally referred to as possessive dative constructions and are analyzed as a distinct category derived syntactically via movement (Lee-Schoenfeld 2006; Deal 2013) or semantically via binding (Hole 2004, 2005). In Haddad (2016), I show that the interpretation of ADs like the ones in (9) through (12) is not arrived at syntactically or semantically but rather pragmatically, and that they belong to the category of TOP/AFF-ADs.

9. Context: A man explains how his father died.
   wiʔiʕ   ʕle-e   lo:h   nha:s ...   ʃaʔʔ-**allo**
   fell   on-him   slab   copper...   split-**him.D**
   ra:s-o   min   wara: w-ma: ʔdirna: naʕmil-lo
   head-his   from   behind   and-NEG we.could   do-him.D
   ʃi: .
   anything .
   'A slab of copper fell on him and split **[him]** his head from behind, and we weren't able to save him.'
   From *ba:b l-ha:ra* 'the neighborhood gate' – Season 1 – Episode 5 – 00:20:40 – SYR

10. Context: A wife is talking about her husband:
    huwwe   byaʕrif   ʔinno   bhibb-o
    he   know   that   I.love-him
    ...
    bas   ma: bhibb-**illo**   ʔixwe:t-o .
    but   NEG   I.love-**him.D** siblings-his .
    'He knows that I love him, but I do not love **[him]** his siblings.'
    From *El Professeur* 'the professor' – 00:26:15 – LEB

11. Context: A woman explains to her neighbor how she underwent four different plastic surgery procedures to make her look like a number of celebrities.
    ʔult-ullu   la-l-dokto:r   ʔismaʕ ,   ʔana:
    I.said-him.D   to-the-doctor   listen ,   I

	biddi:	ʕuyu:n	ʔasˤa:la	w-xdu:d	ʔelissa:
	want	eyes	Asala	and-cheeks	Elissa
	w-ʃafa:yef	hayfa:,	w-biddi:	tʃidd-**illi:**	
	and-lips	Haifa,	and-I.want	lift-**me.D**	
	wiʒʒ-i:	mitil	sˤaba:h.		
	face-my	like	Sabah.		

'I said to the doctor, listen, I want Asala's eyes, Elissa's cheeks, and Haifa's lips; and I want you to lift [**me**] my face to be like Sabah.'

From *nahafa:t ʕaylitna:* 'our family anecdotes' – *tanfi:x* 'inflating' – 00:02:50 – JOR 1.11

12. Context: A mother explains to her son how she converted his ripped jeans into shorts.

	ʕima:d	ya:mma:,	ʕazzalet	xaza:nt-ak	
	Imad	mom,	I.cleaned.up	closet-you	
	lage:t-lak	fi:-ha:	bantˤalo:n	mmazu:ʕ.	
	I.found-you.D	in-it	pair.of.pants	ripped.	
	...				
	gasˤsˤet-o	ʃort...	gasˤsˤet-**lak**	yya:	ʃort	yamma:.[4]
	I.cut-it	shorts...	I.cut-**you.D**	it	shorts	mom.

'Imad, my son, I cleaned up your closet and found a pair of ripped jeans in it. I cut them into shorts. I cut [**you**] them into shorts, son.'

From *watˤan ʕa watar* 'a nation on a string' – *l-ʕa:ʔila* 'the family' – 00:03:40 – PAL 1.12

Before I move to speaker- and hearer-oriented ADs, a point is in order. TOP/AFF-ADs may take the speaker or hearer as a referent, as some of the above examples show. This alone may suggest that they qualify as speaker-oriented or hearer-oriented ADs rather than TOP/AFF-ADs. How can we tell the difference? Context, which is central to this study, is one way to tease apart TOP/AFF-ADs from the other two types. Consider (8) above one more time. In this case, the speaker depicts herself as an affectee of her brother's irresponsible behavior because she ends up having to clean up his mess every time he writes a bad check. If the same sentence is uttered by a stranger – for example, a neighbor – who is not affected by the brother's behavior but who considers himself as cultural police, the same AD will be considered a speaker-oriented AD.

Importantly, the pragmatic function of a first- or second-person TOP/AFF-AD does not change if the utterance in which it occurs is paraphrased into the third person. That is, the referent of the AD will still be portrayed as topic, affectee, and/or object of empathy, regardless of whether it refers to the speaker, hearer, or a third party. Observe (6) again. If I am a neighbor of the family who has suffered the murder of their butler, I may use (13) as a paraphrase of (6) without any change in the function of the AD; that is, the third-person AD, just like its first-person counterpart, portrays its referent as a topic, affectee, and object of empathy. By the same token, if I am an acquaintance of the woman and her irresponsible brother in (8) above, I may tell a friend about them by using the utterance and the AD in (14) to characterize the sister as a topic, affectee, and object of empathy. Whether a TOP/AFF-AD is used to refer to a third party, the speaker, or the hearer, its function does not change. This is not true of speaker- and hearer-oriented ADs, as we will see shortly.[5]

13. ʔatalu:-**lun**   ʒali:l !
    they.kill-**them.D**   Jalil !
    'They killed [**them**] Jalil!'

14. ʃa:tˤer   yiktib-**la:**   ha-l-ʃe:ka:t   min ɣe:r
    smart   he.write-**her.D**   these-the-checks   without
    rasˤi:d , w-hiyye   lli: tsadded   ʃe:ka:t-o .
    funds ,   and-she   who   pay   checks-his .
    'He is only good at writing [**her**] checks without funds, and she is the one who ends up paying off his checks.'

2.2 Speaker-oriented ADs

A speaker may use a speaker-oriented AD (SP-AD) to characterize herself as a form of authority in relation to the hearer and/or the at-issue content of her utterance. The utterances in (15) through (18) are examples.

15. Context: A man visits his sister and her family to check on them. He asks about his brother-in-law. The woman replies with clear annoyance that her husband is on the roof feeding the pigeons. The brother, as well as the whole extended family, is unhappy with the fact that the woman's husband is preoccupied with raising pigeons instead of running his business as a barber. The brother answers with much indignation:
    hallaʔ   msakker   dikka:nt-o   w-milithi:-**li:**
    now   he.closed   store-his   and-preoccupied-**me.D**
    bi-l-hama:m   fo:ʔ !
    with-the-pigeons   up !
    'He is keeping his store closed and wasting [**me**] his time on taking care of the pigeons on the roof!'

1.15   From *ba:b l-ha:ra* 'the neighborhood gate' – Season 1 – Episode 6 – 00:08:30 – SYR

16. Context: The speaker is a private tutor who is homeschooling the son of the Lebanese President and First Lady. In this scene, he explains an academic concept, and he says to the child:
    yalla: ʔe:di: ,   ʒallis-**li:**   ʔaʕidt-ak ,
    go.on   Edy ,   straighten.up-**me.D**   sitting.posture-your ,
    w-sammiʕ-li: lli: ʔilt-o ,   habi:bi
    and-recite-me.D   that   I.said-it ,   sweetheart
    'OK, Edy, sit [**me**] straight and recite to me what I just said, sweetheart.'

1.16   From *l-sayyida l-θa:niya* 'the second lady' – 00:06:15 – LEB

INTRODUCTION 9

17. Context: A man posing as a businessman tries to con an unexperienced young man into handing him all of his own and his parents' money so that he can invest in the stock market on their behalf. When the young man explains that he wants to look for a job instead, he receives the following answer:

    inte   da:yer   tdawwer-**li**:   ʕala: waðʕi:fe ...
    you   going.around   look-**me.D**   for   job ...
    ʕumra: ya: ħabi:b-i: l-waðʕi:fe   ʃabbaʕit
    has.it.ever VOC   darling-my   the-job   satisfied
    ħada: ?
    anyone ?
    'I can't believe you are going around looking [me] for a job. My good man, has a job ever made anyone rich?'

    From *ʔabu: ʕawwa:d* 'Abu Awwad' – Season 1 – Episode 9 – 00:07:20 – JOR   1.17

18. Context: A woman complains about her brother, whom she considers a loser.

    ʕa:mel   ħa:l-o   riʒʒa:l   kbi:r   w-byiħki: ʔalɣa:z .
    pretending   self-his   man   great   and-speak   riddles .
    bala: ʔillet   ʕaʔel   w-ʔillet zo:ʔ .
    without   lack   wisdom   and-lack manners .
    ʔaʕed   bala: ʃaɣle   wala: ʕamle   w-da:yer
    sitting   without   job   nor   work   and-going.around
    ʕamel-**li**:   ʒiva:ra: w-ʔays w-layla
    pretending-**me.D**   Guevara   and-Qays and-Leila
    'He pretends to be a great man, and he speaks in an enigmatic way. Enough with this stupidity and lack of manners. He passes his time jobless, going from one place to another pretending [me] he is Guevara (Ernesto Guevara, the Argentine Marxist, also known as Che) and Qays and Layla (the Arabic pragmatic equivalent of Romeo and Juliet).'

    From *l-mi:ra:θ* 'the inheritance,' a novel by Sahar Khalifeh (1997: 70) – PAL

The speakers in the above examples may also be characterized as affectees. However, affectedness is not a necessary component of the meaning/pragmatic contribution, and even when it is part of the pragmatic function of the AD, it is not the primary one.[6] Importantly, when a SP-AD is replaced by a third-person dative (or when the whole SP-ADC is paraphrased into the third person), the AD loses its pragmatic function as a profile of authority; instead, it is understood as solely characterizing its referent as an affectee. For example, if I say (19) about the brother in (15) above, the AD will only portray its referent, the brother, as affected by the behavior of his sister's husband. The brother is no longer characterized as a form of authority, which in (15) takes the form of cultural police, as we will see in Chapter 3.

19. ʒo:z   ʔixt-o   msakkir   dikka:nt-o
    husband   sister-his   he.closed   store-his

w-milithi:-**lo** bi-l-hama:m !
and-preoccupied-**him.D** with-the-pigeons !
'His brother-in-law is keeping his store closed and wasting [him] his time on taking care of the pigeons.'

2.3 Hearer-oriented ADs

Hearer-oriented ADs (HR-ADs) reference the hearer, as their name indicates, and are used to mark the hearer's involvement or engagement with the at-issue content of an utterance and/or with the speaker as an in-group member. This engagement may take different forms, as we will see in Chapter 4. Examples (20) through (23) are from Syrian, Lebanese, Jordanian, and Palestinian Arabic, respectively.

20. Context: Abu l-Nar is a farrier who owns a business in a poor neighborhood in early twentieth-century Damascus, a time when electricity had not yet reached every house. He is impressed with the concept of electricity. He describes to his friend, Idaashari, how a street light near the house of his employee Abu Draa lights up not only the street but also Abu Draa's house.

    l-ku:ra:n wa:sˁel la-nisˁ be:t-o la-ʔabu: dra:ʕ
    the-electricity reach to-middle house-his for-Abu Draa
    . . .
    l-baladiyye bi-l-ha:ra mrakbe lamba
    the-municipality in-the-neighborhood installed light
    ʕa-l-heːtˁ l-ʕa:li: . ʔawwal ma: bitlayyel l-dinye ,
    on-the-wall the-high . once that get.dark the-world ,
    w-bifaʕlu:-**lak** ha-l-lamba , bithiss wa-kaʔanno
    and-they.turn.on-**you.D** this-the-lamp , you.feel and-as.if
    be:t-o sˁa:r nha:r ya: raʒul ! ya: ʔax-i:
    house-his became day VOC man ! VOC brother-my
    ʃaylet ha-l-ku:ra:n hayy bitmaxwel !
    thing this-the-electricity this be.hard.to.fathom !

    'Electricity reaches the very house of Abu Draa. The municipality in his neighborhood installed a streetlight on the high wall (surrounding the neighborhood). As soon as it gets dark they turn on [you] the light, and you feel as if it is daytime inside his house, man! Brother, this electricity thing is hard to wrap one's head around!'

1.20 From *ba:b l-ha:ra* 'the neighborhood gate' – Season 1 – Episode 12 – 00:47:10 – SYR

21. Context: A Facebook post complains about sectarianism in Lebanon and how some individuals adopt animal imagery to describe themselves as leaders in their respective sects.

    naʔlan ʕan libne:ni: ɣa:dˁib fi: twiter ,
    according to Lebanese angry on Twitter ,
    byitˁlaʕ-**lak** wa:had msammi: ha:l-o ʔasad
    emerge-**you.D** one calling self-his lion

```
l-sunna ,      w-l-te:ni:        nimr  l-ʃi:ʕa ,    w-wa:had
the-Sunna ,    and-the-second    tiger the-Shia ,   and-one
fahad     l-masi:hiyyi:n ,    w-hayde:k     ziʔib   l-dru:z .
leopard   the-Christians ,    and-that      wolf    the-Druze .
fi: maʒe:l      kil       tˤa:yfe    tdˤibb      haywa:ne:t-a: ?
is.it possible  every     sect       put.away    animals-its ?
```
'According to an angry Lebanese on Twitter: There emerges [you] a man calling himself the lion of the Sunna, and another calling himself the tiger of the Shia, and yet another calling himself the leopard of the Christians, and that one calls himself the wolf of the Druze. Could every sect please put away its animals?'

نقلا عن لبناني غاضب في تويتر
بيطلعلك واحد مسمي حاله أسد السنة، والثاني نمر الشيعة، وواحد فهد المسيحيين، وهيداك ذئب الدروز... خيي في مجال كل طائفة تضب حيواناتها؟

22. Context: Abu Awwad has just woken up after having been seriously sick. He tells his daughter:
```
btaʕerfi: ,   ya:     naʒa:ħ,      ħlimit-litʃ         ħilim
you.know ,    VOC     Najah,       I.dreamt-you.D      dream
biwaggif         ʃaʕr    l-ra:s !
make.stand       hair    the-head !
```
'You know what, Najah, I had [you] such a dream, it makes one's hair stand on end!'

From ʔabu: ʕawwa:d 'Abu Awwad' – Season 1 – Episode 5 – 00:11:50 – JOR   1.22

23. Context: A Palestinian man complains on Facebook about women who keep changing boyfriends.
```
biʒu:z                 kil      sine     bitsˤa:ħib-lak       kam
is.it.appropriate      every    year     she.date-you.D       a.few
wa:ħed          ʒda:d   bas    mni:ħ     mi:ʃa:n     taʕref
individual      new     only   well      in.order.to she.know
mi:n   l-ʔasˤi:l           fi:-hum ?       kul       ʕa:m
who    the-of.good.family  among-them ?   every     year
w-intu         ʔasˤa:yel !
and-you.all    of.good.families !
```
'Is it appropriate that a woman should date [you] a few new men every year just to figure out who among them comes from a good family? What a ridiculous excuse!'

بجووز كل سنة #بتصاحبلك كم واحد جداد بس منيح مشان تعرف مين #الاصيل فيهم
كل عام وانتو اصايل

Again, a HR-AD may characterize its referent as an affectee, but this characterization is not a necessary or primary component of its function. If a HR-AD is replaced with a third-person AD, its pragmatic function as marking hearer engagement disappears. If an affectee reading is possible, it applies; otherwise, the utterance sounds pragmatically awkward. For example, a conservative person may say (24) about a young woman and use the AD *-lun* 'them.D' to reference the young woman's parents. Example (24) replicates part of the utterance in (23) but uses a third-person AD instead of a HR-AD. The AD in this case may only characterize the parents as affectees. It does not invoke the parents' engagement; in fact, the parents may not be aware at all of their daughter's behavior.

24. biʒuːz   kil   sine   bitsˤaːħib-**lun**   kam   waːħad ?
    is.it.appropriate every year she.date-**them.D** a.few individual ?
    'Is it appropriate that a woman should date **[them]** a few new men every year?'

2.4 Subject-oriented ADs

Subject-oriented ADs (SUBJ-ADs) refer to the subject of the predicate in an utterance. A speaker uses a SUBJ-AD to characterize an event or a behavior as either insignificant/minor or significant/shocking based on her expectations of and familiarity with the subject. Numbers (25) through (28) are examples. They all mark the depicted events as insignificant or of low cost compared to the potential gain. There is more on this in Chapter 5.

25. Context: Two young men have been guarding the neighborhood all night. They both hold other daytime jobs as well. Around dawn, one man tells another:
    ʔinte   fuːt   nam-**lak**   saːˤteːn   hallaʔ ,
    you   go.in   sleep-**you.D**   two.hours   now ,
    tˤiliˤ   l-sˤibiħ .
    came.up   the-morning .
    'Go in and sleep **[you]** for a couple of hours now. It is almost morning.'

    From *baːb l-ħaːra* 'the neighborhood gate' – Season 1 – Episode 30 – 00:23:00 – SYR

26. Context: A man gives his friend advice about a new tire-repair and oil-change business. He goes on to say:
    leːʃ   laʔ ?   walla: masˤlaħa   mhimme !
    why   not ?   by.God   business   important !
    container   tasˤliːħ   dweːliːb   ˤa-l-autostrad ,
    container   repair   tire   on-the-highway ,
    fxat-**lak**   ʒuːra   ʔiddeːm-o   w-laħħiʔ?   ˤa-ʃiɣil
    dig-**you.D**   pit   in.front.of-it   and-keep.up   with-work
    yaː   mˤallim .
    VOC   master .
    'Why not? It is a great business. Have a tire-repair stand set up on the highway, dig **[you]** a pit in front of it, and keep up with the work, man, if you can.'

    From *El Professeur* 'the professor' – 01:23:00 – LEB

27. Context: A man asks an acquaintance who is travelling to the USA to take a few items to relatives of his who live there. When the acquaintance explains that his bags are already full, the man says:

niftiridˤ   yaʕni:[7]   dafaʕt-**illak**   ʔakam   dina:r
let's.suppose this.mean   you.paid-**you.D**   a.few   pounds
zya:det   miza:n?   tˤab   ma:-ana: wa:xd-ak
additional   weight?   OK   for-I   taking-you
ʕa-l-matˤa:r   bi-bala:ʃ .
to-the-airport   for-free .

'Let's suppose that you ended up having to pay [you] a few pounds for additional weight. So what? I am taking you to the airport for free.'

From *ʔabu: ʕawwa:d* 'Abu Awwad' – Season 1 – Episode 6 – 00:25:15 – JOR   1.27

28. Context: A woman soliloquizes about her single sister-in-law, Nahla, who is not willing to support her brother (the speaker's husband) financially, even though she has the means.

law   ʔinn-ek   mni:ha   w-hanu:ne ,   ka:n
if   that-you   good   and-compassionate ,   you.would
ʔilti:-lo   xid-**lak**   ʔirʃe:n   w-ʃtiri: ʃiʔʔa
say-him.D   take-**you.D**   two.pennies   and-buy   apartment
nsiter   fi:-ha: ʔinte   w-l-wla:d   w-ʔim   ʕya:l-ak .
take-shelter   in-it   you   and-the-children   and-mother   kids-your .

'If you were a good and compassionate person, you would say to him: Take [you] this small amount of money and buy an apartment, a living space for you, your children, and the mother of your children.'

From *l-mi:ra:θ* 'the inheritance,' a novel by Sahar Khalifeh (1997: 118) – PAL

In all four SUBJ-ADCs, the dative references the hearer. The sentences may be paraphrased in such a way that the AD references the speaker or a third party instead, as (29), which is a paraphrase of (27), illustrates. In either case, the SUBJ-AD maintains its pragmatic function. That is, the event in (29) is still portrayed as insignificant in relation to the subject.

ʔiftiridˤ   yaʕni: dafaʕt-**illi:**/dafaʕ-**lo**/
suppose   this.mean   you.paid-**me.D**/you.paid-**him.D**
ʔakam   dina:r . . .
a.few   pounds . . .

'Suppose that I/he ended up having to pay [me/him] a few pounds . . .'

How, then, do we tease apart SUBJ-ADs from the other three types of AD? SUBJ-ADs have two distinctive features. First, if an AD references the subject, it may only function as a SUBJ-AD.[8] This is true even when the subject is also the speaker or hearer. For a dative to be interpreted as a TOP/AFF-, SP-, or HR-AD, its reference may not simultaneously be the subject. Second, constructions with a SUBJ-AD obligatorily contain an adverb or an indefinite object in the form of a vague measure, such as *sa:ʕte:n* 'two hours/a couple of hours' in (25) and *ʔakam dina:r* 'a few pounds' in (27) (Al-Zahre and Boneh 2010: 10; Haddad 2014: 70). No such restriction applies to the other types of AD.

3 Purpose and significance

The main purpose of this study is to provide a sociopragmatic analysis of ADs like the ones we have just encountered in four varieties of Levantine Arabic: namely, Syrian, Lebanese, Jordanian, and Palestinian Arabic, in this order of emphasis. Sociopragmatics is the study of language in its social and cultural context (Leech 1983; Thomas 1983). It investigates the relation between communication and contextual factors; it 'aims to show how social and cultural factors are brought to bear in language practices, and how they influence pragmatic strategies which are manifested by linguistic forms in particular communicative contexts' (Aijmer and Anderson 2012: 1).

This study is an empirical investigation of the social functions of ADs and of the 'specific "local" conditions' on their use, as Leech (1983: 10) would put it, whereby 'use' is 'essentially the function of the linguistic form in communicative interaction' (LoCastro 2012: 19). The study deals with ADCs as social action carried out by language users as social beings in their social context (see Mey 2001; LoCastro 2012). It starts with the premise that language use is 'sensitive to features of the context' (Schiffrin 1987: 4, cited in Aijmer 2013: 10) and that pragmatic markers like the ADs under examination 'do not have a fixed meaning but a meaning potential' that is activated and negotiated in situated use (Aijmer 2013: 12, drawing on Norén and Linell 2007); see also Fraser (1996) and Beeching (2016). The study has four goals:

- to provide as thorough a picture as possible of the phenomenon of ADs in Levantine Arabic by presenting and discussing ample data from a variety of sources; these include soap operas, movies, plays, talk shows, and other audiovisual material
- to explain the meaning contribution of ADs as they are used in particular interactions and examine their attitudinal and relational functions as interpersonal pragmatic markers in their social contexts
- to examine the contextual factors that inform and are informed by the use of ADs
- to put forth a model that captures the cognitive coordination that the speaker and hearer engage in when an AD is used.

The study, to use Culpeper and Haugh's (2014: 11) words, is 'knowingly ethnocentric' in that it focuses on Levantine Arabic to the exclusion of other languages. This constitutes a positive move when viewed from the perspective of Hanks, Ide, and Katagiri (2009). In their introduction to the *Journal of Pragmatics* special issue (volume 41) 'Towards an Emancipatory Pragmatics,' Hanks et al. write:

> It is our shared conviction that pragmatics as an analytic enterprise has been dominated by views of language derived from Euro-American languages and ways of speaking . . . While these research traditions have enriched the field of pragmatics, they also have tended to rely uncritically on the common sense of speakers of modern Western languages, with the attendant premises of individualism, rationality, and market economy. That is, while they are presented as general models of rational language use, they in fact rely heavily on the native common sense of their authors and practitioners. (1–2)

A sociopragmatic analysis of ADs in Levantine Arabic is a departure from what Hanks et al. call 'views of language [that are] derived from Euro-American languages and ways of speaking.'

Research on ADs and non-core arguments in general has, to date, focused predominantly on their role as conventional implicature contributors and on their syntactic and semantic characteristics (for example, Rákosi 2008; Bosse, Bruening, and Yamada 2012; Haddad 2014), with little attention having been paid to their pragmatics; exceptions include Horn (2008, 2013) and Haddad (2013). To my knowledge, there has been no systematic account of the sociopragmatics of non-core arguments as interpersonal pragmatic markers. These markers are used variably in different situations; they interact with elements of the context in order to serve certain functions. In Mey's (2001: 29) words, '[o]ur understanding of utterances like these depends crucially on the worlds in which their speakers live.' A sociopragmatic approach is appropriate in that it means to account in a systematic way for the variability of these markers, the contextual factors they interact with, and the different functions they serve.

Although this study does not deal with the topic of learnability and first- or second-language acquisition, I should point out that a sociopragmatic approach to non-core arguments is important from a learnability point of view. As Mey (2016) maintains, 'language is more than sounds and grammar rules: It is primarily a way of dealing with the world' (19–20). When people learn a language, they learn more than its grammar and lexicon; they also learn how to use language 'meaningfully, appropriately, and effectively (Schieffelin and Ochs 1986 a, b)' (Ochs 1996: 408). This, according to Ochs, means that language learners need to learn not only the structure and mental representation of linguistic forms, but also the rules that inform who may use them, with whom, where, when, and for what purpose, all within the larger sociocultural context. This study takes these rules into account; it means to account for the phenomenon of ADs in Levantine Arabic by focusing on the social and contextual factors that inform their use and that are informed by it. In this sense, it contributes to recent research, such as Aijmer (2013) and Beeching (2016), that underscores the vital role that sociolinguistic factors (for example, social identity and types of social activity) play in the use of pragmatic markers and the influence of context on their function and meaning.

4 Data sources

The focus on Levantine Arabic to the exclusion of other varieties is informed by the observation that the ADs in the four varieties of Arabic under examination behave uniformly in terms of their structure, meaning contribution, and social functions. An ADC that is judged as grammatically acceptable and pragmatically felicitous in one Levantine variety is considered equally readily acceptable by speakers of other Levantine varieties.[9] Preliminary examination shows that this is not necessarily true of other varieties of Arabic. For example, as I mention in Haddad (to appear), unlike SUBJ-ADs in Lebanese Arabic, as well as the other Levantine varieties, Egyptian and Moroccan Arabic SUBJ-ADs may not co-occur with core arguments in the form of recipients or beneficiaries, as (30) and (31) illustrate. The asterisks indicate that the sentences will be ungrammatical if the arguments between parentheses are pronounced. The same sentences are judged as acceptable in Levantine Arabic, with or without the parenthetical material. In Egyptian and Moroccan Arabic, a SUBJ-AD behaves like a reflexive pronoun, an observation that seems to apply to the Eastern Arabic dialects of Bahrain also, as Holes (2016: 436–7) remarks. If this is correct, then SUBJ-ADs in Levantine Arabic are at least syntactically and semantically different from similar datives in other dialects. Other informal observations based on elicitation seem to indicate that other structural, semantic, and pragmatic differences exist with other ADs as well. All this has led to the decision to focus on the sociopragmatics of ADs in Levantine Arabic, deferring the examination of ADs in other varieties until another occasion.

30. Egyptian Arabic (Usama Soltan, personal communication)
    ʔahmad   ʔiʃtra:-**luh**   ʔami:sˁ   gedi:d
    Ahmad   bought-**him.D**   shirt   new
    (*l-ʔibn-u)   ʔimba:rih
    (*for-son-his) yesterday
    'Ahmad bought [**him**] a new shirt (*for his son) yesterday.'

31. Moroccan Arabic (Hamid Ouali, personal communication)
    ħməd   ʃra-**lu**   qamiʒa   ʒdida
    Ahmad   bought-**him.D**   shirt   new
    (*l-bənt-u)   lbarəh
    (*for-daughter-his)   yesterday
    'Ahmad bought [**him**] a new shirt (*for his daughter) yesterday.'

The vast majority of Levantine Arabic ADCs in this study come from soap operas, movies, plays, talk shows, and Facebook. Levantine Arabic is not a single dialect, nor are any of the Levantine varieties. I use the term Levantine Arabic as an umbrella term that encompasses the four dialects of Arabic under examination. I use the terms Syrian, Lebanese, Jordanian, and Palestinian Arabic to characterize the data based on the country of origin of their source. For example, if an example comes from a Syrian show, I label it as a Syrian Arabic example.

In selecting the shows, I have paid special attention to the nationality of the actors, making sure that a Syrian show features Syrian actors, a Jordanian show features Jordanian actors, and so on. I have excluded shows that do not meet this requirement. For example, one Palestinian show called *l-taɣri:ba* 'alienation' features Syrian actors playing the role of Palestinian characters. Although data from this show may not be problematic for the purpose of this study, I have excluded them because shows like *l-taɣri:ba* may place actors outside the comfort zone of their own dialects and thus may allow minimal improvisation as the actors get into their characters (see below for why this is important). As for the data obtained from Facebook, I label a post as Syrian, Lebanese, and so on based on the reported nationality of the Facebook user.

All of the audiovisual materials that I use for this study, including most materials obtained from my personal collection, were accessible on Youtube at the time of research. In order to facilitate access to the data and provide the reader with a feel of how the ADCs I examine sound in context, I have prepared trimmed 5- to 50-second videos of most examples; these audiovisual files are available on a companion website https://edinburghuniversitypress.com/haddad. A video may start 1 or more seconds before the actual example and may continue 1 or more seconds beyond it. The following is a list of the audiovisual sources, other than Facebook, that I consulted for this study:

- The Syrian data come from two sources:
  - the soap opera *ba:b l-ha:ra* 'the neighborhood gate'
  - the soap opera *l-fusˤu:l l-ʔarbaˤa* 'the four seasons.'
- The Lebanese data come from a variety of sources. These include:
  - the soap opera *Meryana*
  - the talk show *ʔahmar bi-l-xatˤ l-ˤari:dˤ* 'a red line with a thick stroke'
  - the documentary show *tahqi:q* 'investigations'
  - other plays and movies, mainly by playwrights George Khabbaz and Ziad al-Rahbani and by movie directors Nadine Labaki, Assad Fouladkar, and Philip Asmar.
- The Jordanian data come from three sources:
  - the soap opera *ʔabu: ˤawwa:d* 'Abu Awwad'
  - the TV show *ha:l l-dunya:* 'this is life'
  - the animated TV show *nahafa:t ˤaylitna:* 'our family anecdotes.'
- The Palestinian data comes from three sources:
  - the 1997 novel *l-mira:θ* 'the inheritence' by Sahar Khalifeh[10]
  - the comedy show *watˤan ˤa-watar* 'a nation on a string'
  - the comedy series *mafru:ˤ tawfi:r* 'a saving project.'

The analysis of the different types of AD in subsequent chapters will always start with data from the first season of the Syrian soap opera *ba:b l-ha:ra* 'the neighborhood gate' before providing further examples from other shows and varieties. The Syrian show is about daily life in a neighborhood (*ha:ret l-dˤabeˤ* 'the neighborhood of the hyena') of early twentieth-century Damascus, Syria. At the time, Syria was under the French mandate. The storyline in the thirty-three episodes of Season 1 revolves around two threads: first, the theft of gold coins from a resident of the neighborhood and ensuing attempts to find the perpetrator, and second, the infiltration of a spy who works for the French and who tries to stymie efforts by leaders of the community to support the Palestinians in fighting for independence from British control. Around these two threads, all types of events and subplots are featured in the show, ranging from family feuds to arranged marriages, and from storytelling to street fights.

ADCs from *ba:b l-ha:ra* 'the neighborhood gate' are an ideal choice for this study for a number of reasons. First, as I mentioned in the previous section, ADCs are common in informal conversations. They are featured in a variety of activities, ranging from household-related activities (for example, conversations around the dinner table, arguments between husband and wife) to workplace-related activities (for example, buying and selling events, visits to the doctor). The Syrian show contains an abundance of these activities and a wealth of data that may otherwise be very hard to access during fieldwork. For example, conversations between husband and wife or between a police chief and a suspect, as well as cases of individuals soliloquizing, are too private to be accessible during fieldwork.

In addition, because the show is about early twentieth-century Damascus, it goes to great lengths to highlight the cultural values, beliefs, and norms considered by the show's writers and producers to be characteristic of Damascene communities of the time. Expectations are often articulated in a way that is not common in shows about contemporary communities and events. For example, at different points in the show, characters explicitly state social expectations of different groups. The following are some expectations of women, men, and community members of the era as presented in the show: women must always cover their faces in public, must obey their husbands, and must be good cooks; men must be brave, must control their wives and children, and must not cry; neighborhood residents must be courteous, must come to each other's aid when needed, and must behave in accordance with their socio-economic status. These sociocultural values and beliefs are important for the sociopragmatic analysis of ADCs. The fact that they are articulated in a show about a specific community at a specific time in history allows the researcher to address them as relevant to the context of the show's storyline, without generalizing over a whole population and thus without the risk of stereotyping.

It is important to note that the aforementioned values and beliefs, and the way they are depicted in the show, may or may not be completely accurate historically, and in fact some of them have been criticized for exactly that. For example, in a 2007 newspaper article, Rima Nazzal criticizes the show for portraying women as objects and for not highlighting the important roles that women historically played in early twentieth-century Syria. For the purpose of the sociopragmatic analysis presented in this study, however, the important question is: how do the sociocultural values, beliefs, and norms that the members of the community in the show live by inform, and how are they informed by, the use of ADs? The question assumes that the values and beliefs apply to the community in the show only and thus interact only with the language used there. It does not assume that they apply to all Syrians, Levantine Arabic speakers, or Arabs of all times. Asking the above question is similar to asking the following one about the movie *A Time to Kill*, discussed in Section 1: how does the use of the lawyer's directive *Now imagine she's white* interact with the sociocultural background depicted in the movie? The question does not deal with the accuracy or ubiquity of the sociocultural background. Even if the movie is in some respect historically accurate, it would be wrong to generalize or assume, based solely on the movie, that no African American may receive a fair trial in the southern states of the USA or that white Americans are incapable of empathizing with a fellow African American citizen.

Using *ba:b l-ha:ra* 'the neighborhood gate' as a baseline serves another purpose as well. It allows for comparison with television shows from different times and with different sociocultural backgrounds to examine how these differences are reflected in the use of ADs. This is where the other audiovisual materials become relevant. In addition to providing data from different dialects, thus showing how prevalent the phenomenon under study is across dialects in Levantine Arabic, the inclusion of additional materials allows us to demonstrate how a different set of sociocultural values and beliefs may lead to variation in who may use ADs, with whom, where, when, and to what end. For example, if a type of AD may be used as a display of authority, one would expect restrictions on its use by women in the public sphere in a strictly patriarchal context, but not so much in an egalitarian context. We will later see that this prediction is correct.

Of course, the study could have focused only on one show. However, this would have meant a focus on one Levantine dialect, overlooking the fact that the phenomenon is prevalent in the Levant as a region. In addition, since *ba:b l-ha:ra* 'the neighborhood gate' is about early twentieth-century Damascus, focusing only on this show would raise the question as to whether the ADs that feature in the dialogs of the show are representative only of the language used at that time alone. This is why I also provide examples from a Syrian show about contemporary Syrian families: *l-fusˤu:l l-ʔarbaʕa* 'the four seasons.'

I have also been sure to select Jordanian shows that were produced in different times. Main Jordanian TV stations, such as Roya TV and the Jordan Radio and Television Corporation, are located in the Jordanian capital, Amman, and their casting is likely to include Ammani residents. As research by Al-Wer indicates, the dialect of Amman has been in the process of formation. Amman historically had no dialect of its own. Most of its older residents 'affiliate themselves with the towns and villages of their forefathers,' while '[t]he youngesters ... call themselves ... "Ammanis"' (Al-Wer 2007: 55). Al-Wer adds that the coinage of the term 'Ammani' is indicative of the formation of a distinctive urban identity and dialect. In order to make sure that ADs in Jordanian Arabic have not been affected in the process, I have included data from three Jordanian shows: one from the 1980s entitled *ʔabu: ʕawwa:d* 'Abu Awwad,' and two recent shows, *ha:l l-dunya:* 'this is life' and *nahafa:t ʕaylitna:* 'our family anecdotes.' Close examination of these shows indicates that the phenomenon of ADs has been robust in the dialect over time.

Finally, unlike ADCs that come from talk shows and Facebook, data that come from soap operas, movies, and plays may be considered too scripted to be valid for analysis as naturally occurring data. There are three reasons why this issue should not undermine the quality of the data as far as ADCs are concerned. First, all ADCs used in the shows sound natural to native speakers; they judge them as something they would also use in similar contexts. Second, the scripts of soap operas, plays, and movies are written for the purpose of relating a story and not as a manifestation of a specific type of construction. ADs, just like intonation or facial expressions, are employed in interaction not as an end in themselves but as subservient to the purpose and function of communication.

Here I should mention that social actors are rarely aware that they use these ADs at all. In interviews with native speakers, when I ask about these ADs or point out that they have just used an AD, more often than not there is a eureka moment. Even when social actors become aware of the fact that they use ADs, they are hardly able to explain why they use them or to articulate their effect.

I mentioned above that I exclude from this study data that come from shows in which actors use a dialect other than their own. This brings me to the third reason why the use of soap operas, movies, and plays as sources should not undermine the quality of the data as far as ADCs are concerned. That reason is improvisation, which is not uncommon in these shows. In an interview on Alsharjah TV with the actor Abbas l-Noury, who plays the role of Abu Esam in *ba:b l-ḥa:ra* 'the neighborhood gate,' he comments that the actors in the show would often improvise the dialog when filming (from a 2009 online article).[11] This observation was confirmed to me independently during an exchange with the actress Laila Sammur, who plays the role of Fawziyye in the same show. When I asked Ms. Sammur if she could share with me the script of one or more episodes of the show, she answered that most of the time the actors were not given scripts but instead broad guidelines, and the dialogs were mostly improvised.

Further support for the role of improvisation in these shows, especially as related to ADs, comes from the utterances in (32) and (33). Both examples are from the Lebanese play *El Professeur* 'the professor,' directed by George Khabbaz. When asked whether the actors in his plays were allowed to improvise, Mr. Khabbaz explained that they did so minimally. He added that he was normally rather strict about the script and that he would ask the actors to follow the written dialog. Mr. Khabbaz kindly shared with me the script of *El Professeur*, which I compared to the actors' actual performance. The two in fact match almost word for word, except for the use of ADs! For example, the ADs in (32) and (33) are featured in the recorded performance but not in the written dialog.

32. Context: Two employees in a shoe store, along with the fiancé of one of the employees, are playfully putting on an act during work hours. Each is pretending to be a different character. While they are acting, the boss walks in. He says in a rather bossy tone:

law btitˁlaʕu:-**li:** min l-ʃaxsˁiyye inta w-iyyeha:
if you.get.out-**me.D** of the-character you and-her

INTRODUCTION   21

    w-kil wa:had   biru:h   ʕa-ʃiɣl-o   bku:n   mamnu:n   ʕayn-kun
    and-each one   go   to-work-his   I.be   thankful   eye-your
    'If you could cut [**me**] out the act and go back to work, I would be very grateful.'
From *El Professeur* 'the professor' – 00:10:30 – LEB   1.32

33. Context: A woman complains about an acquaintance named Adelle; she believes that Adelle is full of herself. She says:
    ha:ʒ   ssit   ʔade:l   re:ffit-**li:**   mne:xi:r-a:
    enough   Ms.   Adelle   raising-**me.D**   nostrils-her
    'Enough with Ms. Adelle acting [**me**] like she is so important.'
From *El Professeur* 'the professor' – 00:50:35 – LEB   1.33

The comments by the Syrian actors about improvisation and examples like (32) and (33) suggest that when actors get into character, they seem to use the datives under examination, as informed by the identity of their character and the type of activity that their character is involved in, among other things. This is so even if the ADs are not in the written dialog and even if the director is strict about the actors' adherence to the script.

5 A roadmap

The rest of the study is organized as follows. Chapter 2 identifies and discusses the analytic tools that are relevant to the sociopragmatic analysis of ADs. These include the elements of the context that interact with the use of ADs and the nature of evaluation that is linked to them. The chapter also puts forth a model that tries to capture the perspectivizing function of ADs and the cognitive coordination that they invoke between the speaker and the hearer. The chapter uses examples of TOP/AFF-ADs in order to illustrate the nature of the analytic tools and the working of the model. TOP/AFF-ADs have been analyzed in more detail in Haddad (2014, 2016), so Chapter 2 is not meant to replicate the analysis presented there. Rather, the discussion of these ADs in Chapter 2 is only for the purpose of making the discussion concrete.

Chapters 3, 4, and 5 discuss SP-, HR-, and SUBJ-ADs, respectively. The chapters present plenty of examples of these ADs and analyze their function in a systematic way. They also highlight the elements of the context that interact with these ADs and the nature of evaluation that they bring about.

Notes

1. Here and throughout this study, I refer to a generic speaker as 'she' and to a generic hearer as 'he.'
2. A 🖥 following the source of an example signifies the availability of an audio-visual file for that example on a companion website https://edinburghuniversitypress.com/haddad.

3. A note about the names used in the examples: we will come across many names that begin with *ʔim/ʔum* (Im/Um) and *ʔabu:* (Abu). These mean 'the mother of' and 'the father of,' respectively. In the Arab world, they are used as teknonyms to refer to an adult by referencing her or his eldest son. If a man is not married, he may still be addressed as, say, *ʔabu: kari:m* 'father of Karim,' with the assumption that his eldest son will be named Karim. This is especially the case if the man's father's name is Karim and he plans to name his future son after his father. Finally, *ʔim/ʔum* and *ʔabu:* may also be used to refer to a salient characteristic that a person may have. For example, *ʔabu: dra:ʕ* 'Abu Draa' in (5) is referred to as such probably because he has strong arms; *dra:ʕ* means 'arm.' In this sense, if we know that *xdu:d* means 'cheeks,' the term *ʔabu: xdu:d* may be used to describe or refer to a person with chubby cheeks, just as the term *cachetón* is used in Colombian Spanish, and perhaps other varieties, to describe a person with big *cachetes* 'chubby cheeks.'
4. The use of *yamma:* 'mom' by the mother to address her son is an instance of a reverse-role vocative, whereby an older relative uses her or his kinship role to address a younger relative. For example, a father may address his daughter or son as 'dad,' and an aunt may address her niece or nephew as 'aunt.' See Rieschild 1998.
5. TOP/AFF-ADs maintain their function in reported speech as well. However, I do not deal with reported speech in this study for two main reasons. First, the remaining three types of AD are rarely used in reported speech. Second, on the rare occasions that ADCs are reported, they are stated as direct speech, whereby the reporter uses the speaker's exact words and even gestures and facial expressions. That is, the reporter tries to deliver the AD, the structure it is embedded in, and the attitude it expresses exactly as the speaker has said or would say them. See (28) in this chapter and (32) in Chapter 3.
6. It is not uncommon for pragmatic markers to fulfil a variety of functions and to do so simultaneously (Beeching 2016: 5). Often, however, a certain function may be foregrounded or backgrounded in an interaction (Aijmer 2013: 10).
7. The word *yaʕni:* is often used as a filler.
8. This is an interesting point from a structural/syntactic perspective, as well as in relation to the syntax–pragmatic interface and the differences between subjecthood and other elements of the left periphery. However, I defer this topic for another occasion.
9. One structural difference exists between Lebanese and Palestinian Arabic, on the one hand, and Syrian and perhaps Jordanian Arabic, on the other hand. Only the former allow ADs to cliticize to the different forms of *ka:n* 'to be'; see example (6) in Chapter 4. This is not possible in Syrian Arabic, as Al-Zahre and Boneh (2016) observe. It does not seem to be possible in Jordanian Arabic either. This structural difference is minor, however, and does not have any sociopragmatic repercussions.
10. The novel is in Standard Arabic, but the interaction among the characters is in Palestinian Arabic.
11. http://alasr.me/articles/view/10983/ (accessed on August 24, 2016).

2

Attitude Datives in Social Context – The Analytic Tools

1 Introduction

As mentioned in Chapter 1, attitude datives (ADs) are interpersonal pragmatic markers that deal with interpersonal attitudes and relations. Interpersonal attitudes may be broadly defined as 'perspectives, usually value-laden and emotionally charged, on others that are mediated by interaction, including generosity, sympathy, like/ dislike, disgust, fear and anger'; interpersonal relations deal with 'mutual social connections among people that are mediated by interaction, including power, intimacy, roles, rights and obligations' (Culpeper and Haugh 2014: 197).

When a speaker uses an attitude dative construction (ADC), she presents the hearer with two entities: first, the AD, including her evaluation of its referent; and second, the at-issue content of the ADC (also known as the main message or propositional content) and her evaluation of it. The two entities are interrelated. The speaker's evaluation of the AD referent involves managing (for example, maintaining, redefining) the identity of the referent or aspects of it that are relevant to the main message of her utterance within the context of interaction. The AD in its turn functions as a perspectivizer, à la Verhagen (2005, 2010), through which the main message is evaluated. By using an ADC, the speaker instructs the hearer to view the propositional content and her evaluation of it from the perspective she identifies via the use of the AD, and invites the hearer to agree with her evaluation. If the AD refers to the speaker or hearer, the evaluation of the AD referent may go beyond managing identities and into managing relationships.

These two functions of ADs are not surprising, given their attitudinal/evaluative nature. Thompson and Hunston (2000: 6) highlight three functions that speakers use evaluation for, two of which pertain to interpersonal pragmatic markers. These are:

- to express an opinion about certain entities or states of affairs, and in doing so reveal, confirm, and/or redefine personal and communal value and belief systems

- to establish, maintain, or negotiate identities (own and hearer's) and interpersonal relationships.

The purpose of this chapter is to identify the main factors that are pertinent to the analysis of ADs within their social context and that can help us understand how these ADs are exploited in different types of interaction. It also puts forth a model that will help visualize how ADs interact with the utterances in which they are embedded, and what role they play therein. In order to make the presentation more tangible, I use examples of topic/affectee-oriented ADCs (TOP/AFF-ADCs). TOP/AFF-ADCs have been analyzed more thoroughly in Haddad (2014, 2016); here they are used to illustrate the contribution of ADs to utterances in general. They are also used to make our discussion of the factors involved in their interpretation, as well as the model I propose for them, more concrete.

In terms of their social functions, TOP/AFF-ADCs are arguably the most straightforward of the four types of ADC introduced in Chapter 1. A TOP/AFF-ADC is an utterance with an optional dative pronominal clitic that places its referent in the spotlight as a topic or a prominent element in discourse. It may characterize the referent as an affectee (benefactive, malefactive), as well as an object of empathy, from the perspective of the speaker. This characterization also applies to ADCs commonly known as possessive dative constructions in which the referent of the dative is additionally construed as the possessor of an argument (for example, subject, object) within the utterance; see Haddad (2016) for more details. For the purpose of this chapter, I will focus on TOP/AFF-ADCs in which the referent of the AD may be characterized not only as a topic but also as an affectee.

Sentences (1) through (3) are examples of TOP/AFF-ADCs from the Syrian soap opera *ba:b l-ḥa:ra* 'the neighborhood gate.' They all make reference to a recent burglary that has taken place in a neighborhood called *ḥa:ret l-dˤabeʕ* 'the neighborhood of the hyena' in early twentieth-century Damascus. Someone broke into the house of one of the residents, a textile store owner named Abu Brahim, and stole fifty Ottoman gold coins. Sentence (1) is taken from one of the scenes in which Abu Brahim talks about the incident to the mayor and other members of the neighborhood board. Sentence (2) is about Abu Brahim, spoken by one of the residents. Most residents in the neighborhood suspect a man named Idaashari, a peddler with a past theft record, is involved in the burglary. Some, however, try to give him the benefit of the doubt. Sentence (3) is a resident's response to a coppersmith who tries to defend Idaashari and cast some doubt on his involvement in the burglary.

1. saraʔ-**li**: dahaba:t-i: , . . .
   he.stole-**me.D** gold-my , . . .
   'He stole [me] my gold, . . . '

From *ba:b l-ḥa:ra* 'the neighborhood gate' – Season 1 – Episode 6 – 00:19:15 – SYR

2. sirʔet ha-l-dahaba:t rah tiksir-**lo** dˤahr-o .
   stealing this-the-gold.coins will break-**him.D** back-his .

'The theft of his gold coins will break [him] his back.'
From *ba:b l-ḥa:ra* 'the neighborhood gate' – Season 1 – Episode 2 – 00:26:50 – SYR

3. kaʔann-ak   nasya:n   ʔinno   huwwe   saraʔ-lak
   as.if-you   forgot   that   he   robbed-you.D
   dikka:n-tak,   w-ma: xalla: fi:-ha: wala: nḥa:se !
   store-your,   and-NEG   leave   in-it   a.single piece.of.copper !
   'You seem to have forgotten that he robbed [you] your store, and that he left nothing in it!'

From *ba:b l-ḥa:ra* 'the neighborhood gate' – Season 1 – Episode 4 – 00:45:00 – SYR

Now the question is: what is the meaning contribution of the optional datives in these examples? The short answer is that the AD places its referent (Abu Brahim in (1) and (2), and the coppersmith in (3)) in the foreground as a topic and affectee, and possibly as an object of empathy. By using an AD, the speaker invites the hearer to view the referent in the same way. In other words, the dative gives its referent a prominent place in discourse and characterizes him as someone who is affected by the event described in the main message of the sentence. In addition, it overtly anchors to the AD any feelings that the speaker may have toward its referent in relation to the event.[1] These feelings may be characterized as benevolence (feeling happy for someone's happiness or sad for that person's sadness) or as malevolence (feeling happy for someone's misfortune or sad for that person's success/good luck).

Importantly, when speakers have no interest in construing the referent as a topic, affectee, or object of empathy, no TOP/AFF-AD is involved. This is illustrated in (4), from the same Syrian soap opera. In this example, Sheikh Abd l-Alim, the religious figure in the neighborhood, confronts the suspect, Idaashari, and asks him in the presence of the neighborhood mayor and board to swear on the Holy Qur'an, the holy book of Islam, that he was not involved in the burglary. The speaker could have used a TOP/AFF-AD and said *saraʔt-illo* 'you.stole-him.D' in order to depict the victim as an affectee on a par with the speakers in (1) and (3), but he does not. The sheikh is more interested in knowing if the hearer is guilty or not than in portraying Abu Brahim as a victim.

4. hitˤtˤ   ʔi:d-ak   ˤa-l-misˤḥaf,   w-hle:f   ʔinn-ak
   put   hand-your   on-the-holy.book,   and-swear   that-you
   ma: nzilit   ˤa-be:t   ʔabu: bra:hi:m,   wala:
   NEG   you.entered   to-house   Abu Brahim,   nor
   saraʔet   dahaba:t-o .
   you.stole   gold-his .
   'Put your hand on the Qur'an and swear that you neither went to Abu Brahim's house nor stole his gold.'

From *ba:b l-ḥa:ra* 'the neighborhood gate' – Season 1 – Episode 4 – 00:21:40 – SYR

Similarly, the dative in (2) above is optional; this is so despite the idiomatic nature of the expression *tiksur dˤahr-o* 'have a bad effect on him,' which literally means 'break his back.' Example (5), a Facebook post by a Palestinian woman, shows that the idiom may be used without the dative. As the example illustrates, the Facebook user is more focused on the person who is shunned than on the 'shunner,' which may explain why she does not use an AD to refer to the shunner.

5. ma: tismaħ la-hada: ytˤanʃ-ak bi-ħiʒʒit ʔinn-o
   NEG allow for-anyone ignore-you in-pretense that-he
   maʃɣuːl! hatta: law kaːn l-ʔinsaːn maʃɣuːl, θaːnye
   busy! even if was the-person busy, second
   min waʔt-o ma: raħ tiksur dˤahr-o!
   of time-his NEG will break back-his!
   'Don't allow anyone to shun you under the pretense that he is busy! Even if a person is busy, a moment of his time will not break his back!'

ما تسمح لحدا يطنشك بحجة انو مشغول! حتى لو كان الانسان مشغول، ثانية من وقته ما رح تكسر ضهره!

This said, it is important to note that the Facebook user in (5) could have chosen to employ an AD to maintain the shunner as a topic. By the same token, the speaker in (2) could have chosen to do without the AD. The outcomes would have the same truth conditions and would not be infelicitous; however, they would direct the gaze of the hearer to different aspects of the interaction. Social actors are tacitly aware of the power of their linguistic choices and they use them accordingly. This observation is in line with Beeching (2016: 5), who holds that pragmatic markers 'guide interpretation rather than have a propositional meaning in and of themselves.'

Identifying the referent of the dative in each of (1), (2), and (3) as an affectee is helpful as far as the meaning contribution of the dative is concerned. However, this characterization is too broad to help us understand how the dative is exploited in interaction. Our social perception of theft as an illegal activity that has negative effects on the victim may make the interpretation of the AD rather transparent. In other words, drawing on our world knowledge and shared understanding about theft, we may fairly conclude that the speaker in (1), Abu Brahim, portrays himself as a maleficiary rather than a beneficiary, and that the speaker in (3) uses an AD to characterize the hearer, the coppersmith, overtly as a victim. This is not the whole picture, though, and things are not always as straightforward. Take another look at (2). Here are a few questions that may have an effect on the social function of the AD in this example.

- Who are the speaker and hearer in terms of their traits, social roles, history, reputation, and so on? What is their relationship? For example, are they like-minded friends or different-minded community members?
- How does the speaker evaluate the burglary event? Does he[2] welcome it as a good thing because, say, it happened to a rich person who shows no compassion toward the poor? Does he consider it as a sin in accordance with his religious beliefs?

- How does the speaker position himself toward that event? Does he reject it or embrace it? Note that people may embrace a behavior that they judge as bad. For example, the speaker may evaluate the event as sinful but still embrace it because he is a thief himself.
- How does the speaker evaluate Abu Brahim, the referent of the AD? For example, does he consider him as a bad man and thus deserving of what happened to him?
- How does the speaker position himself toward the referent of the AD? This may take the form of (dis)like, (dis)satisfaction, and so on. For example, the speaker may dislike Abu Brahim because he is jealous of him. This may be the speaker's position even if he evaluates Abu Brahim as a righteous man who had worked hard for his gold coins.

To be able to determine the function(s) of ADs like the ones employed above, we need to analyze them as pragmatic markers employed in utterances rather than as encoded material used in sentences. That is, we need to observe each AD as it is used in 'a particular piece of language – be it a word, a phrase, a sentence, or a sequence of sentences – spoken or written by a particular speaker or writer in a particular context on a particular occasion' (Huang 2014: 13). We need to approach ADs as pragmatic tools that social actors use to 'create and signal relationships with the propositions they utter and with the people they interact with' (Johnstone 2009: 30–31). This is what is missing in (2). By looking at ADs as encoded material in isolated sentences, we may be able to deal with their semantics, but that only means that we will be able to identify their 'meaning in abstraction from the speakers' intentions, their psychological states, and the cultural and social aspects of the context' in which the sentences are used (Huang 2014: 4–5). The minimal context I have provided for (1) through (3), combined with our experience with and perception of theft, may suffice for (1) and (3), but (2) shows that things are not always this simple.

In order to convert the sentence in (2) into an utterance, we need to spell out the elements of its context. First, we need to situate the ADC, along with the speaker and hearer, in the broader sociocultural context that, in Spencer-Oatey's (2000) words, comprises the 'attitudes, beliefs, behavioural conventions, and basic assumptions and values that are shared by a group of people, and that influence each member's behaviour and each member's interpretations of the "meaning" of other people's behaviour' (4). We also need to gather information about the immediate situational context; this includes who the speaker and hearer are and what activity they are involved in. Finally, we need to locate the ADC in its co-textual or dialogic context in order to understand how it fits with what comes before and/or after, what it is a reaction to, and what the reaction to it is.

Having contextual information of the sort just described helps us determine what kind of evaluation the speakers attach to the referent of the AD and how they position themselves toward it. This in turn helps determine the angle from which the at-issue content is viewed (for example, from an angle that views the AD referent as a bad person or good person), how the speakers evaluate this content, and how they position themselves toward it. Based on all of this, we will be able to infer what kind of attitude the speakers want their hearer to adopt.

The following sections provide further detail regarding these issues. Section 2 discusses the topic of context; it delineates and discusses the contextual factors that are involved in interaction and that have a bearing on the analysis of the social functions of ADs. Section 3 moves on to the topic of evaluation and explains what this involves. Section 4 puts forth a model that will help us visualize what it means for a speaker to present material from a specific perspective and invite the hearer to view the material from the same perspective. The model is informed by Du Bois's (2007) theory of stance and Langacker's (2000, 2008) stage model. Section 5 presents and discusses additional examples of TOP/AFF-ADCs to show how the model applies to different types of context and attitude. Section 6 is a conclusion.

2 ADCs and context

One of the hurdles we face when we look at (2) above as an isolated example is, in general, our inability to determine how to interpret the sentence and, in particular, how to identify the contribution of the AD in relation to an actual situation of use. In order to study the sociopragmatics of ADs – that is, in order to understand how ADs and the structures in which they are embedded are employed in particular interactions (see, for example, Culpeper 2009: 108) – we need to observe them in their social contexts and determine how they interact with the different contextual factors involved. This section delineates and discusses these contextual factors. It also revisits (2) to fill in the contextual blanks.

Culpeper (2009: 180) recognizes three types of context that range from the most general to the most local; these are the sociocultural context, the situational context, and the co-textual context (see also LoCastro 2003). Culpeper goes on to write that 'sociopragmatics should primarily, though not exclusively, concern itself with the medial [situational] context and the phenomena that constitute it.' To him, the sociocultural context is concerned with 'macro, more sociologically-oriented considerations' and may be too broad for sociopragmatics, while the co-textual context is concerned with 'micro, more linguistically-oriented considerations' and as such may be considered too narrow (2009: 180). I agree with this characterization; however, I also agree that the focus should not be exclusively on situational context. As far as this study is concerned, it is important to pay attention to both the macro and the micro aspects of context. With respect to the macro-level sociocultural context, its importance lies in the fact that ADCs are inherently evaluative, often targeting shared values, beliefs, and norms. Or, as Du Bois puts it, they 'invoke presupposed systems of sociocultural value' (2007: 139). To understand this evaluative aspect of ADCs, we often find ourselves having to deal with the broader sociocultural context. Micro co-textual context is also important for our analysis of ADs because part of an AD's contribution may be determined only by looking closely at its most local context: namely, the utterance in which it is realized and often the utterances that come before and/or after.

I now turn to discussing the three types of context separately, beginning with the broader sociocultural context.

2.1 The sociocultural context

This broader cultural milieu is omnipresent in a community and comprises all the social values, norms, and beliefs that members of a given community live by and take for granted. Social values, norms, and beliefs may translate into explicit rules and laws put forth by social institutions (religious, legal, and so on). Such rules and laws may enforce, allow, or prohibit certain behaviors or states of affairs, either in certain situational contexts (in certain types of activity carried out by certain social actors) or across the board in all aspects of community life (Goffman 1967: 7; Fraser 1990: 220; Watts 2003; Spencer-Oatey 2005: 97–8; Culpeper and Haugh 2014: 200). For example, being pious is one of the values of Islam. This translates into a number of rules and expectations. One such rule is the requirement that all Muslims pray five times a day. They may pray more than five times if they wish, but they may not pray without performing *wudhu* (ritual washing performed before prayer). See also Martin and White (2005: 45, 52) and Section 3 on evaluation below.

Values, beliefs, and norms may also take the form of less explicit social expectations as to what sorts of behavior are considered appropriate or inappropriate in any given context. For example, in the context of the Syrian soap opera *ba:b l-ha:ra* 'the neighborhood gate,' women are expected to cover their faces in public places; they are also required to cover their faces in private places if men who are not immediate family members are present. This is why when men enter a house, including their own house, they must announce themselves by saying the reduplicated expression *yalla: yalla:* loudly and clearly; *yalla: yalla:* may roughly correspond to the English expression *A man has arrived*. This allows women other than immediate family members (for example, women who are visiting) to cover their faces.

2.2 The situational context

The situational context pertains to the immediate context in which an interaction takes place. It coincides with Goffman's ([1964] 1972: 63) 'social situation,' which he defines as 'an environment of mutual monitoring possibilities, anywhere within which an individual will find himself accessible to the naked senses of all others who are "present", and similarly find them accessible to him' (cited in Culpeper and Haugh 2014:198).

Drawing on such work as Ochs (1996), Spencer-Oatey (2002, 2005, 2008), and Aijmer and Anderson (2012), I identify two situational factors that will be relevant to the analysis of the social functions of ADs – and arguably of non-core arguments and other interpersonal pragmatic markers in general. These are, first, the identities of the speaker and hearer, and second, the type of activity they are involved in. These factors determine the social actors' rights and obligations in an interaction.

The first situational factor that social actors bring to an interaction is their identities or sense of who they are. More importantly, they bring to an interaction those aspects of their identities that they think others attribute or should attribute to them. These include 'their roles, positions, relations, reputations, and other dimensions of social personae' (Ochs 1996: 424).

Brewer and Gardner (1996) recognize three levels at which social actors define themselves. These are the individual, group, and relational levels. Individual identity encompasses 'those aspects of the self-concept that differentiate the self from all others' (Brewer and Gardner 1996: 83). It includes personality traits (for example, being honest or shy) and acquired skills (for example, being a good chef), among other things. Part of a social actor's individual identity is her reputation, which is based on the person's history, including things she has previously said or done.

Group identity corresponds to group membership and contains 'those aspects of the self-concept that reflect assimilation to others or significant social groups' (Brewer and Gardner 1996: 83). I will include under this category a related type of identity labeled as 'collective identity.' Collective identities differ from group identities in that they involve less 'personalized bonds of attachment' and 'are derived from common identification with some symbolic group or social category' (Brewer and Gardner 1996: 83). To illustrate from the show *ba:b l-ha:ra* 'the neighborhood gate,' an individual may perceive herself as a resident of *ha:ret l-dˤabeʕ* 'the neighborhood of the hyena' (group identity) or as a Damascene, a Syrian, and/or an Arab (collective identity). For our purposes, both group and collective identity will be referred to as group identity.

Finally, relational identity has to do with a social actor's relationships with others and the roles she plays in these relationships. Relational identities are ideally 'derived from intimate dyadic relationships,' such as kinship relations (for example, parent–child); 'they also include identities derived from membership in small, face-to-face groups that are essentially networks of such dyadic relationships,' such as relations between community residents or club members (Brewer and Gardner 1996: 83). They may in addition be derived from more formal dyadic relationships (for example, employer–employee, doctor–patient).

Another situational factor that should be taken into account in analyzing the social functions of ADCs is the type of activity or speech event that the social actors are involved in: for example, a family argument around the dinner table, a committee meeting behind closed doors, or a casual chat during a street encounter. Levinson (1979) defines 'activity' as 'a fuzzy category' that includes 'goal-defined, socially constituted, bounded events with *constraints* on participants, setting, and so on, but above all on the kinds of allowable contributions' (368). Activity types are important, Levinson goes on to show, because they help social actors determine what types of utterance are appropriate and how an utterance will be understood. For example, the term *yalla:* in Levantine Arabic has multiple uses. A speaker may use *yalla:* or, more emphatically, *yalla: yalla:* to indicate that she will be ready shortly (the rough equivalent of *I'll be right there* in English) or to instruct an individual or a group to get going (the equivalent of *Come on, let's go* in English).

However, as I mentioned earlier, when *yalla:* is used by a man during the activity of entering a house in a conservative Muslim community, it is understood as an announcement for women who are not immediate relatives to cover their faces. Men are required to use it every time they enter a house, without exception, and they must utter it loudly and as a reduplicate, *yalla: yalla:*. Women do not use *yalla: yalla:* in this sense.

The identities of the social actors and often the activity type they are involved in determine their rights and obligations or the expectations they have of each other in an interaction. Every social actor comes to an interaction with sociality rights or entitlements that she claims for herself in that interaction (Spencer-Oatey 2002: 540; Spencer-Oatey 2008: 13). Sociality rights may be divided into two types: equity rights and association rights. Spencer-Oatey defines these two types as follows:

> *Equity rights*: We have a fundamental belief that we are entitled to personal considerations from others, so that we are treated fairly: that we are not duly imposed upon, that we are not unfairly ordered about and that we are not taken advantage of or exploited, and that we receive the benefits to which we are entitled. There seem to be two components to this equity entitlement: the notion of cost–benefit (the extent to which we are exploited, disadvantaged or benefitted, and the belief that costs and benefits should be kept roughly in balance through the principle of reciprocity), and the related issue of autonomy–imposition (the extent to which people control us or impose on us). (Spencer-Oatey 2002: 540)

> *Association rights*: We have a fundamental belief that we are entitled to social involvement with others that is in keeping with the type of relationship that we have with them. This principle helps to uphold people's interdependent construals of self, and seems to have three components: involvement (the principle that people should have appropriate amounts and types of 'activity' involvement with others), empathy (the belief that people should share appropriate concerns, feelings and interests with others), and respect (the belief that people should show appropriate amounts of respectfulness for others). (Spencer-Oatey 2005: 100)

Whereas sociality rights as entitlement reflect what a social actor believes she deserves or what she is owed in an interaction, obligations have to do with what she owes others in recognition of their sociality rights; see Brummel and Parker (2015) for a more thorough discussion.

Now we turn to a more local type of context.

2.3 The co-textual context

At a more micro level lies the co-textual context. This may be broadly defined as the actual linguistic interaction that the ADC is a part of. It includes the utterances that come before and after: that is, the utterances that the ADC is a reaction to and the utterances that are a reaction to the ADC. It is also important to recognize the type of social act that the ADC performs, whereby a social act is defined as 'socially recognized goal-directed behavior: for example, a request, an offer, a compliment' (Ochs 1996: 410; LoCastro 2003, 2012). Finally, the co-textual context includes all the contextualization cues that help hearers infer the functions of the different utterances including the ADC itself. These cues may be verbal (for example, a polite *if you don't mind*) or non-verbal (for example, a dismissive tone). Contextualization cues often charge utterances with evaluative meaning as part of the speaker's intention, and thus affect how the hearer may understand these utterances (Alba-Juez and Thompson 2014: 10; Gumperz 1982, in Gumperz 2001: 221). As far as ADs are concerned, the co-textual context, including the utterance they are embedded in, provides the material that makes it possible for the AD to perform its role as an interpersonal pragmatic marker and to be evaluated as one; see Verhagen (2005: 151) for a similar observation.

2.4 ADs in context

Now let us revisit (2), taking into account the elements of context we have just discussed. The example is part of an event that takes place in an early twentieth-century Damascene neighborhood in Syria. Neighborhoods of the time were closed, self-contained entities, each with its own gate. In the series, the neighborhood in question, *ḥa:ret l-dˤabeʕ* 'the neighborhood of the hyena' is a well-off neighborhood, coveted by the surrounding less affluent neighborhoods. There is a strong sense of community in *ḥa:ret l-dˤabeʕ*; if someone needs help, there is a community-wide obligation to help that person out. This sense of community and charity is closely linked to Islamic belief and the teachings of the Holy Qur'an. Based on all this, we can say that, at the sociocultural level, the neighborhood values cooperation and compassion, and condemns wrongdoing.

Now let us take another look at (2) spelled out as an utterance within a larger context in (6). This will allow us to examine more local contextual factors.

6. Context: The sheikh of the neighborhood, Sheikh Abd l-Alim, has just returned from a trip. He learns from the neighborhood mayor, Abu Saleh, about the burglary in Abu Brahim's house. Both social actors are decent, charitable men who are respected and looked up to by all their fellow residents.

    The sheikh: lah lah lah lah !   kil ha-l-ʃi: sˤa:r
    　　　　　　 no no no no !   all this-the-thing happened
    　　　　　　 bi-ɣya:b-i: ?   miski:n ya: ʔabu: bra:hi:m ,
    　　　　　　 in-absence-my ?   poor   VOC   Abu Brahim ,
    　　　　　　 sirʔet   ha-l-dahaba:t   rah tiksir-**lo**   dˤahr-o .
    　　　　　　 robbery   this-the-gold.coins will break-**him.D** back-his .
    　　　　　　 'This is unbelievable! All this happened while I was away? Poor Abu Brahim. The robbery of his gold coins will break **[him]** his back.'

Abu Saleh: ʔe: walla:h, ya: ʃe:x ʔabd l-ʕali:m ... min
            yes by.God, VOC sheikh Abd l-Alim ... from
            le:let l-ha:dse, ʔabu: bra:hi:m ʔaʕed
            night the-incident, Abu Brahim staying
            bi-l-be:t, la: byitʕlaʕ w-la: bifu:t ...
            in-the-house, NEG go.out and-NEG go-in ...
            'Unfortunately, yes, Sheikh Abd l-Alim. Since the incident, Abu Brahim
            has not left the house.'
The sheikh: l-muʔminu mirʔa:tu l-muʔmin. ʔana:
            the-believer mirror the-believer. I
            min raʔy-i: nru:h laʕind-o w-nwa:si-i ...
            in opinion-my go to-him and-console-him ...
            'Believers support each other. I say that we visit him and console him.'
Abu Saleh: w-ha:da: l-ʃi: lli: biddo ysʕi:r, ya:
            And-this the-thing that want happen, VOC
            ʃe:x ʔabd l-ʕali:m.
            sheikh Abd l-Alim.
            'And this is exactly what we shall do, Sheikh Abd l-Alim.'
From *ba:b l-ha:ra* 'the neighborhood gate' – Season 1 – Episode 2 – 00:26:50 – SYR   2.6

At the situational level, the speakers are two good, unselfish, law-abiding men. They are in complementary leadership positions in the community: Sheikh Abd l-Alim is the only religious leader in the neighborhood, and Abu Saleh is the top political leader. The speech event is a semi-official activity. The two men are in a meeting; Abu Saleh is bringing Sheikh Abd l-Alim up to speed about recent events that took place while the latter was away from the neighborhood. At the most local co-textual level, Sheikh Abd l-Alim begins with an expression of disbelief *lah lah lah lah*, which roughly translates to 'I can't believe what I hear,' to express his shock that a burglary took place while he was away. This is followed with an expression of compassion *miski:n* 'poor guy' referring to the victim, Abu Brahim, and an ADC. Abu Saleh's response indicates that the two men are in agreement.

The different contextual factors involved in this example can help us conclude what kind of evaluation Sheikh Abd l-Alim anchors to the burglary event and to Abu Brahim, the referent of the AD. This brings us to the topic of evaluation.

3 ADs and evaluation

I started the chapter by pointing out that ADCs allow a speaker to present the at-issue content of her utterance, along with her evaluation of it or elements in it, from the angle of the AD and her evaluation of its referent. By so doing, the speaker instructs the hearer to view the main message, the referent of the AD, and the evaluations anchored to them from her perspective, and invites the hearer to agree with her. This social function of ADCs reminds us of Leech's (1983: 56) interpretation of Halliday's (1970, 1973) interpersonal function of language. Leech defines this function as follows: 'language functioning as an expression of one's attitude and an influence upon the attitudes and behaviours of the hearer.'

The expression of attitude is also known as evaluation, which is one of the functions that pragmatic markers in general may serve (Östman 1982: 150–2, in Brinton 1996: 39). What does it mean if a linguistic element is evaluative? We start with Thompson and Hunston (2000: 5), who define evaluation as follows:

> [E]valuation is the broad cover term for the expression of the speaker or writer's attitude or stance toward, viewpoint on, or feelings about the entities or propositions that s/he is talking about. That attitude may relate to certainty or obligation or desirability or any of a number of other sets of values.

Alba-Juez and Thompson (2014) adopt the same definition and add that evaluation, as an expression of the speaker's or writer's attitude, is a dynamic phenomenon that often anticipates an evaluative response from the hearer (Alba-Juez and Thompson 2014: 13). The response may be verbal or non-verbal. Of course, the hearer may decide not to share his stance at all, but the stance is bound to be there.

The terms stance, attitude, and evaluation are often used interchangeably in the literature. For the purpose of this study, I adopt Thompson and Hunston's distinction between stance and evaluation in the above quotation. Under this view, '*stance* would be a more abstract concept, and *evaluation* would be the actual verbal realization or manifestation of the stance' (Alba-Juez and Thompson 2014: 10). I take attitude to be synonymous with stance: that is, attitude is more abstract, and evaluation is an expression of attitude.

Stated a little more elaborately, stance is a subjective matter that involves the stance holder's awareness of her own identity, beliefs, and values, as well as the community-wide values, beliefs, and sociocultural norms (Lyons 1982: 102, in Iwasaki and Yap 2015: 3). Stancetaking or evaluation as an expression of stance is intersubjective in that it profiles the subjectivity of the speaker, often in anticipation of the hearer's response, making it available for the hearer to scrutinize in accordance with his belief system. During the act of stancetaking, the speaker and hearer become involved in 'the sharing of experiential content (for example, feelings, perceptions, thoughts, and linguistic meaning)' (Zlatev, Racine, Sinha, and Itkonen, 2008: 1). In other words, stancetaking engages the subjectivity of the speaker with the subjectivity of the hearer (Haddington 2004: 101, 107; Kärkkäinen 2006: 700; Du Bois 2007). When involved in an interaction, if the speaker and hearer know each other – for example, if they are friends, relatives, or members of the same community – this means that they are aware of each other's identities, values, and beliefs. They are also aware of the extent to which their individual values and beliefs coincide or are shared. If the speaker and hearer do not know each other (for example, they are strangers from different cultural backgrounds) or if they do not know each other well enough (for example, if they are strangers from neighboring communities that share some but not all values), this means that they are aware of how much (or how little) they know and of how much (or how little) they can assume about each other's identities, values, and beliefs. This type of awareness is intersubjective par excellence (see Traugott 2010: 33; Traugott and Dasher 2002, in Iwasaki and Yap 2015: 3). Intersubjectivity follows from our ability to view ourselves as intentional and mental beings with goals, beliefs, and thoughts, and our ability to perceive others as intentional and mental beings who may have different goals, beliefs, and thoughts (Tomasello 1999: 14–15; Verhagen 2005: 3–4). Linguistic intersubjectivity is the way a language allows its speakers to express their awareness of their own and the addressee's attitudes and beliefs (Traugott 2003).

What types of stance or attitude do speakers express in communication? Martin and White (2005) recognize three types of evaluation: affect – judgment – appreciation. Affect, they maintain, 'is concerned with registering positive and negative feelings,' such as (un)happiness (for example, *I feel (un)happy about x*), (in)security (for example, *I feel confident/anxious about x*), or (dis)satisfaction (for example, *I feel excited/bored about x*) (Martin 2003: 173; Martin and White 2005: 42, 49). Culpeper and Haugh (2014: 197–8) label this type of evaluation as interpersonal emotions, which they identify as a subcategory of interpersonal attitudes. Du Bois (2007) calls it 'positioning.'

Judgment is concerned with the assessment of behavior as ethical or unethical, praiseworthy or reprehensible, and so on. Such assessment is in accordance with agreed-upon social norms or 'normative principles' (Martin and White 2005: 35). As I stated above, some of these norms take the form of laws and rules put in place by legal or religious institutions, while others are normally monitored and enforced informally by community members, usually via gossip and storytelling, but also through comments and criticism (Martin and White 2005: 45, 52).

Appreciation, on the other hand, deals with aesthetics. It targets objects rather than behavior. The term 'objects' includes all things, living and non-living, abstract and concrete. Appreciation focuses on the value of objects as (un)remarkable, (un) appealing, and so on (Martin and White 2005: 45, 59). Appreciations normally follow from 'our "reactions" to objects (do they catch our attention; do they please us?), their "composition" (balance and complexity), and their "value" (how innovative, authentic, timely, and so on)' (Martin and White 2005: 56).

Judgment and appreciation, Martin and White hold, may be considered as 'institutionalized feelings, which take us out of our everyday common sense world into the uncommon sense worlds of shared community values' (2005: 45). The uncommon sense world also includes social facts, defined as 'cognitive constructs which provide the rules and material for our daily behaviour' (Martin and White 2005: 49; see also Sinha and Rodriguez 2008: 360; Culpeper and Haugh 2014: 197–8).

We should note that the relation between behavior, objects, and individuals, on the one hand, and our judgments and appreciations of them, on the other hand, along with all the shared community values and social facts that these judgments and appreciations are based on, is not always straightforward: thus Martin and White's characterization of shared community values as 'uncommon sense.' As I explain in Haddad (2013), two societies may arrive at two different social facts based on the same social behavior. For example, in some countries, it is conventional for women to cover their hair or faces, but it is acceptable for them to breastfeed their babies in public. Other countries may have a pretty liberal social dress code in the sense that there are very few restrictions on how people – both women and men – may or may not dress, but women may have to carry out campaigns to promote women's right to breastfeed in public (see, for example, Riordan 2005).

This said, we should add that evaluation not only relies on the presence of shared values and social facts but also constitutes them by helping to confirm, redefine, negotiate, or introduce them. If this were not the case, the shared values and social facts of a given community would be forever the same.

Evaluation or stancetaking as an expression of affect, judgment, or appreciation is done intersubjectively rather than subjectively, whereby the speaker is aware not only of her own subjectivity (attitudes, values, beliefs, and so on) but also of the hearer's subjectivity. In addition, the speaker is aware of the situatedness of her utterance, along with all the contextual factors involved, and of how much of that situatedness the hearer is aware of. In this sense, evaluation becomes more a matter of social relationships than of truth conditions, as Martin and White (2005: 94) observe.

When applied to ADCs, appreciation is normally the form of evaluation that targets the AD embedded in these constructions. The speaker invokes aspects of the individual, social, and/or relational identities of the AD referent that are relevant to the context of interaction in order to accomplish one of the following:

- maintain and reinforce existing identities
- challenge and redefine existing identities
- explore the status of uncertain identities, or
- introduce and negotiate new identities.

Concerning the at-issue content of ADCs, if it designates a behavior, the speaker's evaluation of it takes the form of judgment. If it designates a state of affairs, the evaluation takes the form of appreciation. The speaker evaluates the at-issue content from the angle of the AD and the appreciation she anchors to its referent in order to accomplish one of the following:

- maintain and reinforce a shared belief, value, or norm
- challenge and redefine a shared belief, value, or norm
- explore the status of an uncertain belief, value, or norm, or
- introduce and negotiate a new (probably personal and not yet shared) belief, value, or norm.

For related discussions, see Brinton (1996: 31 and works cited there); Ochs (1996: 424); Thompson and Hunston (2000: 6); Iwasaki and Yap (2015: 1).

Let us now take another look at (2) and the expanded version of the same example in (6), along with the contextual factors discussed in Section 2. Our task is to identify the types of evaluation that Sheikh Abd l-Alim anchors to the burglary and to the referent of the AD, Abu Brahim. Sheikh Abd l-Alim evaluates the burglary event as devastating in terms of its effect: it breaks one's back, he holds. He feels sad about what happened. He states that Abu Brahim will most likely be hurt by the event, and by doing so reinforces the identity that Abu Brahim has just acquired as a victim. He also reinforces the shared cultural understanding that illegal behavior, like the discussed burglary, is destructive and that individuals targeted by such behavior need the compassion of their community. Sheikh Abd l-Alim is aware of his hearer's stance on these issues. He invites his hearer to evaluate the burglary and its effect from the perspective of the AD referent, Abu Brahim, as a victim and fellow resident.

This brings us to the next topic: how can we model, in Leech's words, the speaker's attempt to exercise 'influence upon the attitudes and behaviours of the hearer' by using an ADC?

4 ADCs and the stancetaking stage model

We established above that when two people engage in an interaction, they each bring their own subjectivities to the communicative event. The interaction is in fact their opportunity to share their subjectivities (Haddington 2004: 107) and to participate in what Verhagen (2005: 9) calls 'intersubjective coordination.' To explain how this happens, I adopt a combination of Du Bois's (2007) theory of stance and Langacker's stage model. I start with an overview of the former.

4.1 Theory of stance

Du Bois's theory of stance is an interdisciplinary theory informed by research in linguistics, sociology, anthropology, and cognitive science, among other fields. Linguistically, it subscribes to Halliday's systematic functional linguistics, a theory of language and grammar that deals with linguistic structures and forms in contextualized discourse and explains the particular functions that these structures and forms serve in discourse situations. In his discussion of stancetaking, Du Bois holds:

> One of the most important things we do with words is take a stance. Stance has the power to assign value to objects of interest, to position social actors with respect to those objects, to calibrate alignment between stancetakers, and to invoke presupposed systems of sociocultural value. (2007: 139)

This power is exercised in contextualized interactions. That is, it is exercised via utterances, which are 'inherently embedded in their dialogic contexts,' rather than sentences, understood as decontextualized structures (Du Bois 2007: 148).

Du Bois (2007) further maintains that a stancetaking act involves at least two individuals or social actors, *Subject 1* and *Subject 2*, and an object of stance that could be a thing, an individual, an event, or a state of affairs, and that serves as a target of evaluation. These three entities form what Du Bois calls the stance triangle in Figure 2.1. *Subject 1* and *Subject 2* are presented as SP (speaker) and HR (hearer), respectively,

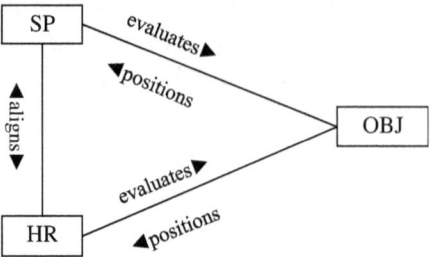

Figure 2.1 Stance triangle

and the object of stance as OBJ. The speaker introduces an object of stance; she evaluates it (for example, as good or bad) and positions herself toward it (for example, whether she is satisfied with it or not). She invites the hearer to attend to the same object of stance and to evaluate it and position himself toward it in the same way. If the hearer agrees with the speaker, the result is positive alignment or convergence. Otherwise, the result is negative alignment or divergence. Convergence and divergence do not need to be viewed as a dichotomy of alignment; rather they may be viewed as a range of possible positions (see Haddington 2004).

Using the stance triangle to capture what is happening in (2)/(6) above, we can say that Sheikh Abd l-Alim presents the burglary and its effect on the victim as an object of stance, and invites his hearer, Abu Saleh, to attend to the same object as a shared focus. He epistemically evaluates the effect of the burglary as devastating by speculating that it will break Abu Brahim's back, and he positions himself as shocked and saddened by it. He invites his hearer, Mayor Abu Saleh, to evaluate the object of stance and to position himself toward it in the same way. In (6), Abu Saleh responds by confirming that the effect of the burglary on Abu Brahim has in fact been devastating, stating that Abu Brahim has not left the house since his gold coins were stolen. The outcome of this intersubjective coordination is positive alignment between the speaker and hearer. Convergence in this case goes beyond a nod of agreement and leads to action: the speaker and hearer decide to visit the victim to console him.

How does the AD feature in all this? The AD, I argue, is another object of stance that triggers its own stance triangle. Together with the main message of the ADC, they form a relationship of interdependence. The interpretation of the AD, as well as its evaluation, is contingent not only on the speaker's familiarity with its referent (in the case of (2)/(6), the referent is Abu Brahim) but also on the different types of context: co-textual – situational – sociocultural. In (2)/(6), the interpretation and evaluation of the AD depend not only on the speaker's acquaintance with its referent, Abu Brahim, but also on the at-issue content and the burglary it depicts, on the identities of the speaker and hearer, and on the overall sociocultural values that they share and live by. It is in this context that the AD referent is portrayed as a victim who deserves the interlocutors' compassion.

At the same time, the AD is a linguistic tool of perspectivization à la Verhagen (2005, 2010). By using an AD, the speaker construes the main message from the angle of the dative and invites the hearer to attend to it in the same way. In (2)/(6), the burglary is lamented as a sad event, not in absolute terms but from the perspective of the victim and the effect it has on him. Note that the speaker could alternatively portray the burglary as outrageous from the perspective of the neighborhood as a community and the potential threat that it poses to its residents.

In order to capture this interdependence between the AD and the rest of the utterance that it is embedded in, I adopt a hybrid of Du Bois's (2007) stance triangle and Langacker's (2000, 2008) stage model. The stage model will also help us incorporate the contextual factors discussed in Section 2.

4.2 The stage model

The stage model was proposed by Ronald Langacker as part of his comprehensive usage-based theory of language, Cognitive Grammar. It is meant to mirror our perceptual experience when we engage in an interaction (Langacker 2000: 24; Langacker 2008: 354–60; see also Taylor 2010; Maldonado 2002). Langacker holds that our perceptual experience with the world is similar to watching a play. He adds:

> We cannot see everything at once, so viewing the world requires the directing and focusing of attention. From the maximal field of view, we select a limited area as the general locus of attention (the analog of looking at the stage). Within this region, we focus our attention specifically on certain elements (analogous to actors and props). (Langacker 2008: 356)

The stage model contains an off-stage region and an on-stage region. The social actors, our speaker and hearer, are labeled as 'conceptualizers' or 'subjects of conceptualization' in this model. They reside in the off-stage region and function as viewers of a play. The object of stance is labeled as 'object of conceptualization' in the stage model. It occupies the onstage region and as such is the center of attention. The speaker (SP) presents an object of conceptualization (OBJ) and invites the hearer (HR) to attend to it in a specific way. This is illustrated in the general stage model in Figure 2.2; see also Haddad (2013).

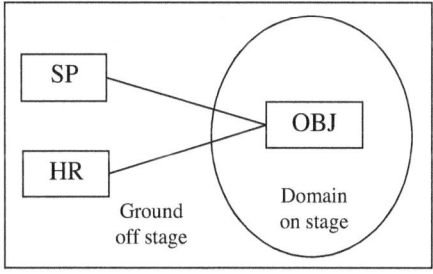

Figure 2.2 General stage model

The stage model accommodates the contextual factors discussed in Section 2. The off-stage region is labeled the Ground. It contains more than just the conceptualizers (SP and HR) and the speech event or interaction that they are involved in. It also contains the immediate circumstances of the interaction, such as the time and place of speaking, the social identities of the speaker and hearer, their shared knowledge of social norms and sociocultural values, and so on (Taylor 2010: 346; Verhagen 2005: 5). Importantly, the Ground portion of the stage model signifies that the speaker and hearer do not come to an interaction with tabula rasa backgrounds; rather, they engage in an interaction as social actors with a sociocultural package. If these social actors belong to the same culture or community, which is the case in all the data in this study, they are aware not only of their own identities and sociocultural package, but also of the other interlocutors' identities and sociocultural package. They are also aware of the fact that their interlocutors come to the interaction with similar presuppositions. As Ochs (1996) maintains, social actors take these social dimensions and sociocultural backdrop, along with 'their conceptualization of the social situation at hand,' into account when they make linguistic choices (410).

The on-stage region is the focus of attention. It is a virtual spot to which the gaze of the speaker and hearer is directed. It contains the object of conceptualization profiled by the speaker's utterance. It also comprises an appropriate domain of instantiation against which the object of conceptualization is established as an event distinct from other events of the same type (Langacker 2008: 132–6; Taylor 2010: 346–9). For our purposes, an utterance's domain of instantiation is the time and space in which the utterance takes place and the type of activity in which its speaker is engaged, along with the sociocultural expectations linked to the activity at this specific time and in this specific space. The domain of instantiation helps delimit the scope of an AD. For example, if an AD profiles an individual, the maximal scope of the AD referent is the individual as a whole, along with every identity (trait, role, relation, and so on) she has. However, only specific aspects of that identity, and thus the immediate scope of the AD, are relevant for the profiled event. Within the domain of instantiation, only the immediate scope of an AD is foregrounded (see Langacker 2008: 63).

One way to illustrate how the domain of instantiation as described here delimits the scope of a pronoun referent is to visualize a wedding ceremony. The identity of the person performing the ceremony encompasses more than just the role of an officiant; she may be also a sister, a daughter, and a friend. However, when she says during the ceremony, 'By the power vested in me . . . ,' only the speaker's role as an officiant is instantiated by the pronoun *me* within that domain. For a more detailed breakdown of the stage model, see Langacker (2010: 425–6).

To combine the two models, the stance triangle and the stage model, I propose the stancetaking stage model in Figure 2.3. In this model, SP (speaker) and HR (hearer) stand for *Subjects/Conceptualizers 1 and 2*. The roles of the speaker and hearer will be specified shortly. For our purposes, the object of conceptualization (OBJ) comprises the at-issue content or main message of an ADC: that is, it refers to the whole utterance minus the AD. It may designate – or profile – an event, a situation, a request, or a threat, among other things, directing the hearer's attention to it.

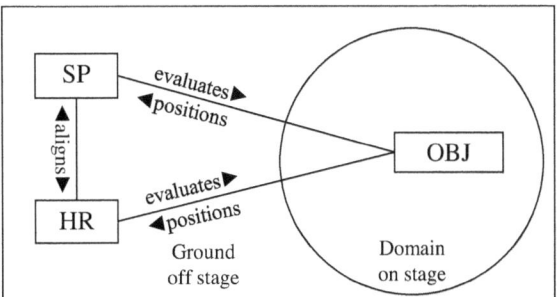

Figure 2.3 Stancetaking stage model

In future figures, the terms 'evaluates,' 'positions,' and 'aligns' will be deleted from the model. The following relations continue to hold, however. The line connecting SP and OBJ signifies that the speaker profiles the object, evaluates it, and positions herself toward it. Evaluation is understood as Martin and White's (2005) 'judgment' and 'appreciation,' while positioning corresponds to Martin and White's 'affect' which is concerned with registering positive and negative feelings; see Section 3 for more details. The line connecting HR and OBJ signifies that the hearer's attention is directed to the profiled object; it also signifies that the hearer engages with OBJ from the perspective that the speaker presents. The line joining SP and HR stands for mutual engagement and the resultant alignment between the two. Alignment may be convergent, divergent, or anywhere in between (Du Bois 2007: 163).

To elaborate, the speaker initiates the stancetaking act by profiling an event or a situation – that is, by presenting it on stage as an object of conceptualization. By so doing, she directs the hearer's gaze to it. The speaker also evaluates the object of conceptualization and positions herself toward it and with respect to the social value that it invokes. For example, the speaker may profile a friend's financial contribution to an orphanage, evaluate it as admirable, and position herself affectively as touched and impressed. Stancetaking events like this have broader sociocultural implications. They allow the speaker to confirm, redefine, or negotiate the value linked to a specific event or behavior. For example, in this case, the speaker may confirm the positive social value attached to the friend's act of charity. Importantly, she invites the hearer to attend to the profiled event in a special way: that is, she invites him to look at it from her perspective.

The hearer is the recipient of the stance initiated by the speaker and a respondent/reactant to it. By being a respondent/reactant, the hearer is also a stancetaker who positions himself toward the object of conceptualization. In addition, he may choose to agree or disagree with the speaker. In the example about the speaker's friend's financial contribution to an orphanage, the hearer may question the charitable act by casting some doubt on how the money may be handled in charitable organizations and suggest that a contribution in the form of goods (for example, diapers, food) may have been wiser. By doing so, the hearer positions himself affectively as touched but epistemically as uncertain about the effectiveness of the friend's behavior. In terms of alignment, the hearer shows that he is not in total agreement with the speaker.

As the example illustrates, from the perspective of the hearer, the target of evaluation includes not only the profiled event, behavior, or individual but also the speaker's attitude toward these elements. The speaker invites the hearer to attend to this attitude as an object of evaluation in itself, to consider it as valid, and to adopt it (Du Bois 2007: 141). This remark is in line with the following observation by Langacker (2009: 266):

> [I]f a conceptualizer adopts an epistemic stance toward an event or situation, that itself constitutes an event or situation at a higher level of organization. . . . That is, the situation of a conceptualizer adopting an epistemic stance toward a process can itself function as an object of conception toward which an epistemic stance can be adopted.

How does this work? The on-stage object of conceptualization is one of the entities or propositions (small squares in Figure 2.4) that the speaker accepts as valid. Collectively, these propositions constitute the speaker's dominion or 'view of reality' (Langacker 2009: 130–1). The dominion includes the speaker's attitudes toward the propositions and all underlying beliefs.

Importantly, when the speaker presents an object of conceptualization on stage and evaluates it, she places both the object and her evaluation of it in the hearer's field, or 'scope of potential interaction,' as Figure 2.5 demonstrates. Of course, the hearer also has his own dominion or view of reality. He considers whether he wishes to accept or reject the profiled object and/or the evaluation as a part of his dominion. This tension is presented as a broken line in Figure 2.5. The result may be acceptance or rejection, depending, among other things, on the linguistic choices that the speaker makes. The speaker may make certain linguistic choices in order to present the object of conceptualization from a certain perspective or vantage point. In this way, she manipulates the viewing arrangement or the way the hearer would view the object being profiled (Langacker 2008: 73–8). The purpose is to influence the hearer's 'thoughts, attitudes, or even immediate behavior' (Verhagen 2005: 10).

The whole cycle, including the introduction of the object of conceptualization and the speaker's evaluation of it into the hearer's field, the tension this induces,

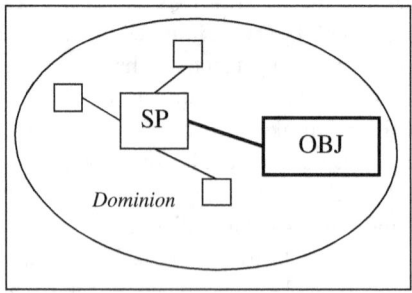

Figure 2.4 Speaker's dominion

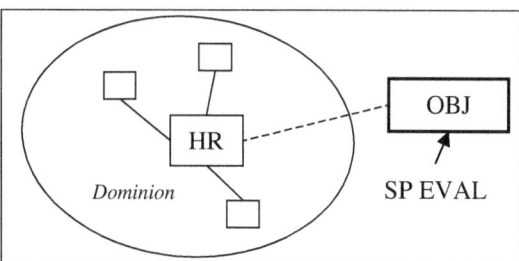

Figure 2.5 Hearer's dominion

and the result (acceptance or rejection, which Du Bois labels as alignment), is what Langacker (2009) calls the control cycle. He further holds that

> we can see the control cycle as being utterly ubiquitous in our own experience. . . . At the cognitive level, we entertain new ideas, assess them for their possible validity, and resolve the matter by either accepting them in our conception of reality or else excluding them. (Langacker 2009: 259–60)

Upon the hearer's response/reaction, the speaker in her turn becomes a recipient of the hearer's stance and may choose to align or disalign with him.

In all this, stancetaking is not only about the stancetakers each positioning themselves with respect to a stance object but also about them aligning with each other. It is about a speaker and hearer using language both for informative purposes and for argumentative purposes in order to achieve convergent alignment (or divergent alignment if they so desire) with each other; see, for example, Verhagen (2005: 9–10, building on Owings and Morton 1998 and Anscombre and Ducrot 1989) and Johnstone (2009: 31). Social actors opt for linguistic choices that best help them achieve this goal. We will see in the next subsection that ADs are one of the choices that speakers make in order to manage the way hearers view a profiled object. In this sense, the AD helps boost the argumentative potency of their utterances.

Before we proceed, a word about the roles of the speaker and hearer is in order. *Speaker* and *hearer* are complex terms that involve multiple subroles or footings (Goffman 1981; Levinson 1988; McCawley 1999). The speaker and hearer do not assume the same participant roles all the time; rather, they 'constantly change their footing' (Goffman 1981: 128). According to Goffman, a speaker may assume one or more of the following roles:

- animator or 'the sounding box from which the utterances come'
- author or 'the agent who puts together, composes, or scripts the lines that are uttered'
- principal or 'the party to whose position, stand, and belief the words attest' (Goffman 1981: 226).

Ideally, a speaker can be all three, but she does not have to be. For example, if I read another linguist's paper aloud at a conference because she could not physically be there, I am only the animator of that paper; I am neither the author nor the principal. If I answer questions on behalf of my colleague, trying to say what she would say if she were there, even if I do not agree with her views, I am the animator and the author of the answers, but I am not the principal.

For the purpose of this study, I will assume that the speaker is the initiator of the stancetaking act; in Levinson's (1988) terms, this is the person who assumes the production role. Also, the speaker is always an animator, author, and principal unless there is a reason to consider her differently. Regarding the role of the hearer, I will assume the following unless otherwise specified. The hearer is always a ratified participant who is expected to hear the speaker's utterances. He is channel-linked, where channel linkage is defined as 'the ability to receive the message' (Levinson 1988: 174). He is an addressee: that is, he may assume the speaking role in response to the speaker (Goffman 1981: 133). Finally, the hearer is a target: he is a person whose thinking the speaker may be trying to influence with the hope that he would align with her.

4.3 ADCs in the stancetaking stage model

When a speaker uses an ADC, she places the entity that the expression refers to on stage and makes it the focus of attention. In the previous section, we referred to this entity as an object of conceptualization or a profiled object. A profiled object may be abstract or tangible; it may be a living or non-living thing. If an expression is uttered with the intention of giving an order, we will consider the order itself to be the expression's conceptual referent or its profile.

In addition to entities, expressions may also profile relationships (Langacker 2008: 67). Consider, for example, the two expressions *the books by the table* and *the table by the books*. Each profiles two elements, *the books* and *the table*, as well as the relation between them: they are next to each other. The two elements do not have the same prominence in both expressions, however. In *the books by the table*, *the books* is the primary focus of attention; Langacker (2008, 2010) refers to such elements as the trajector (*tr*). *The table*, on the other hand, is the less prominent participant in the relation; it is of secondary focal prominence and is referred to as the landmark (*lm*). The opposite is true of the same elements in *the table by the books*.

Similarly, when a speaker uses an ADC, she profiles two entities, as well as the relationship between them. The two entities are, first, the at-issue part of her utterance (for example, an order, a request, a suggestion, an assertion), which we will continue to refer to as OBJ; and second, the referent of the AD (that is, topic/affectee, speaker, hearer, or subject of at-issue predicate). Both entities are prominent but to varying degrees. The OBJ or the at-issue content is the primary focus or the trajector (*tr*) that is being described and evaluated. The AD is the non-at-issue entity; it is the secondary focus or landmark (*lm*). The ADC profiles the relationship between the OBJ and the AD. The two are anchored to each other and are viewed as

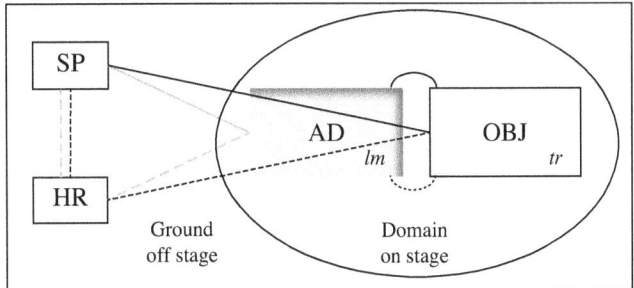

Figure 2.6 Stancetaking stage model for ADCs

interdependent rather than independent. As the model in Figure 2.6 demonstrates, the speaker places the OBJ and AD on stage in a special viewing arrangement. She places the AD, along with her evaluation of its referent, as a screen through which the OBJ must be viewed and evaluated. The AD in this model may be considered, in Verhagen's (2005: 50–1, 78) words, as an 'argumentative operator' and the element 'expressing the relevant perspective,' while the OBJ is 'the thought being perspectivized.' The AD does not alter the truth condition of the at-issue content of the ADC – that is, the OBJ – but it influences the conclusion to be drawn from it; see Verhagen (2005: 60–9) for a similar discussion of *let alone* as an argumentative operator.

The solid lines connecting the speaker to the AD and the OBJ signify that she already accepts them and accepts the relation between them as part of her dominion. She instructs the hearer to attend to the AD and OBJ and invites him to identify with her perspective on them and on the relationship between them. The broken lines connecting the hearer to the AD and the OBJ, as well as the AD and the OBJ, represent the tension that the hearer experiences as he decides whether to accept or reject either of the profiled entities, the relationship between them, and/or the speaker's evaluation of them as a part of his dominion. The broken lines connecting the speaker and hearer stand for the pre-alignment tension between the two social actors during interaction; the outcome may be positive or negative alignment, or something in between.

Now let us re-examine (2)/(6) and the conversation between Sheikh Abd l-Alim and Abu Saleh about the burglary in the light of the model in Figure 2.6. In his ADC, Sheikh Abd l-Alim profiles two entities: first, the burglary and its effect on Abu Brahim as the OBJ/trajectory, and second, the AD referent, Abu Brahim, as a landmark. He is shocked and saddened by the burglary and he evaluates it negatively. As to the AD/landmark, within the context of the dialog and the construction in which it is embedded, its referent is instantiated primarily as a victim of the burglary. The speaker feels bad for him as a victim and evaluates him as worthy of compassion. Any other identity that the AD referent may have, be it his individual identity (for example, as a fair and pious person), his group identity (for example, as a resident of the community), or his relational identity (for example, as a friend or a father), may contribute to the interpretation and evaluation of the AD in (2)/(6), but it remains subservient to the new victim identity instantiated in this context. That is, these other identities may only contribute to making the AD referent a more serious victim, but they are not the primary reason the speaker uses an AD.

In all this, the speaker invites the hearer, Abu Saleh, to evaluate the profiled AD referent and OBJ and to position himself toward them in the same way. He employs the AD as an argumentative operator that expresses the perspective through which the OBJ must be viewed. Without the AD, the conversation may still have proceeded in the same way, but it also may have proceeded differently. The speaker and hearer could have continued to focus on the burglary and its effect in general rather than focusing on the victim and the effect that the burglary has on him. For example, as a response to Sheikh Abd l-Alim's statement that the burglary will break Abu Brahim's back, Abu Saleh could have responded by delineating other damages that the burglary would cause; these include instilling fear among the residents and giving an excuse to the local police department to interfere in the neighborhood's affairs. By using an AD, however, Sheikh Abd l-Alim makes sure that the conclusion drawn from his comment about the burglary is related to the AD referent as a victim, and in fact he is successful in this; Abu Saleh's response focuses on how the victim is homebound and hardly functional in the aftermath of the burglary. In this case, the hearer's positive alignment with the speaker allows the latter to continue the discussion and propose that they visit and console the victim. As Verhagen (2005: 9–10) puts it, engaging in cognitive, intersubjective coordination of this type 'comes down to, for the speaker/writer, an attempt to *influence* someone else's thoughts, attitudes, or even immediate behavior'.

5 Putting it all together

ADs as interpersonal pragmatic markers play an argumentative and perspectivizing role in interaction. They are a choice that speakers make depending on the stance they would like to take within a given context, and depending on the conclusion they want their hearer to draw. To illustrate further how speakers employ ADs in interaction, I present a few additional examples of TOP/AFF-ADCs.

First, however, I start by revisiting (3) above, presenting it in its context as (7). In this excerpt, the coppersmith, Abu Khater, tries to play devil's advocate and presents the possibility that Idaashari, the man everyone thinks is behind the recent burglary, could be innocent. The barber and herbal doctor, Abu Esam, thinks that this is unlikely. He believes that Idaashari is guilty. To drive this argument home, he mentions that Idaashari has a criminal record. However, instead of providing a list of this record (for example, in 1909 he stole from your store; in the same year he broke into Abu Samir's house), he refers only to the one time Idaashari broke into his hearer's store. Importantly, by placing his hearer on stage via the AD, he instructs him to evaluate the event from the perspective of his identity as a victim. In all this, Abu Esam wants Abu Khater to arrive at the same conclusion: Idaashari is likely to be guilty.

7. Context: Abu Khater, the coppersmith, is having his beard shaved by Abu Esam, the neighborhood barber and physician. Meanwhile, the two men are discussing the recent burglary in the neighborhood and the likelihood that Idaashari, the suspect, is guilty.

Abu Khater: barkatan   ha-l-riʒʒa:l   mazlu:m ?
           perhaps   this-the-man   unjustly.accused ?
           'Perhaps this man has been unjustly accused.'
           ...
Abu Esam: zalame   sˤa:heb   sawa:be?   ha:d .
           man   of   criminal.record   this .
           walla: kaʔann-ak   nasya:n   ʔinno
           by.God   as.if-you   forgot   that
           huwwe   saraʔ-lak   dikka:n-tak ,   w-ma:
           he   robbed-you.D   store-your ,   and-NEG
           xalla: fi:-ha: wala: nha:se !
           leave   in-it   a.single piece.of.copper !
           'The man has a criminal record. I swear you seem to have forgotten that he robbed [you] your store, and that he didn't leave a single piece of copper in it!'
Abu Khater: laʔ   ma:-ni: nasya:n ,   bas   l-riʒʒa:l
            no   NEG-me   forgot ,   but   the-man
            ʕam-biʔu:l   ʔinn-o   ta:b   w-htada: .
            PROG-say   that-he   repented and-found.guidance .
            'No, I didn't forget, but the man is saying that he has repented and found God.'

From ba:b l-ḥa:ra 'the neighborhood gate' – Season 1 – Episode 4 – 00:44:40 – SYR   2.7

Abu Khater proves difficult to influence. As the stage model in Figure 2.7 illustrates, he accepts as part of his dominion the conceptualized AD and at-issue content, and he briefly accepts the perspective. However, he does not believe that the thought being perspectivized is enough of an argument to convict Idaashari. Thus, in terms of alignment, the outcome is divergence.

Example (8) is from a Jordanian show. In this excerpt, the protagonist of the show, a family man called Abu Awwad, expresses discontent to his wife Um Awwad because she and their daughter Najah went shopping and spent money on what he considers unnecessary things. The speaker uses a first-person plural dative -*lna:* 'us.D'

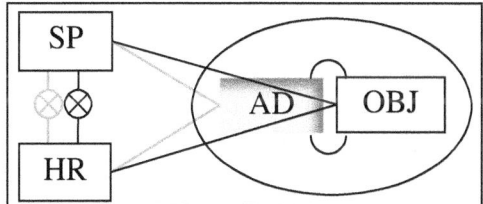

Figure 2.7 Stancetaking stage model of (7)

(in italics) as an argument in *tiʃtiru:-lna:* 'buy-us.D' to refer to all the members of the family as beneficiaries and recipients. However, he uses a first-person singular dative as a non-core argument to profile himself as an affectee. This is so because he believes that he is the only one concerned about the money and thus the only one affected by his wife and daughter's purchases. By using a TOP/AFF-AD, he invites his wife to evaluate her and Najah's behavior from his perspective as the main breadwinner of the family who is concerned about the family budget. By doing so, he affirms this role as part of his relational identity with respect to them. Interestingly, as Figure 2.8 demonstrates, the wife does not discredit his financial concern or his role in the family; thus, she accepts the profiled AD. However, she disagrees with main message of his utterance, believing all the purchases that she and Najah made were necessary.

8. Context: Um Awwad and her daughter Najah went to the market and did some shopping. They bought things for the house, but they also bought personal things (for example, make-up products). When they arrive home, Abu Awwad is shocked by the amount of merchandise they bought.

    Abu Awwad: wadde:na:-kun   ʕa-l-muʔassase   tiʃtiru:-*lna:*   kammen
    　　　　　　　we.sent-you   to-the-institution buy-*us.*D   a.few
    　　　　　　　ɣaradˤ   byilzam   bi-l-be:t .   ʔiʃi: byilzam
    　　　　　　　things   be.useful in-the-house . something be.useful
    　　　　　　　w-ʔiʃi: ma: byilzam ,   ʒa:ybi:n-**li:**
    　　　　　　　and-something   NEG   be.useful , you.brought-**me.D**
    　　　　　　　yya:ha: kul-ha: yaʕni: ?
    　　　　　　　it   all-it   this.mean ?
    　　　　　　　'We sent you to the market to buy a few things for the house. I see things we need and things we do not need. Is it reasonable that you bought [**me**] it all?'

    Um Awwad: kul l-ʔaɣra:dˤ   lli: ʃtare:na:-ha: btilzam-na: .
    　　　　　　All the-merchandise that   we.bought-it   be.useful-us .
    　　　　　　'All the things we bought are things we need.'

From *ʔabu: ʕawwa:d* 'Abu Awwad' – Season 1 – Episode 6 – 00:02:50 – JOR

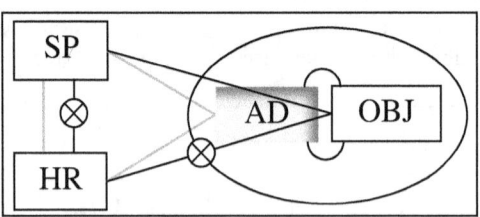

Figure 2.8 Stancetaking stage model of (8)

The ADC in (9) comes from a Lebanese talk show that deals with social problems. This specific episode focuses on daughter-in-law/mother-in-law relations.

The speaker tries to explain why she has interfered with her son's marriage and made him divorce his wife. According to her, if the wife is not a good person, an early divorce before the couple have any children is better than a divorce later on when there are children involved. Interestingly, the speaker chooses to use a TOP/AFF-AD that profiles her as an affectee. The reference to potential grandchildren instantiates only one part of her identity: her role as a potential grandmother. By placing herself on stage as an affectee, she invites the audience in the studio and the viewers at home to evaluate her behavior and her positive evaluation of it from her perspective as a potential grandmother of grandchildren in a broken family. The AD in (9) serves another function. The speaker is aware that mothers-in-law are usually characterized as malicious, and in fact the younger women in the show make constant remarks to this effect. By using an AD in the capacity just described, the speaker justifies her interference with her son's marriage and characterizes it as a necessary evil: that is, the speaker uses an AD in order to redefine the individual and relational identity that the show has given her, up to this point, as an abusive mother-in-law. By using an AD, she portrays herself as a concerned potential grandmother instead.

9. Context: A mother-in-law has managed to get her son to divorce his wife after five months of marriage. When criticized, she says:

   ʔiza: min   ʔawwal   ma: ʃift-a: ,   ʔaxle:ʔ-a: miʃ
   if   from   beginning that   I.saw-her,   morals-her   NEG
   mni:ħa , w-muʕa:mlet-a: miʃ   mni:ħa (.) baddi:
   good,   and-treatment-her NEG   good (.)   should.I
   ʔintˤur   baʕd   sine,   la-tʒib-**li:**   wle:d ,   walad
   wait   another year,   till-she.bring-**me.D**   children ,   child
   w-walade:n ,   w-baʕde:n   ʃamʃitˤ-un   la-l-wle:d ,
   and-two.children ,   and-then   drag-them   for-the-children ,
   ʃamʃitˤ-un   maʕ-i: ,   w-nizˤab-a: la-l-mara:?
   Drag-them   with-me ,   and-kick.out-her   for-the-woman?
   'If from the outset I could see that she had no morals and that she did not treat us well, would it have been better for me to wait another year until she begot [me] children – one or two children – that I would have to drag along with me (in all this mess) and kick the woman out?'

From *ʔaħmar bi-l-xatˤ l-ʕari:dˤ* 'a red line with a thick stroke' – Season 5 – *Daughter-in-Law and Mother-in-Law* – 01:00:20 – LEB

2.9

The speaker in (9) could have made other AD choices that would have perspectivized the main message differently. As Figure 2.9 shows, the speaker had at least three other options. She could have profiled herself as the mother of a divorced son who would have to raise his children without a wife; as such, she would be placed on stage as a concerned mother instead of a concerned grandmother. Alternatively, she could have used an AD that refers to her son as an affectee. In both cases, her behavior would have been evaluated as an attempt to spare her son the consequences

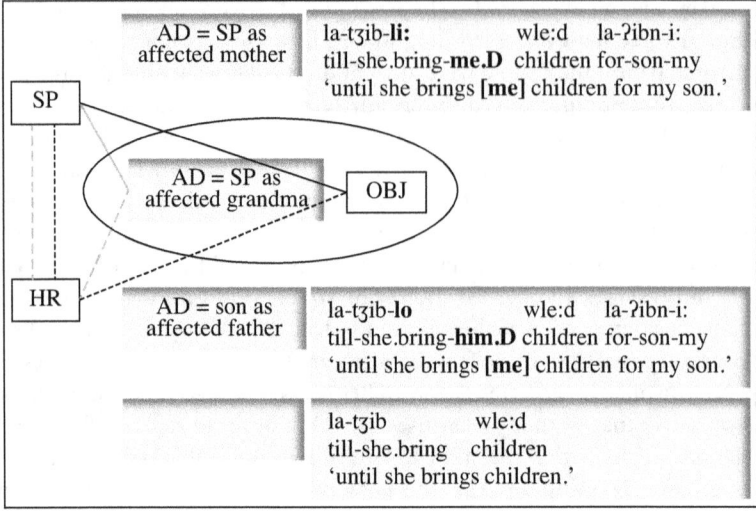

Figure 2.9 Stancetaking stage model of (9)

of a bad marriage. Had she done so, it would have been easier for the guests to point out that the issue was her son's problem and that she should not have interfered. A third option would be for her not to use an AD at all, in which case the gaze would have been exclusively focused on the potential children. Given that the show is about daughter-in-law/mother-in-law relationships and given that the speaker is interested in redefining her identity as a concerned grandmother rather than a bad mother-in-law, she portrays herself as an affectee and an object of empathy in relation to the most vulnerable: namely, the unborn grandchildren.

Finally, (10) is an excerpt from a play by the Lebanese director and playwright George Khabbaz. The example is interesting because it contains two TOP/AFF-ADs that reference the same person: Farah. Yet, each instance negotiates a new identity of the same individual in order to provide a different perspective on the at-issue content of the utterance. Issa, a policeman, brags about all the information he gathers about the residents' private lives in the areas he patrols while he is on duty. When Farah asks him to stay away from his house, he tries to make an argument that he should be allowed near Farah's house in order to protect him and his property. He uses an AD in order to place Farah on stage as a potential victim of property theft and to present his suggestion more convincingly. Farah makes a counterargument, namely, that Issa should stay away from him and his house. He uses an AD to place himself on stage as a potential victim of privacy theft, and he instructs Issa to evaluate his concern from this perspective. That is, in each case the speaker invites the hearer to evaluate his proposal (the main message of his utterance) from the perspective of the new identity. Note that Farah does not reject the potential identity that Issa negotiates for him. In other words, Farah tacitly accepts that if there is no police officer around, he may in fact be a victim of property theft. Nevertheless, he is willing to take on this new identity in order to avoid one he considers worse: victim of privacy violation.

10 Context: Farah, a vendor in a shoe store, finds out during a conversation that Issa, a policeman and an acquaintance, passes the time during his service at night eavesdropping on people's conversations while lurking outside their houses, only to gossip about them later. The conversation continues as follows:

Farah: ʔuːʕa   tʔaddim   sˤoːb   bayt-i: haː !
        don't.you   come.close   toward   house-my   INTER !
        'Don't you come close to my house, I am warning you!'

Issa: w-barki   feːt   haraːme   w-saraʔ-**lak**
        and-maybe   entered   thief   and-stole-**you.D**
        ʃiː ?
        something ?
        'What if a thief broke in and stole [you] something?'

Farah: miʃ   ahsan   maː   yfuːt   haraːme   teːne
        NEG   better   that   enter   thief   another
        w-yisriʔ-**liː**:   xsˤuːsiyyeːt-iː ?
        and-steal-**me.D**   privacy-my ?
        'Wouldn't that be better than having another thief steal [me] my privacy?'

Issa: ʔanaː   haraːme   yaː   farah ?
        I   thief   VOC   Farah ?
        'Do you consider me a thief, Farah?'

From *El Professeur* 'the professor' – 00:6:10 – LEB   2.10

6 Conclusion

This chapter started with the premise that to understand the social function of ADs, we need to look at ADCs as utterances embedded in their social context. We identified three types of context, ranging from the broadest to the most local. These are the sociocultural context, the situational context, and the co-textual context. Additionally, given that ADCs are inherently evaluative – there are no neutral ADCs – we took a closer look at evaluation and what it constitutes. We found out that evaluation as an expression of stance or attitude is an intersubjective matter made possible via interaction. By using an ADC, the speaker presents an object from a specific perspective and invites the hearer to attend to it in the same way. To capture how this works, I put forth the stancetaking stage model. In this model, when a speaker uses an ADC, she places two objects on stage: the at-issue content of her utterance and an AD. She invites the hearer to attend to the at-issue content as the primary focus of her utterance; at the same time, she instructs him to view the at-issue content through the AD as a filter. In this sense, the AD becomes a perspectivizer and the at-issue content becomes the perspectivized thought.

In the following chapters, we will use the tools presented here in order to analyze speaker-oriented, hearer-oriented, and subject-oriented attitude datives.

Notes

1. To visualize better how the presence of the AD allows the speaker to anchor her feelings overtly to its referent, compare the two expressions *I'm glad!* and *I'm happy for him!*, both uttered authentically/non-sarcastically by a speaker upon learning that a friend has just bought a new car. While both may mean roughly the same thing, only the latter overtly anchors the speaker's happiness to the friend. The former remains vague as to whether the speaker is happy for her friend or whether she is happy that the friend will finally stop asking her for a ride.
2. All the speakers in 1 through 3 are men.

3

Speaker-Oriented Attitude Datives in Social Context

1 Introduction

Social actors are normally responsible for what they say or write, unless they indicate explicitly that they are not because they are reporting another person's words, or saying what they believe another person would say in the same situation. Despite this inherent responsibility, speakers often remain off stage, profiling only their utterance and its conceptual reference on stage. Sometimes, however, they choose to place themselves on stage as well via the explicit mention of a first-person pronoun. For example, a speaker may choose to make a comment in reference to an experience by saying *I am exhausted* as opposed to *This is exhausting*. The affective stance profiled in the former expression is explicitly anchored to the speaker, unlike the stance profiled in the latter expression which may be anchored not only to the speaker but also to anyone who is or could be in the same position (Langacker 2008: 78; Langacker 2009: 145).

More specific to our purposes are situations in which speakers assume responsibility for their utterance by highlighting a certain aspect or aspects of their identity. Take the exchange between a father and his daughter in the English example in (1).

1. Father: 'I'm your legal guardian, and this is me ordering you to tell us what happened.'
   Daughter: 'Since when have you ever cared about being my dad?'
   Father: 'Just answer the question! Aria, please.'
   Daughter: 'No,' she spit out. 'There is nothing to tell. Nothing happened . . .'[1]

The main message of the father's utterance is the order *tell us what happened*. The rest of the utterance contains material not immediately relevant to the main message: namely, the profile of the father as an authority figure who is legally qualified to give the order and who is entitled to receive a response from his daughter.

By using the expression *legal guardian*, the father profiles himself as representing an institutionalized form of authority. Importantly, as the stancetaking stage model in Figure 3.1 demonstrates, he invites his daughter to evaluate the directive (the object or OBJ in our model) from the perspective of himself as her guardian; he instructs her to take the directive seriously because of who he is or what he represents. The daughter as a hearer (HR) may now evaluate the OBJ, the speaker (SP), and the relation between the two, and decide how she wishes to position herself with regard to them. The daughter's first response is an explicit evaluation of the father's profile of himself; she questions the authenticity of the role he attributes to himself and aligns negatively with him, as the x-marks in Figure 3.1 indicate. This is when the father abandons this profile of himself and asks the question again, this time pleading rather than legally requiring an answer. Only now does the daughter deal with the order itself, indicating that she does not want to obey it.

Languages may offer their speakers different means to place themselves on stage in some capacity. These means allow the speakers to highlight an aspect of their identity that is relevant to the context. Placing themselves on stage also makes it possible for speakers to anchor the main message of their utterance and their evaluation of it explicitly to themselves as participants in the communicative event. One option that is available to speakers of Levantine Arabic, in its different varieties, is the insertion of an optional speaker-oriented attitude dative or SP-AD, exemplified in (2) through (5). The SP-ADs are in boldface.

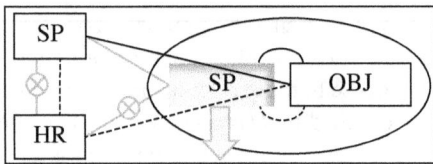

This is me giving you this order by virtue of my identity as your legal guardian.

Figure 3.1 Stancetaking stage model of the first half of (1)

2. Context: A boss is giving instructions to his employee.
   bitdˤabdˤib-**li**:   ʔardˤ   l-dya:r   mni:ћ ,
   you.arrange-**me.D** ground   the-house   well ,
   w-bitzˤabbitˤ   l-ʔahwe   miʃa:n   l-tiʕza:ye .
   and-you.fix   the-coffee   for   the-funeral.reception .
   'Put [me] the house in order and fix the coffee for the funeral reception.'
   From *ba:b l-ha:ra* 'the neighborhood gate' – Season 1 – Episode 10 – 00:11:30 – SYR

3. Context: A grandmother explains to her grandson how she felt when he moved to Canada.
   dayman   ydˤall   ʔalb-i: ʕle:-k. . .   ʔu:l   ki:f
   always   remain   heart-my   on-you . . .   I.say   how

```
baʕatu-u,      ki:f    ʔimm-o       ʔila-a     ʔalb    tiʔʕud    bale-e .
they.sent-him, how     mother-his   to-her     heart   stay      without-him .
ma:   fi:     ɣayr-o,       baʕatit-li:    yye:h    ʕa-Canada !
NEG   there   other-him,    she.sent-me.D  him      to-Canada !
```
'I was always worried about you. I would ask myself: how could they let him leave? How could his mother have the heart to stay without him? She has no other son, she sent [me] him to Canada!'

From *te:ta: ʔalef marra* 'grandma, a thousand times' – 00:27:00 – LEB

4. Context: A mother finds out that her son, Raad, uses Facebook. When she asks what Facebook is, her daughter explains that it is an internet application that people may use to learn what is going on in other people's lives. The mother answers:

```
yaʕni:       ha:da:   raʕed,   ga:ʕed    biʃamʃim-li:    ʔaxba:r
this.mean    this     Raad,    sitting   sniff-me.D      news
l-na:s        mitl    l-nasa:wi:n    ?!
the-people    like    the-women      ?!
```
'Do you mean to tell me that this Raad of mine spends his time sniffing [me] other people's news the way women do?!'

From *nahafa:t ʕaylitna:* 'our family anecdotes'– Facebook – 00:01:00 – JOR   3.4

5. Context: A man complains about how some Palestinians express their patriotism by taking photos of themselves at destroyed sites.

```
w-illi:       bigul-lak,    kulma:      tinhadd     <tˤa:ga>
and-who       say-you.D,    whenever    destroyed   <window>
bi-l-guds,          biru:h    yitsˤawwar-li:     fo:g      l-hʒa:r
in-the-Jerusalem,   he.go     take.photos-me.D   above     the-stones
ta:ʕ-a: .
POSS-it .
```
'And then there are those who, whenever a small structure is destroyed in Jerusalem, they go and take [me] photos of themselves on top of its debris.'

From *watˤan ʕa-watar* 'a nation on a string' – *ʔiftita:h l-xa:zu:q* 'the opening ceremony of the screw' – 00:00:50 – PAL   3.5

So what does a SP-AD in Levantine Arabic profile? A SP-AD, like all ADs in Levantine Arabic, and arguably interpersonal pragmatic markers in general, functions primarily as a perspectivizer that instructs the hearer to view the at-issue content of an utterance from a specific point of view. More specifically, a SP-AD performs two functions, as Figure 3.2 schematically illustrates. First, it allows the speaker to conceptualize herself explicitly as a form of authority by virtue of an aspect of her identity that is relevant to the context. Additionally, by using a SP-AD, the speaker assumes responsibility for the attitude she expresses toward the main message. In other words, the attitude may no longer be attributed to a generalized experiencer or generalized attitude holder, but instead is necessarily attributed to the speaker herself. Recall the contrast discussed earlier between *I am exhausted* and *This is exhausting*.

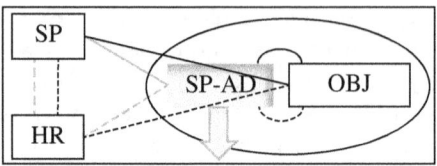

- This is me telling you this in my capacity as a *form of authority*.
- I own the attitude I express toward OBJ.

Figure 3.2 Stancetaking stage model of SP-ADCs

Languages in general allow speakers to project aspects of their identity that are relevant to the context, so Levantine Arabic is not exceptional in this respect. On occasion, speakers may even overtly state the aspect or aspects of their identity that they wish to project, as the English example in (6) demonstrates; see also (1) above.

6. 'Before you even start, **this is me talking to you as a friend, not your boss**. I don't want to see either of you burn out, so I'm expecting you to take some time off . . . '

From Nulli Para Ora's 2012 *Dragon Moon*

A SP-AD is not as explicit, however, and its semantic contribution is limited to profiling the speaker as having or representing a form of authority. The nature of this authority is not invariant. It is contingent on a number of contextual factors and their interrelation. These factors are discussed in Chapter 2 and fall into three categories: first, the broad sociocultural context (shared values, beliefs, and norms); second, the immediate situational context (speaker and hearer identities; activity type); and third, the co-textual context (speech act; contextualization cues).

Before we proceed, a word on 'authority' is in order. Authority is defined as 'a form of legitimation [that is] legally, culturally, and interactionally constructed' (Wilson and Stapleton 2010: 50). The legitimation is based on a person's individual identity (for example, physical strength, level of expertise), group identity (for example, gender, institutionalized role), and/or relational identity (for example, kinship). Thus, a police officer's order to a driver to pull over is taken seriously because she represents a legal authority. Similarly, a professor's input on a topic related to her field of study is often deemed worth considering because it comes from an individual with academic authority. A statement by the Food and Drug Administration (FDA) that a new medicine is safe for humans to consume is considered legitimate because it comes from an appropriate voice of authority (Wilson and Stapleton 2010: 50–1).

The definition of authority sounds very similar to Brown and Gilman's (2003) definition of power. However, here I distinguish the two. Authority is an attribute that a social actor claims for herself and that society acknowledges based on the social actor's identity or identities. A social actor may choose to exercise her authority or not. If she does, the exercise of authority may result in power, but it does not have to. For example, a police officer has the legal authority that allows her to order a driver to pull over; however, whether this authority results in power is to be determined on a case-by-case basis. If the driver disobeys, the police officer's authority does not translate into power. Similarly, a medical doctor has the professional authority that allows her to prescribe a treatment for her patients. However, whether every patient allows this authority to translate into power and thus lead to action, such as the taking of medication as prescribed, may be up to the patient (Wilson and Stapleton 2010).

Authority manifests itself in daily interactions and is affirmed, redefined, or negotiated via linguistic choices that social actors make during these interactions (Wilson and Stapleton 2010: 50–1). We will see in the following sections that a SP-AD is one of the choices that Levantine Arabic speakers may make to profile themselves as possessing authority within a given context. The use of SP-ADs is dictated by the form of authority that a speaker believes she has. At the same time, employing a SP-AD contributes to the social construction of this authority.

Now we turn to the analysis of specific instances of SP-ADCs. I will organize the discussion according to the illocutionary domain. We will start with the most local co-textual context before we move on to discuss broader situational and sociocultural contexts.

2 SP-ADCs as directives

Speakers may use SP-ADCs as directives. Simply put, directives are 'attempts . . . to get the hearer to do something' and include requests, orders, invitations, and advice (Searle 1976: 11; see also Huang 2014: 133). When a speaker uses a SP-ADC as a directive, she profiles three entities: first, the directive; second, herself as a form of authority; and third, the relation between the first and the second. She construes herself as responsible for the directive and qualified to give it. She also construes herself as entitled to the action that it requires the hearer to take, whereby entitlement is defined as the individual's belief that she deserves 'the time, resources, and considerations' of others (Brummel and Parker 2015: 130). All this is in accordance with the speaker's and hearer's rights and obligations as dictated by their respective identities and the requirements of the context. A SP-ADC used as a directive is a reflection of the speaker's belief that she has the right to expect her instructions to be followed by the hearer, and as such it is the hearer's obligation to comply. Specifically, use of this type of SP-ADC instructs the hearer to evaluate the directive from this perspective.

Activities in which SP-ADCs are used as directives range from public activities (for example, in the workplace) to private, household activities. Let us refer to these SP-ADCs as SP-AD directives. In order to organize the discussion in this section, I will divide SP-AD directives into categories based on the type of authority that the SP-AD profiles. These are hierarchical authority, knowledge authority, and reciprocal authority.

2.1 SP-AD directives and hierarchical authority

I define hierarchical authority as a form of legitimation derived from at least one aspect of a social actor's identity that ranks her legally or socioculturally superior to other social actors in an interaction. Hierarchical authority is potentially coercive. It allows the social actors who have it to force those whom they outrank to comply with their desires. If the latter refuse to comply, hierarchical authority allows the former to penalize them in one way or another: for example, by firing or grounding them. This form of authority, and the superiority it bestows upon those who have it in relation to those who do not, are normally activity-specific and culture-specific. For example, age as a group identity feature may rank one group superior to another and accordingly be relevant in household activities but not so much so in workplace activities. Similarly, gender may be a relevant identity feature in relation to hierarchical authority in early twentieth-century Damascene household activities but less so in contemporary household activities in the same or a different region.

SP-AD directives may profile the speaker as a form of hierarchical authority. They are normally uttered with an assertive tone and a falling contour; see, for example, Wichmann (2012: 195), who observes that a falling contour is characteristic of requests spoken by 'more powerful participants'.

2.1.1 SP-AD directives and hierarchical authority in the public sphere

We begin with SP-ADCs used as orders and requests in interactions in the public sphere. These are workplace-related or community-related interactions that take place outside the nuclear and extended family. One of the most common cases of such SP-AD directives occurs between supervisors and subordinates (for example, employer and employee). The exchanges in (7) and (8) are examples from the Syrian soap opera *ba:b l-ha:ra* 'the neighborhood gate.' In both exchanges, the employer speaks with an assertive tone.

7. Context: Abu Shihab owns a barn. In this scene, he gives instructions to Nader, one of his employees, to take care of a customer.

    Abu Shihab: ya: na:dir .
                VOC   Nader .
               'Nader.'
    Nader: ʔmo:r ,   mʕallem .
            order ,   boss .
            'Tell me, Boss!'
    Abu Shihab: hammil-**li**:   ʕaʃr   ʃwa:la:t   hintʕa   w-ʕaʃr
               load-**me.D**   ten   bags   wheat   and-ten
               ʃwa:la:t   ʃʕi:r   la-ʕamm-ak   ʔabu: yu:sef   ʔawa:m
               bags   hay   for-uncle-your   Abu Youssef   immediately
               ʕa-l-sari:ʕ .
               on-the-quick .

SPEAKER-ORIENTED ATTITUDE DATIVES IN SOCIAL CONTEXT 59

'Load **me** ten bags of wheat and ten bags of hay for Mr. Abu Youssef immediately, right away.'
Nader: ha:dʕer , mʕallem .
          'At your service, Boss!'
From *ba:b l-ha:ra* 'the neighborhood gate' – Season 1 – Episode 6 – 00:28:20 – SYR   3.7

8. Context: Abu Esam is the neighborhood physician and barber. His son Esam works for him. A patient comes to Abu Esam with a hemorrhoid problem. Abu Esam asks his son to prepare a treatment for the patient:

Abu Esam: ʔab-i: ,   ʔalla: yirdʕa: ʕle:k ,   zʕabbit-**li:**
           father-my ,   may.God.be.pleased.with.you ,   fix-**me.D**
           dawa: l-bawa:si:r ,   w-ʕtʕi:-na: ʃaʔfet
           medicine   the-hemorrhoid ,   and-give-us   piece
           ze:t xarwaʕ   ...
           laxative   ...
           'Son, may God bless you, put [**me**] together the hemorrhoid medicine and bring us a piece of laxative.'
Esam: ʔamr-ak , ʔamr-ak .
           'At your service, at your service.'
From *ba:b l-ha:ra* 'the neighborhood gate' – Season 1 – Episode 9 – 00:24:50 – SYR   3.8

In both examples, the speakers Abu Shihab and Abu Esam place themselves on stage as authority in relation to the hearers Abu Nader and Esam. They anchor their order to their profile of themselves as bosses and instruct the hearers to evaluate the order from this perspective, as Figure 3.3 illustrates.

By using a SP-AD directive, the speakers in (7) and (8) do a number of things. They evaluate their orders as consistent with their rights and obligations, as well as the rights and obligations of their hearers. Additionally, they evaluate themselves as qualified (that is, they have the identity requirements) to give the orders they give, in the contexts where they give them, and to the persons they give them to. Accordingly, they feel entitled to the action that their orders require of the hearers.

The speakers in (7) and (8) also assume responsibility for the directives. In each case, the boss orders his employee to carry out an action that serves a third party (Abu Shihab's customer, Abu Esam's patient). By using a SP-AD, however, each

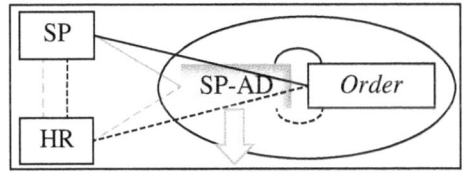

This is me telling you this as your boss.

Figure 3.3 Stancetaking stage model of (7) and (8)

speaker anchors the order to the profile of himself as boss. He instructs the hearer to evaluate the order from this perspective: that is, the hearer is instructed to view the order as coming from his boss as opposed to the individual that benefits from the action. In a possible world where Abu Shihab's customer and Abu Esam's patient would make their requests directly to the employees, one could imagine Nader and Esam directing their gaze to their bosses to get a nod of approval from them before they carry out any action. The SP-AD is the verbal form of that nod.

In all of this, each speaker invites his hearer to align with him positively in relation to three entities:

- the content of his order
- a conceptualization of himself as an authority figure
- the relation between points one and two above.

The hearer may choose to align with the speaker positively or negatively (or anywhere in between) with regard to these entities. As evident in their responses, the hearers in (7) and (8) position themselves positively in relation to all three points above, and thus the outcome is positive alignment in both cases.

Further evidence of how the speaker's authority is recognized by the hearer comes from (9). In this case, the speaker Abu Shihab uses a SP-AD directive, not to give his hearer an order but to offer him a hot beverage as a token of appreciation. As in the above examples, the use of a SP-AD profiles the speaker as an authority figure. This authority takes the form of a caring boss who is conscious of the hearer's right to fair consideration and to empathy. At the same time, even if the hearer does not wish to have tea, the SP-AD directive makes it hard for him to turn the offer down.

9. Context: In addition to owning a barn, Abu Shihab is the second-in-command in the neighborhood after the mayor, Abu Saleh. He asks Abdo, a young man who works at the public bath, to sub for the night guard, Abu Samo, who mysteriously disappeared. At one point before midnight, Abu Shihab stops by the gate and offers Abdo tea:

Abu Shihab: mse:k mse:k , rawwiʔ-**li**: ra:s-ak
hold hold , relax-**me.D** head-your
bi-ka:set ʃa:y , raḥ tdˤallak
with-cup tea , will you.remain
sˤaḥya:n la-l-sˤibiḥ .
awake till-the-morning .
'Here here, relax [me] yourself with a cup of tea. You will be awake till morning.'

. . .

((Abdo soliloquizing))
Abdo: walla: kbi:re ha:y . . . l-ʕadi:d bi-za:t
by.God big this . . . the-boss of-self
nafs-o , yʒib-lak barra:d l-ʃa:y , w-ka:se ?
self-his , bring-you.D kettle the-tea , and-cup ?

	ʔe:	walla:	ma:	sˤa:ret	la-ḥada:	ha:y .
	INTER	by.God	NEG	happened	to-anyone	this .

'I swear this is huge. The boss himself has brought you a kettle of tea and even a cup? I swear no one has had this privilege before.'

From *ba:b l-ḥa:ra* 'the neighborhood gate' – Season 1 – Episode 2 – 00:17:30 – SYR   3.9

It is important to note that the SP-ADs in the above examples, as well as in the examples we will examine below, are optional. If any or all of the speakers in (7) through (9) choose to use a directive without a SP-AD, the effect of the AD may still be there, but it will be part of the ground and thus not explicitly profiled. As Holtgraves (1994) observes, the speakers' high status is enough to prime the hearer to view their remark as an order. Since a SP-AD is used, however, its referent and effect are explicitly profiled by virtue of it being mentioned.

There are restrictions on who may use a SP-AD as a reflection of hierarchical authority. While a directive given by an employee to a colleague of equal or even higher rank is not inappropriate, a SP-AD directive is. Take (7), for example. The same directive to load the bags of wheat and hay may be given to Nader by a fellow employee of an equal rank as long as it does not contain a SP-AD. Only Nader's boss, however, may give the order in the form of a SP-ADC without being challenged. Both groups, employers and employees, are aware of each other's respective identities, as well as their rights and obligations. By using a SP-AD, the speakers affirm their identity as bosses in relation to their employees, and maintain in the process the shared sociocultural values and norms that inform their relationship.

Supervisor–subordinate relations are not limited to employer–employee interactions but also include interactions between employees of different ranks. This is evident in (10) and (11) from Lebanese Arabic. The speakers in both examples are employees themselves, but they outrank the hearers and are in charge of supervising them in the workplace. By using a SP-AD, the speakers affirm and maintain their identity and the form of authority linked to it.

10. Context: The head of the servants in a household tells his subordinates that he is unhappy with their work. He then adds, first addressing everyone, then addressing a female employee:

ʃiddu:-**li:**	ha:l-kon	ʃway
toughen-**me.D**	self-your	a.little

    . . .

ma:	tinsi:	tɣasli:-**li:**	maktab	l-ʔiste:z .
NEG	forget	wash-**me.D**	office	the-sir .

    'Work [me] harder. Don't forget to wash [me] the boss's office.'

    From *kizze:b kbi:r* 'a big liar' – 00:03:45 – LEB   3.10

11. Context: A psychiatrist in a psychiatric hospital gives a nurse instructions.

ʒmaʕi:-**li:**	ʕadad	min	l-mmardˤa:t
gather-**me.D**	number	from	the-female.nurses

	wi-l-mmardˤi:n,	w-nazliyy-un	ˤa-ʔisim	tle:te...
	and-the-male.nurses,	and-send.down-them	to-department	three...

'Gather [me] a number of nurses and send them to Department Three.'

3.11 From *fi:lm ʔameriki: tˤawi:l* 'a long American movie' – 01:48:15 – LEB

By using a SP-AD, the speakers in (10) and (11) instruct the hearers to deal with the directive as something they should take seriously, not only because it is necessary to maintain order in the workplace or to get the job done but also because it comes from them. In these examples, the presence of a SP-AD makes it so that a refusal to carry out an order would be considered a direct act of defiance against the speaker, unless properly justified. To illustrate, reconsider Abu Shihab's order to his employee, Nader, in (7) above. Let us assume that Nader has a bad history with Abu Youssef, the client. When Abu Shihab instructs Nader to take care of Abu Youssef's order, Nader could not just offer the answer in (12) without risking losing his job. He would have to show respect to his boss first, saying something along the lines of (13). With an answer like (13), Nader would acknowledge Abu Shihab's authority and thus positively align with him in this regard. His refusal to fulfill his boss's desire would only mean negative alignment with the boss regarding the order, as Figure 3.4 demonstrates.

12. ʔabu: yu:sef   ʔana: ma: ʔili: muˤa:tˤa:t   maˤ-o
    Abu Youssef   I   NEG   have   dealing   with-him
    'I refuse to serve Abu Youssef.'

13. ʔinte   ˤala: ra:s-i: mˤallem   bas
    you   on   head-my   boss   but
    ʔabu: yu:sef   ʔana: ma: ʔili: muˤa:tˤa:t   maˤ-o
    Abu Youssef   I   NEG   have   dealing   with-him
    'I have so much respect for you, Boss, but I refuse to serve Abu Youssef.'

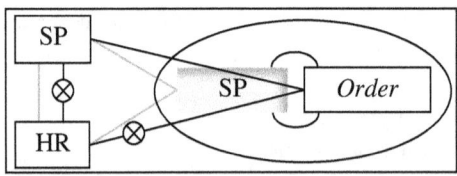

Figure 3.4 Stancetaking stage model of the order in (7) and the reaction in (13)

It should be noted that a speaker's right to fair consideration and involvement alone may be enough to qualify her to perform a directive, such as a request or an order, but it is not enough to qualify her to use a SP-AD directive. Consider the utterance in (14) from Lebanese Arabic, for example. In this case, a woman named Mazzika uses a SP-ADC and a rather offensive tone to ask the First Lady of Lebanon, who is giving a speech in a poor neighborhood, to speak up because she cannot hear. One could argue that Mazzika as a Lebanese citizen has the right to have access to the speech of the First Lady and to be involved in an activity that is meant for all citizens. If the First Lady does not speak more audibly, Mazzika will be denied this access; thus, she will not be treated fairly (equity right) and she will be denied her right of involvement in the activity (association right). All this, however, does not give Mazzika the right to instruct the First Lady to speak up via a SP-AD directive. By using a SP-AD, Mazzika incorrectly profiles herself as an authority in relation to the First Lady.

14. Context: The Lebanese First Lady visits a poor neighborhood in Beirut to talk to its residents. She barely starts talking when Mazzika, a woman on the third floor, says to her:
    ma: ʕam-bismaʕ-ik .   ʕalli:-**li**:   sˤawt-ik   ʃwayye !
    NEG   PROG-I.hear-you .   raise-**me.D**   voice-your   a.little !
    'I cannot hear you. Raise [me] your voice a little!'
    From *l-sayyida l-θa:niya* 'the second lady' – 01:02:30 – LEB   3.14

It should be noted that Mazzika's directive is inappropriate even without the SP-AD. Mazzika should have used a polite formula or at least a polite tone in order to frame her directive as a request rather than as an order. However, according to native speakers of the four varieties of Levantine Arabic, a SP-AD directive in cases like this is markedly more inappropriate than a directive without a SP-AD.

Mazzika's SP-ADC in (14) is followed with grunts of disapproval from her fellow citizens. Importantly, however, the First Lady evaluates the order as fair and caters to Mazzika's desire, agreeing to use a loudspeaker in order to make herself more audible. In other words, she aligns with Mazzika positively regarding the content of her order. However, unlike the hearers in (7) and (8) above, she does not directly respond to Mazzika; she only casts a quick and dissatisfied look at her. Thus, she tacitly aligns with Mazzika negatively with respect to her profile of herself as a form of authority, as Figure 3.5 illustrates, evaluating her as unqualified for the authority role she claims for herself via the SP-AD.

A speaker's hierarchical authority is rarely, if ever, absolute. Consider (15), for example. The exchange contains a TOP/AFF-AD that depicts a third party as an affectee (see Chapter 2 and Haddad 2016). However, this dative may easily be replaced with a SP-AD, placed between curly brackets in (15). Let us assume that (15) does in fact contain a SP-AD. The interaction involves a boss, Abu l-Nar, asking his employee, Abu Draa, to divorce his wife Shafiqa as an act of revenge against her

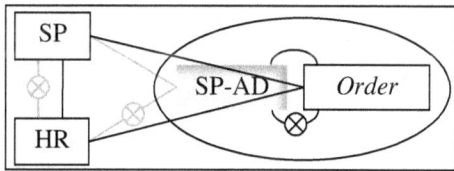

Figure 3.5 Stancetaking stage model of (14)

father, Idaashari. In the context of *ba:b l-ḥa:ra* 'the neighborhood gate,' only a man's father has the authority to perform a directive like this, something that viewers may witness in the first few episodes of Season 2 of the show. This means that Abu l-Nar's directive in (15) falls outside the scope of his authority in relation to the hearer. In his response, Abu Draa does not directly address the order or the authority of the speaker. Rather, he questions the relation between the two. In other words, it is not the nature of the order that Abu Draa questions; the order itself may, under the right circumstances, be evaluated as acceptable, even ethical, in the world of *ba:b l-ḥa:ra* 'the neighborhood gate.' Neither is it Abu l-Nar's authority that Abu Draa has trouble with; Abu Draa has been given many orders by Abu l-Nar before and has been happy to be of service. It is the relation between the order and the profiled authority that Abu Draa refuses to embrace, as Figure 3.6 illustrates.

15. Context: Abu l-Nar and Idaashari are close friends. The former has helped the latter out through many difficulties, and even arranged for the marriage of his employee, Abu Draa, to Idaashari's daughter. In this scene, Abu l-Nar finds out that Idaashari has betrayed him. He becomes furious and orders Abu Draa to divorce Idaashari's daughter as a way to retaliate against Idaashari.

    Abu l-Nar: ʔiza: baddak   tdˤall   ʕam-btiʃtiɣil
                if   you.want   continue   PROG-work
                ʕind-i: , baddak   ttˤlliʔ-**lo/{li:}**   bint-o
                place-my, you.must   divoce-**him/{me}.D**   daughter-his
                la-ha-l-waːtˤi: !
                for-this-the-lowlife !
                'If you want to continue to work for me, you have to divorce [**him/{me}**] the daughter of this lowlife!'
    Abu Draa: ʃu: ʕam-tiħki: ʔabadˤaːy ?   ma: tʕawwadna:
                what   PROG-say   tough.guy ?   NEG   we.are.used
                ʕa-l-rʒaːl   tʒiːb   siːret   l-ħariːm   bi-kalaːm-ha: .
                to-the-men   bring   topic   the-women   in-speech-their .
                'What are you saying, Boss? We are not used to men bringing up women in conversation.'

3.15 From *ba:b l-ḥa:ra* 'the neighborhood gate' – Season 1 – Episode 21 – 00:24:20 – SYR

In (15), Abu l-Nar tries but fails to redefine the scope of the authority that his identity and the sociocultural norms that inform boss–employee relationships

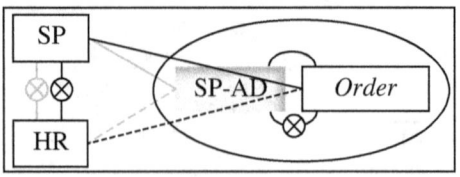

Figure 3.6 Stancetaking stage model of (15)

normally allow. This is so because he tries to use his public role as boss in a private activity that is family-related rather than work-related. Thus, a social actor may have authority in one type of activity but may not qualify as an authority in another type of activity, even if both activities involve the same hearers.

Example (16) provides further evidence of how the identities of social actors and the type of activity that they are involved in interact. In this scene from a Jordanian show, a daughter becomes an entrepreneur and employs the members of her family. As we will see in the next subsection, a daughter may not use a SP-AD directive of this type with her parents without violating social norms. As an entrepreneur and boss, however, she addresses her parents with a SP-AD directive in a work-related activity without being challenged, and thus she successfully profiles herself as a form of hierarchical authority.

16. Context: Amani, a young woman, decides to start a business making clothes. She employs the rest of the family (mother, father, and brothers) and starts bossing them around. When the father asks if they could receive an advance payment on their salary, she says with a patronizing tone:
ma: fi: muʃkile . yalla: ʃiddu:-**li**: he:l-kum .
NEG there problem . go.on toughen-**me.D** self-your .
xalli:-ni: ʔaʔbadˤ, w-baʔabbidˤ-kum .
let-me receive.payment , and-I.pay-you .
'Not a problem. Get [me] your act together. Once I get paid (from selling merchandise), I'll pay you.'
From *nahafa:t ʕaylitna:* 'our family anecdotes' – *Entrepreneur* – 00:03:35 – JOR   3.16

All the examples so far involve the use of SP-AD directives in a workplace where the speaker is either an employer or a high-ranking employee. Similar uses of SP-AD directives are possible in military-style contexts as well. Examples (17) through (19) demonstrate this.

17. Context: The head of the district police, Abu Jawdat, gives a direct order to his second-in-command, Nuri:
sma:ʕ nu:ri: (.) bitfattiʃ-**li**: be:t-o (.)
listen Nuri (.) you.search-**me.D** house-his (.)
bi-l-le:l , bi-l-nha:r , b-kil l-ʔawʔa:t .
in-the-night , in-the-daytime , in-all the-times .
bithitˤtˤ-**illi**: ʕinsor . . . ʔidda:m ba:b be:t-o .
you.put-**me.D** soldier . . . in.front.of door house-his .
'Listen, Nuri, search [me] his house at random times, day and night, and place [me] a soldier in front of his house.'
From *ba:b l-ḥa:ra* 'the neighborhood gate' – Season 1 – Episode 7 – 00:14:50 – SYR   3.17

18. Context: A man comes to the American Embassy in Beirut to apply for a visa. He brings his cello along with him. An officer gives a direct order to a lower-ranking guard to search the cello.

fattiʃ-**li:** hayda: mazˤbu:tˤ .
search-**me.D** this well .
'Search [me] this (cello) well.'

3.18 From *matˤlu:b* 'wanted' – 00:19:00 – LEB

19. Context: A detective and a lower-ranking officer are investigating a murder in a rich household that has a butler and a crew of maids and servants. The lower-ranking officer becomes involved with a maid who is also a murder suspect. The detective says to the officer:
trik-**li:** ha-l-bint , w-fakir-**li:** bi-wazˤi:f-tak
leave-**me.D** this-the-girl , and-think-**me.D** of-job-your
labaynama: nixlasˤ .
until we.finish .
'Leave [me] this girl alone and focus [me] on your job until we're done.'

3.19 From *Meryana* – Episode 7 – 00:49:40 – LEB

Note that the detective in (19) orders the lower-ranking officer to stop seeing the woman he likes until the investigation is concluded, which makes his directive work-related. Otherwise, he does not have the right to give the directive or profile himself as an authority in relation to it.

Examples (20) and (21) include utterances by community members who are endorsed with community-wide authority and who decide to profile their status as such. These are also clear examples in which the speakers are not affectees.

20. Context: Abu Shihab, the second-in-command in the community, arrives at the neighborhood early in the morning only to find the main gate open and the guard, Abu Samo, asleep. Abu Shihab reprimands the guard and reminds him of his responsibility. The conversation ends with Abu Shihab telling Abu Samo the following:
ʔinte ha:res l-ha:ra . mwa:l w-ʔarwa:ḥ
you guard the-neighborhood . money and-souls
l-na:s ʔama:ne bi-raʔibt-ak
the-people trusted.responsibility in-neck-your
. . .
sakkir-**li:** ba:b l-ha:ra , w-dir-**li:**
close-**me.D** gate the-neighborhood , and-pay-**me.D**
ba:l-ak mni:ḥ , yirdˤa: ʕle:-k .
attention-your well , may.God.be.pleased.with.you .
'You are the neighborhood guard. The property and souls of the residents are entrusted to your care. Close [me] the neighborhood gate and pay [me] good attention/be very alert, may God be pleased with you.'[2]

3.20 From *ba:b l-ha:ra* 'the neighborhood gate' – Season 1 – Episode 1 – 00:12:10 – SYR

21. Context: In a remote village in Lebanon, the community gathers in a square to watch TV, using the only TV set in the village. While searching for something to watch,

some young men come across a show that is not appropriate for children. The mayor's wife, Yvonne, yells this utterance from the back seat, to the dismay of all the men present, including her husband:

ɣayru:-**li**:   ha-l-maḥḥatˤa ,   fi: wle:d
change-**me.D** this-the-station ,   there.are children
ˤam-btiḥdˤar .
PROG-watch .

'Change [me] this TV station; there are children watching.'
From *halla? la-we:n* 'where do we go now' – 00:21:00 – LEB

While Abu Shihab in (20) has authority over his hearer, he is not personally affected by his negligence. Similarly, Yvonne in (21) has the authority to boss everyone around but she is not affected by the inappropriate content on TV. Abu Shihab's role is more of a protector than a protectee, and Yvonne is an adult with no underage children of her own.

The situations presented thus far include institutionalized forms of authority that are also culturally endorsed. Sometimes, however, speakers grant themselves a form of hierarchical authority based on an aspect of their individual identity that makes them superior to other social actors in an interaction. Clear cases of this type of hierarchical authority are presented in (22) and (23). In these examples, the speakers use a SP-AD to place themselves on stage as an authority by virtue of their physical strength. In other words, they place themselves on stage as 'tough' people who may penalize their hearer by inflicting physical harm upon him if he refuses to comply. In the scenes building up to (22), we know that the speaker, Idaashari, has made friends with a man from an adjacent neighborhood, Abu l-Nar, who is notorious for being belligerent and dangerous. This friendship has given Idaashari a similar reputation that allows him to engage in the scene depicted in (22). The hearer outranks Idaashari on the socio-economic scale. However, the aforementioned events have given Idaashari the upper hand in his relations with the neighborhood residents, so that (22) goes unchallenged. The SP-AD, combined with elements of the ground, such as the speaker's recent reputation, and contextualization cues (for example, his condescending tone), explicitly profiles the speaker as a tough guy who demands respect. Abu Marzuq, the hearer, recognizes this authority and backs off.

22. Context: After having moved out of the neighborhood because he felt he was treated unfairly, Idaashari comes back for a brief visit to pick up some medication for his sick wife. Abu Marzuq, a grocer who is notorious for being a busybody, tries to pry. Idaashari replies with this directive.

    kitret   l-ɣalabe   tabaˤ-ak   bitbatˤtˤil-**li**:   yya:ha: .
    abundance   the-curiosity POSS-your   give.up-**me.D**   it .

    'This bad habit of yours of sticking your nose into other people's business, quit [me] it.'
    From *ba:b l-ḥa:ra* 'the neighborhood gate' – Season 1 – Episode 15 – 00:42:00 – SYR   3.22

Example (23) provides a similar scenario. The main difference between (22) and (23) is that the profile of the SP-AD referent in the latter is an affirmation and enhancement of an already established identity. The speaker in this case is already known as a 'tough guy' and he uses a SP-ADC to maintain his reputation. The profile of Idaashari in (22), on the other hand, is a redefinition of the speaker's identity; in the context of the Syrian show, we know that Idaashari tries to negotiate and redefine this new identity as a tough guy in light of his recent connections.

23. Context: During the war in Lebanon, it was common for men with weapons and connections to act tough in public. In this scene, a tough guy in a pub has become upset with one of the waiters. He is about to start a fight when the pub manager tries to calm him down. The customer says with indignation and a patronizing tone:
fahhim-**li**:   ʃayyi:l-tak ,   ʔana   ma: hada: byitʕa:tʕa:
explain-**me.D**   workers-your ,   I   no one   interfere
maʕ-i: ʔabdan .
with-me   ever .
'Explain [**me**] to your employees that they should never mess with me.'

3.23 From *bi-l-nisbe la-bukra ʃu:* 'what are the plans for tomorrow' – 00:52:20 – LEB

The use of SP-AD directives as a reflection of hierarchical authority in the public sphere is constrained by a number of factors; these include the speaker's and hearer's identities and the type of activity they are involved in. Both factors may be restrictive with respect to who may use SP-AD directives and where and when they may use them. We have seen that a speaker must outrank the hearer on some identity scale that is relevant to the interactional activity in order to qualify for the use of a SP-AD as a profile of authority.

While identity-related factors such as the speaker's and hearer's socio-economic status, their respective role and rank, or their physical strength play a part in the public sphere when it comes to SP-AD directives and hierarchical authority, two identity-related factors that do not seem to have a say are gender and age. For example, the speakers in (16) and (21), Amani and Yvonne respectively, are women. Their hearers include women and men of different ages, some older and some younger. Similarly, the speakers in (17) and (20), Abu Jawdat and Abu Shihab, are men who are younger than their hearers, Nuri and Abu Samo. Yet, this does not stop the former from giving direct orders to the latter. Of course, sociocultural values and norms are always taken into account. For example, (16) and (21) take place in more egalitarian sociocultural contexts where there is no gender segregation. This is unlike the sociocultural context of the Syrian soap opera *ba:b l-ha:ra* 'the neighborhood gate,' where women are restricted to the private sphere. This is why we do not come across any examples in Season 1 of the show of women performing SP-AD directives as a reflection of their hierarchical authority in the public sphere.

Age and gender may not be instrumental in workplace or community-wide activities, but they do play a role in private household activities. The next subsection shows how.

2.1.2 SP-AD directives and hierarchical authority in the private sphere

The interactions presented in the previous subsection take place outside the household in what may be labeled as the public sphere. Things are a little different in the private sphere. Within the household, identity factors like kinship relationships, age, and gender, which play little role in the public sphere, may be factors when it comes to the use of SP-ADs and the speaker's self-conceptualization as hierarchical authority in family and family-like interactions. We start with parent–child relationships. Consider examples (24) and (25).

24. Context: Im Khater has two daughters, Zahra and Khayriyye, and one son, Khater. Zahra has a disability. She was seriously ill when she was little, and she lost her hearing and her ability to talk, but she can read lips. Khayriyye often abuses Zahra in matters related to housekeeping. One day, Im Khater catches Khayriyye bossing Zahra around in the kitchen. She reprimands Khayriyye and sends her away to do something else. She then turns to Zahra and tells her in a loving tone:

    ya:mo   zahra,   tiʔibri:-ni:,³   bas   txalsˤi:
    mom   Zahra,   bury-me,   when   you.finish
    taʔʃi:r l-batˤaːtˤa,   bitxartˤi:-**li:**   l-banduːrat,
    peeling the-potatoes,   you.dice-**me.D**   the-tomatoes,
    w-bitʔaʃri:-**li:**   l-xyaːrat,   ʔe: ...
    and-you.peel-**me.D**   the-cucumbers, OK   ...

    'Sweetheart Zahra, when you are done peeling the potatoes, dice [me] the tomatoes and peel [me] the cucumbers, OK?'

    From *baːb l-haːra* 'the neighborhood gate' – Season 1 – Episode 9 – 00:33:15 – SYR   3.24

25. Context: Idaashari has two sons, Sobhi and Maarouf. One night Idaashari comes home drunk and decides that his donkey is cold and needs to be covered. He calls Sobhi and says:

    Idaashari: nitˤtˤ   ʒib-**li:**   lha:f,   w-ɣatˤtˤi:-**li:**
                 jump   bring-**me.D**   blanket,   and-cover-**me.D**
                 ha-l-ʔasˤi:l,   yallaː.
                 this-the-well-bred,   go.on.

    'Go bring [me] a blanket and cover this well-bred (normally used for horses). Go on now.'

    ((Sobhi questions his father's order, so Idaashari becomes upset and tries to beat him up. Maarouf steps in in an attempt to resolve the problem.))

    Maarouf: hallaʔ   ʔana: bʒib-lo   lha:f
                immediately   I   bring-him.D   blanket
                la-l-ħmaːr,   w-bɣatˤtˤi:-*lak*   yyaː:
                for-the-donkey, and-I.cover-*you.D*   it
                bi-ʔiːday-i:.
                with-hands-my.

'I will immediately bring a blanket for the donkey and cover *[you]* him with my own hands.'

3.25 From *ba:b l-ha:ra* 'the neighborhood gate' – Season 1 – Episode 17 – 00:22:30 – SYR

In both examples, the speakers profile themselves as parental authorities but of different forms. These forms of authority are determined by elements of the ground, such as the identities of the speakers (including their history) and contextualization cues (including the speakers' tone). Im Khater in (24) is generally a caring mother, especially with Zahra. Her loving tone, sweet facial expressions, and endearing remarks make it clear that she is using her authority but not abusing it. The outcome of her interaction with Zahra is positive alignment across the board, as Figure 3.7 schematically illustrates.

The details and outcome of (25) are different. In this case, the speaker Idaashari profiles himself as a cruel form of authority. He does not care how his children feel about his directive or whether his directive is reasonable or not; he cares only about being obeyed. This is why he grows indignant when he is defied by Sobhi. I should add that Sobhi does not question his father's authority; he only evaluates the order as irrational and aligns with his father negatively with regard to it, as Figure 3.8 demonstrates. To Maarouf, Sobhi's brother, the father's authority is enough reason to obey the order, no matter how unreasonable, which is evident in his use of a hearer-oriented attitude dative, or HR-AD (in italics), to be discussed in Chapter 4.

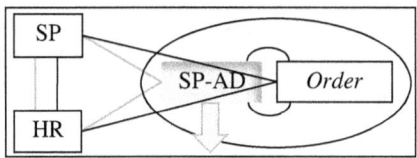

This is me telling you this as your loving mother. I know that you love me and that you will do this for me.

Figure 3.7 Stancetaking stage model of (24)

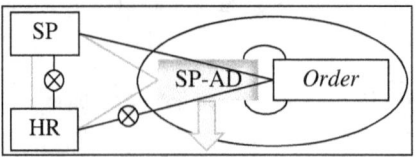

This is me telling you this as your bossy father; I don't care how you feel. You have to do this because I said so.

Figure 3.8 Stancetaking stage model of (25)

Similar examples may be found in other Levantine Arabic dialects, as (26) and (27) illustrate. In both cases, the speaker addresses the hearer with an assertive tone, profiling herself as a firm mother that must be taken seriously.

26. Context: In a village inhabited by Christian and Muslim families, a young Christian man, the youngest of two brothers and a sister, is killed while running an errand outside the village. The mother decides to keep his death a secret for a while because she believes the elder brother may assume that Muslims were responsible for his death and go after the Muslims in the village. She says to her daughter:
rita,   ma baʔaʃ   baddi: ʃu:f-ik   ʕam-btibki: (.)
Rita,   no longer I.want   see-you   PROG-cry (.)
ɣasli:-**li**:   wiʒʒ-ik,   tˤlaʕi: hitˤtˤi:-**li**:   ʃi
wash-**me.D**   face-you,   you.go.up   put-**me.D**   something
ʕa-ʕinay-ki (.)   w-ɣayri:-**li**:   tye:b-ik,
on-eyes-your (.)   and-change-**me.D**   clothes-your,
lbisi: mlawwan
wear   colorful (clothes)
'Rita, I don't want to see you crying anymore. Go upstairs, wash [**me**] your face, put [**me**] some makeup on your eyes, change [**me**] your black clothes and wear colorful clothes.'
From *hallaʔ la-we:n* 'where do we go now' – 01:06:00 – LEB   3.26

27. Context: A young woman refuses to get dressed to meet the family of a prospective groom. She tells her mother that she does not want to get married. She is traumatized by the way her father mistreats her mother. The mother tells her to stop acting up and adds:
ʔu:mi: ɣayri:-**li**:   l-T-shirt   ha:d,   w-hal   l-jeans...
get.up   change-**me.D**   the-T-shirt   this,   and-this-the-jeans...
tharraki: yalla: ʔumi:!
move   go.on   get.up!
'Get up, change [**me**] this T-shirt and these jeans. Move, hurry up!'
From *ha:l l-dunya:* 'this is life' – *fa:res ʔahla:mi:* 'my prince charming' – 00:04:00 – JOR   3.27

Note that the SP-AD in (26) strictly depicts the mother as authority and not as affectee. The utterance is not about the mother being affected by the daughter's sadness over the loss of a family member; the mother herself is devastated by the loss. Rather, the utterance is a direct order to the daughter to hide her feelings in order to keep the death of the son/brother a secret and to avoid bloodshed in the village.

In the private sphere, age and relationships override gender. Thus, we find that older women (for example, mothers) may use SP-AD directives to exercise hierarchical authority over younger men (for example, their sons). This observation is true in contexts with gender segregation, like the context of *ba:b l-ha:ra* 'the neighborhood gate,' as well as in less segregated contexts, as (28) through (30) illustrate. The examples show that mothers may use SP-AD directives with both their daughters and their sons, explicitly placing themselves on stage as a form of hierarchical authority that must be respected and obeyed. The mother in (30) is the same mother as in (26) above, and the hearer is the young man who is later killed.

> 28. Context: Im Esam is assigning chores to her daughters in the house. Her son Esam is about to leave. This conversation takes place between the two right before he leaves.
> Im Esam: ʕisˤa:m, la: tinsa:-**li:** l-labana:t
> Esam, NEG forget-**me.D** the-yogurt
> 'Esam, don't forget [**me**] the yogurt.'
> Esam: ha:dˤer, ya:mo.
> at.your.service, mother.
> 'Okay, mother.'

3.28 From *ba:b l-ha:ra* 'the neighborhood gate' – Season 1 – Episode 24 – 00:21:50 – SYR

> 29. Context: A mother addresses her daughter and son:
> smaʕu: ya: wla:d. ʕmilu: ħsa:b-kun,
> listen VOC children. make calculations-your,
> lyo:m masa: ʕind te:te, ha:!
> today evening at grandma, INTER!
> lyo:m ʕi:d mi:la:d-a:. ma: hada: yirtibitˤ-**li:**
> today birthday-her. no one commit-**me.D**
> ʔirtiba:tˤa:t ɣe:r ʕa:ʔiliyye! smiʕit-ni:, ma:zen?
> commitments NEG familial! you.heard-me, Mazen?
> 'Listen, kids! Remember this evening we will be at Grandma's. Today is her birthday. No one is allowed to make [**me**] non-family-related commitments! Do you hear me, Mazen?'

3.29 From *l-fusˤu:l l-ʔarbaʕa* 'the four seasons' – Season 1 – Episode 1 – 00:13:15 – SYR

> 30. Context: A mother addresses her son:
> ʃlaħ-**li:** yye:ha: ha-l-ʒake:t l-mʕafne
> take.off-**me.D** it this-the-jacket the-rotten
> 'Take [**me**] off this rotten jacket of yours.'

From *halla? la-we:n* 'where do we go now' – 00:18:00 – LEB

Members of the community who may usurp the role of parents could also use SP-ADCs in the same way. The criterion in this case is age: that is, the speaker must be of the same age as the hearer's parents or older. In (31), the speaker Im Khater is the same woman featuring in (24) above. In (24), Im Khater performs a SP-AD directive to give instructions to her own daughter, while in (31) she uses the same type of directive to give instructions to both her daughters and their peers. Example (32) from Palestinian Arabic shows that acquaintances (relatives and other members of the community) may also parent a child. The example is interesting because it shows the speaker's awareness of the fact that elder members of the community may exercise authority over her. The SP-AD is used in a direct quotation. It is not clear whether people say these exact words to her or not, but she knows that they could. The second dative (in italics) cliticized to *tidrisi:* 'study' is a subject-oriented attitude dative (SUBJ-AD), to be discussed in Chapter 5.

31. Context: Im Khater has a social gathering in her house. She has several neighbors (women and their daughters) over for tea, sweets, and fruit. The younger women, including Im Khater's two daughters, Zahra and Khayriyye, are in the kitchen getting things ready, while the mothers are in the living room. Im Khater comes into the kitchen and says:
    yalla: , ya: sˤaba:ya: , ʒahzu:-**li:** l-fawa:ke
    go.on , VOC young.women , prepare-**me.D** the-fruit
    w-l-hilu .
    and-the-sweets .
    'Go on, girls. Prepare [me] the fruit and sweets.'
    From *ba:b l-ha:ra* 'the neighborhood gate' – Season 1 – Episode 8 – 00:06:40 – SYR   3.31

32. Context: One of the three main characters in a short Youtube show introduces herself.
    marḥaba: . ʔana: ʔism-i: li:n . ʕumr-i:
    hello . I name-my Lynn . age-my
    sabaʕtaʕʃar sine . tˤa:lʕa ʕa-l-tawʒi:hi: li-l-ʔasaf .
    seventeen years . going.up to-the-secondary unfortunately .
    ʕan ʒad ʕan ʒad ʕindi: xo:f rahi:b min
    for real for real I.have fear great of
    l-tawʒi:hi: . w-l-muʃkile , l-na:s ma: bitsa:ʕed .
    the-secondary . and-the-problem , the-people NEG help .
    'yalla: ʃidi:-**li:** ha:lek , l-sana l-ʒa:y tawʒi:hi:
    'go.on work.hard-**me.D** , the-hear the-next secondary
    ... biddik-ʃ tidrisi:-*lik* ʔiʃi: bi-l-sˤe:f ? '
    ... you.want-NEG study-*you.D* something in-the-summer ? '
    'Hi! My name is Lynn. I am seventeen years old. I am about to start high school, unfortunately. I am seriously scared of high school, and the problem is that people don't help. They are like, "You have to work [me] hard; next year you will be in high school. Don't you want to study [you] a little in the summer (to be better prepared)?"'
    From *maʃru:ʕ tawfi:r* 'a saving project' – Episode 1 – 00:02:25 – PAL   3.32

The use of SP-AD directives is common between parents or parent-like individuals (legal guardians, teachers, older people) and children. The former may use SP-ADCs with the latter; however, children, including adult children, do not use SP-AD directives with their parents or other parent-like individuals without being challenged for doing so.

Now we turn to SP-AD directives of the same type as used between spouses. When these are used in contexts like *ba:b l-ha:ra* 'the neighborhood gate' in which men are considered categorically superior socioculturally to women, they are far more likely to be used by men to address women and not the other way around. The exchange between Abu Esam and Im Esam in (33) illustrates this power relation between husband and wife. In this example, Abu Esam explicitly profiles himself as a hierarchical authority in the household, placing himself on stage as the individual in the relationship who has the final say. This type of profile matches the shared belief in the community that a husband must control his wife and that a wife must obey her husband, a belief that both women and men explicitly state as a social fact at different occasions in the show. In (33), Im Esam defies Abu Esam, and so he pronounces her divorced.[4]

33. Context: After a disagreement, Im Esam has kicked her son's soon-to-be mother-in-law, Firyal, out of the house. Firyal is also the niece of Abu Saleh, the neighborhood mayor, whom Abu Esam holds in high esteem. When Abu Esam learns of his wife's treatment of Firyal, he becomes upset. He grabs Im Esam by the arm and demands that she go to Firyal's house and apologize to her.

Abu Esam: bitruːhi: laˈ-ʕind   l-maxluːʔa   bi-raːs-ek ,
you.go   to-place   the-person   with-head-your ,
bitdiʔʔi: baːb-aː ,   w-btiʕtizri: minn-aː ,
you.knock   door-her ,   and-you.apologize   to-her ,
w-bitsakri:-**li:**   ha-l-ʔisˤsˤa: kill-aː !
and-end-**me.D**   this-the-story   all-it !
'You go to Firyal's house, you knock on her door, you apologize to her, and you end [me] this issue completely!'

Im Esam: ʔana: ʔiʕtizir   min-ha: ?   laː ,   la-had hoːn w-bas !
I   apologize   to-her ?   no ,   enough is enough !
'You want me to apologize to her? No way! Enough is enough.'

Abu Esam: la-had hoːn w-bas ?   ʃuː   haːy   la-had hoːn w-bas ?
enough is enough ?   what   this   enough is enough ?
'Enough is enough? Are you out of your mind?'

Im Esam: msˤaːlaha   maː   rah   saːleh-aː ,   w-haːda:
making.up   NEG   will   make.up.with-her ,   and-this
l-mawdˤuːʕ   ʔinta   laː   *titdaxxal*   fiː-i ,
the-topic   you   NEG   *interfere*   with-it ,
laʔann-ak   maː   btaʕrif   ʃuː   fi:
because-you   NEG   know   there   is
beːn-i: w-beːn   Firyaːl .
between-me   and-between   Firyal .
. . .
ʔinte   laː   *tihʃer*   haːl-ak   beːn   l-niswaːn ,
You   NEG   *insert*   self-your   between   the-women ,
w-*titdaxxal*   bi-ʔisˤasˤ-un . . .
and-*interfere*   with-stories-their . . .
'I will never make up with Firyal. This topic is none of your business and you have no idea what is going on between Firyal and me. Don't

insert yourself in women's business and concern yourself with their issues.'

From *ba:b l-ha:ra* 'the neighborhood gate' – Season 1 – Episode 33 – 00:42:30 – SYR

3.33

The interesting part about (33) is that Im Esam actually uses very strong language with her husband, even yelling at him at times. She could have easily used a SP-AD with either of the two instances of *titdaxxal* 'interfere' and/or with *tihʃer* 'insert' (presented in italics in (33)), but she does not. In fact, I was not able to find any scene in any of the 33 episodes that make up the first season of this series where a woman uses a SP-AD directive as a reflection of hierarchical authority when speaking with her husband.

In contexts where relations between husband and wife are more egalitarian, SP-AD directives may be used by either partner in the relationship. Examples (34) and (35) feature wives addressing their husbands with SP-AD directives. In both cases, the wife is fed up with her husband's attitude and/or behavior and expects him to change it. Example (34) is from the Lebanese show *Meryana*. The speaker is one of the main characters. A strong woman who likes to be in control, she is often manipulative and does not hesitate to express her opinion. Example (35) from the Lebanese movie *l-sayyida l-θa:niya* 'the second lady' is different. In this case, the wife uses a SP-AD directive with her husband, not because she is angry or offended but to encourage him to improve his mood and let go of the negative emotions he has been dealing with.

34. Context: A formerly wealthy family is now on the verge of bankruptcy because of their extravagant lifestyle. The family's only hope for financial assistance is the wife's rich brother. In a conversation between the husband and wife, the wife says:

    xaffif-**li:**   min   ɣuru:r-ak ,
    diminish-**me.D** of   arrogance-your ,
    w-hki: maʕ   xayy-i: .
    and-talk   with   brother-my .
    'Get rid [**me**] of your arrogance and go talk with my brother.'

Meryana – Episode 2 – 00:39:40 – LEB

3.34

35. Context: A woman addresses her husband, who is worried they may lose their apartment and have to live in public housing.

    ʕisse:f ,   frid-**li:**   wiʒʒ-ak   ʃway .
    Assaf ,   spread-**me.D** face-your   a.little .
    xalli:-na: nithanna: bi-finʒe:n   l-ʔahwe .
    let-us   enjoy   in-cup   the-coffee .
    'Assaf, put [**me**] a smile on your face. Stop looking grumpy. Let us enjoy this cup of coffee.'

From *l-sayyida l-θa:niya* 'the second lady' – 00:07:00 – LEB

3.35

I should point out here that, based on the data I collected for this study, SP-AD directives used between spouses are the least common. They are rather marked, and they often occur in arguments and moments of indignation. They stand in contrast with SP-AD directives used in the workplace (for example, employer–employee) or between parents and children. These are very common and rather unmarked, and they need little motivation.

Before we turn to SP-AD directives and reciprocal authority, a word about directives and facework is in order.

2.1.3 SP-AD directives, hierarchical authority, and facework

I mentioned at the beginning of Section 2.1 that SP-AD directives used to profile the speaker as a form of hierarchical authority are normally spoken with an assertive tone and a falling contour. A directive spoken in this way 'has more affinity prosodically with a command' than a request, as Wichmann (2012: 195) observes. As such, it may be considered a face-threatening act in the sense of Brown and Levinson because it imposes on the hearer's 'want to maintain claims of ... self-determination' and on his desire that his actions be 'unimpeded' by others (1987: 70). This is especially true of SP-AD directives because they are often uttered as bald on record, without redress (Brown and Levinson 1987: 68–9): that is, these directives are unambiguous commands, often without any modification or additional expressions that mitigate their effect and make them sound less authoritative or less imposing. Such directives are considered the most face-threatening, even without a SP-AD. Therefore, the question becomes: does the SP-AD have an additional effect or countereffect on directives as face-threatening acts? If so, how?

To answer this question, I adopt Spencer-Oatey's (2002, 2005, 2008) model of rapport management, which builds on the model introduced by Brown and Levinson (1987). Recent research has shown that social acts are not inherently face-threatening or impolite. Instead, decisions about face threat and impoliteness need to be made on a case-by-case basis, taking into account context and expectations of the social actors involved; see Culpeper (2011), Culpeper and Haugh (2014), and research cited there. This means that the same directive may be evaluated differently as a face-threatening act or a non-face-threatening act, depending on such contextual factors as the identities of the social actors, the expectations they have of each other, and the type of activity they are involved in.

Spencer-Oatey maintains that communication is not only about facework and counterbalancing threats, as Brown and Levinson argue, but rather about rapport management. She defines rapport as 'the relative harmony [or disharmony] and smoothness of relations between people,' and rapport management as 'the management (or mismanagement)' of these relations. She maintains that the management of rapport includes 'not only behavior that enhances or maintains smooth relations, but any kind of behavior that has an impact on rapport, whether positive, negative, or neutral' (Spencer-Oatey 2005: 96). To Spencer-Oatey, the negotiation of face in social interaction plays an essential role in rapport management, but it is not the only factor involved. Social actors' interactional goals and their corresponding rights and obligations must also be taken into account. We discussed rights and obligations above in terms of sociality rights. I will now discuss face and interactional goals.

Face is the interactional aspect of identity or, as Scollon, Scollon, and Jones (2012) maintain, 'the interpersonal identity of the individuals in communication' (46). Spencer-Oatey (2002, 2005, 2008) recognizes three types of face that social actors attend to or are concerned about in interaction: 'quality face,' 'social identity face,' and 'relational face,' corresponding to the three types of identity (individual, group, and relational) discussed in Chapter 2.

Quality face is related to our individual identity and is concerned with 'the value we effectively claim for ourselves' in terms of 'our personal qualities' and those aspects that distinguish us from others. This type of face follows from 'our fundamental desire for people to evaluate us positively in terms of our personal quality' and 'is closely associated with our sense of self-esteem' (Spencer-Oatey 2002: 540).

Social identity face is related to our group identity. It 'is concerned with the value that we effectively claim for ourselves in terms of social or group roles, and is closely associated with our sense of public worth' (Spencer-Oatey 2002: 540). Social identity face follows from our 'fundamental desire for people to acknowledge and uphold our social identities or roles' (Spencer-Oatey 2002: 540).

Relational face is related to our relational identity. When we are members of a group (for example, a family, community, club), we are involved in relations with other members in different capacities (for example, as a mother, as a group leader). Relational face is concerned with the value we claim for ourselves in terms of our role in these relations (Spencer-Oatey 2008: 15).

Social actors have specific goals, also known as interactional goals, when they communicate. Spencer-Oatey (2005: 107) recognizes two types of interactional goal: transactional and relational. Transactional goals are task-oriented and require the completion of specific tasks (for example, taking care of a customer's order). Relational goals focus less on tasks and 'aim at effective relationship management, such as peace-making, promoting friendship, currying favour, or exerting control.' These goals, Spencer-Oatey adds, 'can affect rapport management judgments.'

Most of the directives we have seen in this section are transactional; they are performed by speakers in order to get a job done. In these cases, a directive which is bald on record is more practical and can be expected by all parties involved. As such, it is not judged negatively in terms of rapport management. We asked above whether the use of SP-ADs has an additional effect or countereffect on rapport management. The short answer is that a SP-AD adds a relational undertone to a transactional directive. As such, it is evaluated as a welcome addition from the perspective of the hearer under two conditions: first, the directive is performed in accordance with the rights and obligations of the speaker and hearer; and second, the speaker and hearer have positive feelings toward each other (for example, respect, love). Examples (7) and (8), as well as (24), fall in this category. Native speakers judge these directives as kinder and more motivational for the hearer, while their counterparts without a SP-AD are judged as aloof and abrupt. A SP-AD directive like (7) or (8) corresponds to an English directive that starts with the expression *I want/need you to do something for me*, said by a caring boss to an employee. The employee appreciates being trusted by the boss and appreciates being involved in the boss's activities. In this case, a SP-AD is evaluated as a boost to the hearer's quality face and his desire to be evaluated as trustworthy. It is also a boost to his social identity and relational face because it makes him feel that he is a vital member of the speaker's group, it affirms and enhances his relation with the speaker, and it acknowledges his right of involvement. In fact, Season 1 of the Syrian soap opera *ba:b l-ha:ra* 'the neighborhood gate' contains at least two scenes in which an employee is offended if his boss has an important task to assign but does not assign it to him.

In contrast, if a directive is performed in contradiction with the rights and obligations of the speaker and hearer, a SP-AD makes the directive more offensive. One example is (14) above, in which a citizen addresses the First Lady of Lebanon with a SP-AD directive. The directive itself is offensive without the AD, and the SP-AD makes it even more so because it relationally tries to exert control on the hearer by an unqualified speaker. Similarly, if the speaker and hearer have a negative relation that lacks mutual respect, a SP-AD directive becomes the equivalent of an English directive that ends with the expression *because I said so*. We have seen a few relevant examples, such as (22) and (23). Native speakers judge these directives as offensive in the sense that they are damaging to the hearer's self-esteem (quality face). Everything else being equal, native speakers prefer directives like (22) and (23) to be performed without a SP-AD. The SP-AD gives the directive an *in your face* effect, which makes it more confrontational, more disrespectful, and more damaging to the relation between speaker and hearer.

All in all, when a SP-AD is employed in a directive for the purpose of profiling the speaker as a hierarchical authority, it also makes the directive more personal. If the speaker and hearer enjoy a good relationship based on mutual respect and each recognizes the other's rights, a SP-AD enhances this relationship. If, on the other hand, the speaker and hearer have a bad relationship, a SP-AD can only challenge the rapport between them and make the relationship worse.

2.2 SP-AD directives and reciprocal authority

We saw in the previous section that hierarchical authority is asymmetrical. Social actor A may use a SP-AD directive to exercise authority on social actor B only if A outranks B in terms of socio-economic status, physical strength, or some other aspect of their respective identities. This superiority gives the social actor a unilateral sense of entitlement, a sense that she deserves the time, effort, and consideration of those around her, including her interlocutor, and that she may penalize him if she is not given what she believes she is owed.

There is another form of authority that is more symmetrical, which I call reciprocal authority. One social actor may use a SP-AD directive in order to exercise reciprocal authority over another social actor, not based on the speaker's sense of entitlement but rather based on the hearer's sense of obligation. In this case, the hearer may choose to refuse to abide by the speaker's directive without fear of being penalized by her, which is one reason why this form of authority is not considered hierarchical. When the hearer complies, he may do so for at least one of four reasons, which the speaker is also aware of:

- he considers his relationship with the speaker solidary enough to allow her to exercise authority over him
- he is bound by the group solidarity invoked by the speaker and is expected to comply with her desires
- he owes the speaker a debt for something she did for him in the past and this is an opportunity to pay her back
- he wants the speaker to be in debt to him so that he can ask her for a favor in the future.

The first and second may be grouped under the topic of solidarity, while the third and fourth deal with mutual indebtedness. Throughout all of this, both the speaker and hearer know that the roles may be reversed at any time: that is, the speaker is aware that the hearer may exercise authority over her under similar circumstances.

We start with reasons one and two and the topic of solidarity. Drawing on Brown and Gilman (2003) and Bayertz (1999), I define solidarity as the social closeness or cohesion among members of a community. This cohesion may be the outcome of 'frequent contact,' 'like-mindedness,' and 'similar behavior dispositions' (Brown and Gilman 2003: 160), as well as 'a common descent and history, a common culture and way of life, and common ideals and goals' (Bayertz 1999: 9). Bayertz adds that solidarity as social cohesion and 'mutual attachment between individuals' entails 'mutual obligations [between these individuals] to aid each other, as and when should be necessary' (1999: 3). I add that solidarity may also entail mutual obligation among individuals to comply with each other's desires and to compromise their own in order to preserve their relationship.

Example (36) contains a SP-AD directive as a reflection of reciprocal authority. The driving factor in this case is solidarity between two brothers. The speaker uses a SP-AD directive with his brother, Abu Shihab, whom the reader may recall is politically second-in-command in the community. In the entire show only one other man gives him a direct order in the form of a SP-AD directive: Abu Saleh, who is the mayor and Abu Shihab's superior. In this unique case the SP-AD directive is received as normal/unmarked because it is triggered by reciprocity and solidarity.

36. Context: Abu Shihab, the mayor's second-in-command, is troubled by rumors he has heard from his brother's employee, Abdo. His brother believes that he should not be concerned, telling him to dismiss the issue and attend to other business: in this case, an invitation to lunch.

    ʔax-i: (.)   l-kala:m   lli: ʕa:l-o   ʕabdo ,
    brother-my (.) the-talk   that   said-them   Abdo ,
    ʔi:m-o   min   ra:s-ak ...   w-halla?   ʒahhiz-**li:**
    remove-it   from   head-your ...   and-now   prepare-**me.D**

ḥa:l-ak,   ʔixt-ak   suʕa:d   ʕa:zmit-na: ʕa-l-ɣada: .
self-your,   sister-your Suaad   invited-us   to-the-lunch .
'Brother, forget what Abdo said and get [me] yourself ready. Your sister Suaad has invited us over to lunch.'

3.36 From *ba:b l-ḥa:ra* 'the neighborhood gate' – Season 1 – Episode 9 – 00:34:00 – SYR

Another example featuring reciprocal authority is (35) above, in which a wife instructs her husband to dismiss his worries and have a cup of coffee instead. The relation between the wife and husband in this example may be considered egalitarian rather than hierarchical. Just like in (36), the speaker in (35) acts as an equal rather than as a superior, with the understanding that the hearer may refuse to comply and that the hearer may treat her in the same way under similar circumstances. For this reason the hearers in both examples do not challenge the speakers as a form of authority, and align with them positively in this regard, as Figure 3.9 illustrates.

When a speaker of Levantine Arabic is in doubt that her directive may be understood as a reflection of hierarchical rather than reciprocal authority, she may add a clarifying expression like *bi-l-ʔamaliyye*, which roughly means 'in the hope that you will comply' but which has come to mean 'in the name of the familiarity between us.' Example (37) illustrates how this expression may be used. When a speaker employs this or similar expressions in a directive, she indicates that the directive is a request that she allows herself to perform by virtue of the solidary relationship she has with the hearer and that she is simply hopeful that the hearer will comply.

37. Context: A Facebook user shares this post:
    ʔasˤdiqaʔ-na: l-ʔaʕiza:ʔ ,   ʔiza: ʔamkan   taʕemlu:
    friends-our   the-dear ,   if   possible you.make
    share   la-l-page ,   laysa   ʔamran   ʕale:-kum ,
    share   for-the-page , not   order   on-you ,
    ʔinnama: bi-l-ʔamaliyye .
    but   in.the.name.of.the.familiarity.between.us .
    'Dear friends, please share this page. This is not an order, I just ask in the name of our relationship.'

    اصدقائنا الاعزاء اذا ممكن تعملوا شير (share) للبيج. ليس امر عليكم انما بالأملية

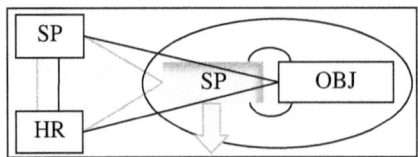

This is me allowing myself to tell you
this by virtue of our good relation.

Figure 3.9 Stancetaking stage model of (35) and (36)

Solidarity may be based on a mutual, exclusive relation between the speaker and hearer. Alternatively, it may be invoked by their group membership. In the latter case, the speaker may not qualify – that is, she may not have the identity requirements, in general or in a specific context – to address the hearer with a SP-AD directive of the form we have seen so far. One way around this is for the speaker to use a plural SP-AD – that is, 'us.D' instead of 'me.D' – to include everyone present as a carrier of the same attitude and to invoke solidarity in the name of group membership. If no member of the group contradicts the speaker, the hearer feels a pressure to comply because his refusal would mean going against the group's wish. If the hearer cares to be a member of the group himself, solidarity generates an obligation for him to accept the directive and align positively with the speaker.

Examples (38) and (39) illustrate this point. In (38), the hearer Im Ziki is older than the speaker Fawziyye. For Fawziyye to address Im Ziki with a SP-AD directive similar to those we have seen in the previous sections would be inappropriate, based on the criterion of age alone. By using a plural SP-AD, however, she effectively says, 'This is not only me posing as an authority on this topic. This is collective wisdom. Everyone here (in this house or in the neighborhood) thinks the same, and I speak on behalf of all of us.'

38. Context: Two women in the neighborhood, Firyal and Im Esam, are archenemies. Im Ziki, the neighborhood midwife, wants the two to get along. She visits Im Esam while another neighbor, Fawziyye, is there. Im Ziki tries to defend Firyal in front of Im Esam. Fawziyye sides with Im Esam and says:
batˤli:-**lna**: ha-l-ˤa:de , ʔim Ziki: .
quit-**us.D** this-the-habit , Im Ziki
kil ˤimr-ek bitda:fˤi: ˤann-a:
all life-your you.defend on-her
w-ma: btiħki: dˤami:r-ek , ʔe: .
and-NEG speak conscience-your , yes .
'Quit [**us**] this habit, Im Ziki. You always defend her and do not say what you actually believe.'

From *ba:b l-ha:ra* 'the neighborhood gate' – Season 1 – Episode 29 – 00:13:00 – SYR   3.38

In (39), the speaker addresses his father-in-law. If the speaker uses a directive with a singular SP-AD, he may be understood as profiling himself as a form of hierarchical authority in relation to his father-in-law, which would be inappropriate. By using 'us.D' instead of 'me.D,' the speaker invokes group solidarity and effectively says, 'This is not only my desire; this is the group's desire.' No one contradicts the speaker in this case, so the father-in-law finds himself having to succumb to the group's wishes.

39. Context: A man has written a poem about his mother-in-law. He plans to read it to her on her birthday while the rest of the family is present. His father-in-law is playing records on a phonograph, a present he bought for his wife. The son is

excited to read his poem, and wants his father-in-law to stop the phonograph.
He says:

ʕamm-i: ,   waʔʔif-**ilna**:   ha-l-ʒihaːz   ʃway   haːd .
uncle-my,   stop-**us.D**   this-the-device   a.little   this .

'Uncle (used to address a father-in-law), stop [**us**] this device for a second!'

3.39 From *l-fusˤuːl l-ʔarbaʕa* 'the four seasons' – Season 1 – Episode 1 – 00:41:15 – SYR

The interesting thing about SP-AD directives like (38) and (39) is that any member of the group may potentially use them, and this makes the form of authority profiled in these examples reciprocal rather than hierarchical. The requirement is not a superior identity feature; rather, the requirement is a group identity that allows the speaker to be perceived as a member of the group she represents via a plural SP-AD. This type of SP-AD directive is normally uttered with a rising tone characteristic of requests rather than commands.

We now turn to indebtedness. A speaker who promises or has already done the hearer a favor can be said to have the hearer indebted to her. The indebtedness of the hearer, whether actual or promised, qualifies the speaker to use a SP-AD directive that profiles her as a form of reciprocal authority in relation to the hearer. There is a mutual understanding that the hearer may use a SP-AD directive of the same type under similar circumstances. This type of SP-AD directive often takes the form of a whispered secret, with the speaker and hearer featuring as accomplices. The unspoken agreement between the two is along the lines of 'you scratch my back and I scratch yours.' A clear example of this type of SP-AD directive is given in (40). The hearer in this case is already indebted to the speaker. She often visits the speaker's home and is always invited to join for meals. This alone could make the hearer feel obligated to comply with the speaker's desires. However, the speaker's request is rather unusual, and in order to ensure that the hearer will comply, she immediately offers a gift in return.

40. Context: Suaad (also known as Im Esam) learns about her husband's intentions to arrange the marriage of their eldest son to the daughter of her archenemy, Firyal. She asks Im Ziki, the midwife and matchmaker in the neighborhood, to find a husband for Firyal's daughter before her husband carries out his plan.

   Suaad: biddi: tdabri:-**li**:   ʕariːs   la-binit   Firyaːl .
             I.want   you.find-**me.D**   groom   for-daughter Firyal .
   'I want you to find [**me**] a husband for Firyal's daughter.'
   . . .
   Im Ziki: tˤayyeb   ʔuli:-li: ,   leːʃ ?
             Okay   tell-me.D ,   why ?
   'Okay, but why?'
   Suaad: ʔinti   ʕmili: mitil   ma: ʕam-ʔil-lek ,
             you   do   like   that   PROG-I.say-you.D ,
             w-ʔil-ek   min-ni: lli: biddik   yyaː .
             and-to-you from-me   what   you.want it .

'Just do as I say and I'll give you whatever you want in return.'
From *ba:b l-ḥa:ra* 'the neighborhood gate' – Season 1 – Episode 13 – 00:42:20 – SYR

3.40

In my personal experience, SP-AD directives that are motivated by indebtedness are common in government transactions that require *wa:stˤa* to be completed. The term *wa:stˤa* literally means 'an intermediary.' It refers to the use of a third party as a connection in order to get a government transaction done. It often involves bribery and favoritism, and as such is a form of corruption. For example, let us say I want to renew my passport and I want to expedite the process. If expedited requests are done via *wa:stˤa* instead of a legal form, I may need to find someone (who knows someone) who knows the officer that will work on my passport. That person will be my *wa:stˤa* and may require 'a fee.' At the passport renewal office, the person serving as my *wa:stˤa* may then say something like (41) to the officer in charge. By saying this, my *wa:stˤa* also puts himself in the hearer's debt, and the hearer knows that. Either my *wa:stˤa* will have to pay the hearer 'a fee' immediately, or the hearer may one day come to the *wa:stˤa* with a favor of his own. Importantly, it is only by evaluating the directive from the perspective presented via the SP-AD that the hearer is willing to comply and thus align positively with the speaker.

41. htamm-**alli:**   bi-l-ʃabb
    take.care-**me.D**   of-the-young.man
    'Take care [**me**] of the young man.'

We now turn to the third and last type of authority profiled by SP-ADs in directives.

2.3 SP-AD directives and knowledge authority

Another form of authority that a SP-AD may profile is knowledge authority. In this case, the speaker may use a SP-AD directive to instruct a hearer on a topic on which she is an expert. For example, she could be a physician prescribing a treatment for a patient, an experienced salesperson training a new employee, or an older person that has been married for a long time giving advice to a newlywed. In all these scenarios, the speaker knows better than her hearer, and this knowledge qualifies her as an authority. If the hearer chooses not to abide by the speaker's directives, the speaker may not penalize him. The hearer may, however, be penalized by the consequences of his own choices, eliciting an 'I told you so!' from the speaker.

The following are a few examples to illustrate this point. In (42), the speaker Abu Esam is an herbal doctor; he uses a SP-AD directive in this capacity to give his patient instructions about how he should implement a treatment. The speaker in (43), Abu Samir, stands for a different type of knowledge authority. He is a restaurant owner and an expert on fava beans and chickpeas. He uses a SP-AD directive in this capacity to indicate that he knows what he is doing and to instruct his customer Abdo to be patient. He believes that Abdo should trust him if he wishes to receive a serving of fava beans that is to his liking. In both cases, the speakers affirm their identities as experts, simultaneously affirming the cultural belief that one should trust those who know best.

> 42. Context: Abu Esam, the neighborhood doctor, prescribes an ointment for the garbage collector and explains how to apply it onto his foot. At one point, Abu Esam says:
> ʕind ʕala: bukra:, bitfikk-**illi:** ha-l-ʃa:ʃe . . .
> at on morning, you.remove-**me.D** this-the-dressing . . .
> 'First thing in the morning, you remove [me] the wound dressing . . .'

3.42 From *ba:b l-ha:ra* 'the neighborhood gate' – Season 1 – Episode 20 – 00:46:20 – SYR

> 43. Context: Abdo, an employee at the public bath in the neighborhood, enters Abu Samir's fava bean restaurant. He orders a plate of fava beans.
> Abdo: ʔabu: sami:r . . . ħitt-ilna: faremte:n banadu:ra .
> Abu Samir . . . put-us.D two.pieces tomato .
> 'Abu Samir, let's add some tomato.'
> Abu Samir: wlik tikram ʕyu:n-ak . tawwel-**li:** ba:l-ak
> INTER welcome eyes-your . stretch-**me.D** patience-your
> ʃwayy, bas la-nassiʔ-lak yya: ʕala: ke:f-i: .
> a.little, only to-fix-you.D it to liking-my .
> 'Of course! Be [me] patient and I will fix your fava beans exactly as I think they should be.'

3.43 From *ba:b l-ha:ra* 'the neighborhood gate' – Season 1 – Episode 6 – 00:21:20 – SYR

Not all forms of knowledge authority are formal or endorsed by the whole community. Some forms of knowledge authority are self-proclaimed. Consider (44), for example. The speaker Im Ziki uses a SP-AD directive to profile herself as someone who knows better than her hearer, Firyal, about wedding preparations. Firyal refuses to accept the profile and the result is negative alignment, at least as far as Firyal's immediate response to Im Ziki is concerned. We learn later that she eventually takes Im Ziki's advice and seeks the help of professional tailors but refuses to admit it.

> 44. Context: Firyal wants to sew all her daughter's dresses herself in preparation for the wedding. Im Ziki is trying to convince her that she will not be able to finish on time and that she should seek help from professional tailors.
> fikki:-**li:** ki:s-ek, w-laʔi:-lek
> open-**me.D** bag/purse-your, and-find-you.D
> kam xayya:tˤa ysaʕdu:-ki, ʔaħsan-lek .
> a.few tailor help-you, better-you.D .
> 'Open [me] your wallet and pay a few tailors to help you out with this. That would be better for you.'
> ((When Firyal does not take the advice, Im Ziki says:))
> ʔe: tistʕifli: . ka:net l-nasˤiħa bi-ʒamal .
> OK suit.yourself . was the-advice for-camel .

'OK, suit yourself. A piece of advice used to be worth a camel (and people were willing to pay for it. My advice is for free and you're unwilling to take it).'
From *ba:b l-ḥa:ra* 'the neighborhood gate' – Season 1 – Episode 19 – 00:8:30 – SYR   3.44

In (45), an example from another Syrian show, the speaker prides himself as a world traveler and as an expert in vacation destinations. At some point, he recommends Turkey to his in-laws as an excellent place for a vacation. Once they are back from their trip, he asks his father-in-law about his impression of Turkey. The SP-AD he uses in the question profiles the speaker as an expert. In a way, he is not only asking about his in-laws' opinion of Istanbul; he is also seeking positive acknowledgment of his expertise.

45. Context: A couple have recently travelled to Istanbul, Turkey, upon a recommendation from their son-in-law. After their return, the son-in-law asks:
    ʔill-i: ʕamm-i: (.)   ʃlo:n   ʃift-**illi**:   stˤanbu:l?
    tell-me   uncle-my (.)   how   you.see-**me.D**   Istanbul?
    'Tell me, Uncle, how did you find [**me**] Istanbul?'
From *l-fusˤu:l l-ʔarbaʕa* 'the four seasons' – Season 1 – Episode 5 – 00:04:50 – SYR   3.45

This section has dealt with SP-ADs as used in directives. We will now turn to SP-AD representatives.

3 SP-ADCs as representatives

Representatives are speech acts that 'commit the speaker (in varying degrees) to something's being the case, to the truth of the expressed proposition,' and their content may be assessed as true or false (Searle 1976: 10). A SP-ADC used as a representative may take the form of a commendation or a complaint/criticism. These acts do more than commit the speaker to 'the truth of the expressed proposition'; they also indicate that the expressed proposition is of interest to the speaker (Searle: 1976: 10).

Consider the constructed examples in (46) and (47). The former is a commendation addressed to a female student, and the latter is a complaint addressed to a male student. Let us say that the speaker is an older relative (for example, an aunt) who feels compelled to express her opinion, but who is not necessarily affected, positively or negatively, by the hearers' performance. Both representatives may be realized without a SP-AD. By using a SP-AD, the speaker assumes responsibility for the attitude she anchors to the utterance: that is, she may not attribute the attitude to a general experiencer, and she may not claim that the statement is simply neutral, non-attitudinal. In addition, the SP-AD places the speaker on stage as a form of moral authority or cultural police who feels both entitled and qualified to praise or criticize others' conduct and judge it as laudable or reprehensible, based on culturally shared beliefs, values, and rules of conduct.

46. smiʕit ʔinn-ik   ʕam-btihtammi:-li: bi-dars-ik.
    I.heard that-you PROG-take.care-**me.D** of-studies-you.
    ʕafe:-ke !
    may.God.give.you.good.health !
    'I heard that you are taking care [me] of your studies. Good job!'

47. smiʕit ʔinn-ak   he:mil:-**li:**   dars-ak   w-ʔe:ʕid-**li:**
    I.heard that-you neglecting-**me.D** studies-your and-keeping-**me.D**
    tilʕab games . ma: bisʕi:r   he:k .
    play games .   NEG   happen   like.this .
    'I heard that you are neglecting [me] your studies and wasting [me] your time on games. This is not good.'

The hearers in (46) and (47) may align positively or negatively with the speaker regarding both the proposition and the form of authority that she profiles. Alternatively, the alignment may be convergent with regard to one but divergent with regard to the other. Importantly, for the speaker to qualify as a form of moral authority or cultural police and thus minimize the risk of negative alignment with regard to this profile of herself, she needs to have the identity requirements associated with the role. For example, if the hearer in (47) knows that the speaker was not an impressive student herself when she was young, based on this reputation alone he could challenge the speaker with (48). As Figure 3.10 illustrates, the hearer accepts the speaker's evaluation of his academic performance, but he does not believe she is qualified to assume the role of cultural police in relation to it.

48. te:ta   bitʔu:l ʔinno inti ma: kinti ʔaħsan .
    grandma   says   that   you   NEG   were   better .
    'Grandma says that you were no better.'

Although SP-AD representatives may serve as either commendations or complaints, the vast majority that I have observed in my data are complaints. These complaints often involve the speaker's judgment of a behavior as culturally inappropriate, reprehensible, and so on. They may also involve evaluation of an individual as incompatible with the ideals that society finds acceptable. In addition, it is common

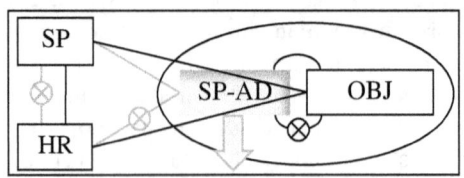

This is me evaluating your behavior in
my capacity as cultural police.

Figure 3.10 Stancetaking stage model of (47) and (48)

for the speaker to have a tone of indignation when she uses a SP-ADC as a complaint; this corresponds to 'affect,' as discussed in Martin and White (2005).

These complaints may take one of two forms:

- second-person complaints in which the hearer and his behavior are the target of evaluation
- third-person complaints in which a speaker evaluates an absent individual or individuals and their behavior.

The first may additionally serve as an implied directive, pointing out that the hearer's behavior or the state of affairs is unacceptable, in order to invite him to remedy it. The second is typical of gossip. I will address these two types separately.

3.1 SP-AD representatives as second-person complaints

SP-ADCs as second-person complaints do more than just assert the truth of a proposition and express dissatisfaction with its content; they also invite the hearer, albeit indirectly, to take action to fix the source of the complaint. In this respect they are similar to directives, and in fact the contextual conditions that inform the use of SP-AD directives also inform the use of SP-AD complaints. When a speaker employs a SP-AD complaint, she profiles herself as responsible for and entitled to the profiled attitude by virtue of certain aspects of her and the hearer's identities relevant to the interactional context. All is done in accordance with the shared values, beliefs, and norms that constitute the sociocultural context in which the interaction takes place. Normally, these factors cumulate in a profile of the speaker as two forms of authority: first, as a moral authority who is dissatisfied with a given behavior or a state of affairs; and second, as a hierarchical, reciprocal, or knowledge authority who believes some action must follow to remedy an unacceptable situation.

One aspect of the speaker's identity that is saliently relevant to SP-AD complaints is her reputation. The speaker may not criticize a behavior as inappropriate or unacceptable if she has ever been known to be guilty of the same offense. If she does, she is likely to be challenged by her interlocutor. If the complaint does not include a SP-ADC, as is the case in (49), the speaker may be able to excuse herself by claiming that the statement is merely descriptive and informative, especially if the statement is uttered in a neutral tone. Once the speaker uses a SP-AD as in (50), however, she may not deny the attitude or her responsibility for it, even if the statement is uttered in a neutral tone. This is so because SP-ADCs are inherently attitudinal, and the SP-AD overtly places the speaker on stage as responsible for her utterance and for the evaluation that she anchors to it. It profiles the speaker as a cultural police who is entitled to make an evaluative statement by virtue of occupying a higher moral ground. If she herself is found guilty of the thing she complains about – in the case of (50), smoking – such authority is less likely to pass unchallenged. See Johnstone (2009) for a discussion about the speaker's credibility in terms of her history and her moral and epistemic authority.

49. Kari:m   bidaxxin   ʕilibte:n   dixxa:n   kil   yo:m
    Karim   smoke   two.packets   cigarettes   every   day
    'Karim smokes two packets of cigarettes a day.'

50. Kari:m   bidaxxin-li: ʕilibte:n   dixxa:n   kil   yo:m
    Karim   smoke-me.D   two.packets   cigarettes   every   day
    'Karim smokes [me] two packets of cigarettes a day.'

Now let us turn to some attested examples. Observe (51) through (53). In each of the three examples, the speaker judges the hearer's behavior as unacceptable and complains about it in an attempt to get the hearer to modify it. In all three cases, the [male] speaker profiles himself as a form of moral authority. We start with (51); in this case, the speaker Abu Shihab puts himself on stage as a moral–hierarchical authority, whose job is to enforce good social practices in the neighborhood. He speaks in his capacity as the neighborhood guardian. Example (51) is uttered with rising intonation, which is characteristic of complaints in general.

51. Context: Abu Satur is an ex-convict and friend of Abu l-Nar's, a resident of another neighborhood. Both are notorious for being belligerent troublemakers. Abu Satur recently rented a house in the neighborhood of Abu Shihab, ḥa:ret l-dˁabeʕ 'the neighborhood of the hyena,' and is using the house to slaughter sheep and sell their meat. Abu Shihab confronts him after some neighbors have complained.
    ʃu: ,   ʔabu: sa:tˁu:r ,   fa:teh-li: l-be:t   maslax ?
    what ,   Abu Satur ,   you.opening-me.D   the-house   slaughter.house ?
    'What is going on, Abu Satur? You are using [me] the house as a slaughterhouse!'

3.51 From ba:b l-ḥa:ra 'the neighborhood gate' – Season 1 – Episode 19 – 00:12:50 – SYR

In (52), the same speaker, Abu Shihab, now profiles himself as a reciprocal authority and cultural police. Over the course of the show, he and the hearer, Idaashari, have built up a relationship of mutual respect after having been enemies for a long time. Here he addresses Idaashari as a friend and a fellow resident. Idaashari has been ill and refuses to leave the house. Abu Shihab considers this behavior a violation of the cultural expectations of men as conceived in the context of the show. The speaker feels entitled to make the complaint by virtue of his individual identity as a strong man who is never idle and who never gives in to hardship.

52. Context: Abu Shihab visits Idaashari in his house. Idaashari has been unemployed for weeks, spending all his time at home. From the perspective of this soap opera, only women are expected to stay at home all the time (a sentiment that is repeated at different times throughout the program). Abu Shihab decides to offer Idaashari a job in order to get him out of the house.
    ha:bis-li: ha:l-ak   be:n   ha-l-ḥi:tˁa:n ,
    you.trapping-me.D   self-your   between   these-the-walls ,

```
w-ha-l-ʃi:           ma:     biʒu:z ...
and-this-the-thing   NEG     allowed ...
```
'You are trapping [me] yourself between these walls (staying at home), and it's not OK.'

From *ba:b l-ḥa:ra* 'the neighborhood gate' – Season 1 – Episode 28 – 00:29:35 – SYR   3.52

In (53), the speaker is a doctor addressing a patient. By using a SP-AD, the speaker profiles himself as a form of knowledge authority as well as cultural police. The complaint is an invitation to the hearer to change his behavior. The SP-AD indicates that the speaker is responsible for the complaint and entitled to it in two capacities: as a doctor who knows what is better, and as a community member who believes that a cobbler who sells shoes to others should have good shoes himself.

53. Context: Abu Esam is talking to the neighborhood cobbler and shoemaker, who has calluses on his feet.

```
ya:      ʕamm-i:,    ʔabu: maḥmu:d,   l-dama:mer      lli:
VOC      uncle-my,   Abu Mahmud,      the-calluses    that
tˤa:lʕa       bi-riʒle:-k     ha:y,    sabab-a:     l-sˤara:mi:   l-dayʔa
appeared      on-feet-your    these,   reason-its   the-shoes    the-tight
lli:    ʕam-btilbis-li::       yya:ha:.   yaʕni:      sˤada?        lli:
that    PROG-wear-me.D         them.      this.mean   he.was.right  who
ʔa:l,    l-ska:fi:      ha:fi:      w-l-ḥa:yek      ʕarya:n !
said,    the-cobbler    barefoot    and-the-tailor  naked !
```
'Abu Mahmud, you have calluses on your feet because the shoes you wear [me] are too tight. It is true what they say: the cobbler is barefoot and the tailor is naked!'

From *ba:b l-ḥa:ra* 'the neighborhood gate' – Season 1 – Episode 16 – 00:43:30 – SYR   3.53

In (51) through (53), the speakers affirm their identities via the use of SP-ADs. They also affirm the cultural values linked to their complaints and invite the hearers to adopt these values or re-embrace them after having temporarily abandoned them.

There is no clear list of the values, beliefs, or norms that a community or a group (for example, the residents of a neighborhood in Aleppo, university female students in Amman) may share. To provide an idea about the breadth of behaviors and objects that may be the target of complaints featuring SP-ADs, I present additional examples from other shows. Consider the Jordanian Arabic example in (54). The speaker criticizes the hearer, who has just been elected to public office, for wearing expensive clothes. This behavior, he suggests, is unacceptable because it may send the wrong message, giving people the impression that the hearer can afford such clothes because he accepts bribes. In reality, the speaker is simply jealous because he ran against the hearer for the same office and lost. In this case, the speaker pretends to be a moral authority, but the hearer sees through it immediately, resulting in negative alignment. The first AD in the example (in italics) is subject-oriented; SUBJ-ADs will be discussed in Chapter 5.

54. Context: Fawwaz, a respectful and hardworking young man, has just won a city election after running against Abu Awwad, a respected elder in the neighborhood. A few days later, the two men run into each other in the neighborhood. Fawwaz is dressed up in a nice suit. Abu Awwad criticizes him for being extravagant and for spending money on clothes. He continues:

ʔana: gasˤd-i: ya: habbu:b-i: tistanna:-*lak*
I intention-my VOC darling-my you.wait-*you.D*
ʃwayye . miʃ tˤibb tˤabbatak lʕa:fye , tru:h tnazzig-**li:**
a.little . all.of.a.sudden , you.go you.dress-up-**me.D**
walla: inte la:bis-**li:** badle ʒdi:de . habi:b-i: ,
and you wearing-**me.D** suit new . darling-my ,
ʔa-bisˤi:r-iʃ tidˤhar ʔaddaːm l-na:s
NEG-becoming-NEG you.go.out before the-people
bi-badle ʒdi:de .
in-suit new .

'What I mean, my good man, is you should wait a little. You shouldn't all of a sudden start dressing [me] up and wearing [me] new suits. My good man, it is not appropriate to present yourself to the people in a new suit.'

3.54 From ʔabu: ʕawwa:d 'Abu Awwad' – Season 1 – Episode 4 – 00:03:50 – JOR

Examples (55) and (56) present additional situations from contemporary Syrian and Jordanian shows. In (55), a young woman criticizes her brother for what she thinks is unacceptable behavior, while (56) features a married son criticizing his father for being stingy and inconsiderate. These examples are interesting because they stand in stark contrast with possible utterances in the early twentieth-century Damascene context of *ba:b l-ha:ra* 'the neighborhood gate.' Although in *ba:b l-ha:ra* it is possible for children and sisters to criticize their parents and brothers, I have not come across any scene in which they do so by using a SP-AD complaint, which would profile them as an authority and cultural police. The fact that such utterances are possible in contemporary Syrian and Jordanian society is indicative of a set of redefined identities and cultural values and beliefs which differ from those portrayed in *ba:b l-ha:ra* .

55. Context: A sister criticizes her brother for not being involved in family affairs.

le:ʃ inte ʃu: btaʕref bi-ha-l-dine
why you what know in-this-the-world
ɣe:r l-sayya:ra w-l-bana:t ...
other.than the-car and-the-girls ...
w-tisraʕ-**li:** bi-ha-l-sayya:ra ?
and-speed-**me.D** in-this-the-car ?

'Do you care about anything in this world other than cars and women, and speeding [me] around in the car?'

3.55 From *l-fusˤu:l l-ʔarbaʕa* 'the four seasons' – Season 1 – Episode 6 – 00:08:40 – SYR

56. Context: A man is in an ambulance with his sick wife on their way to the hospital. It is after midnight. He calls his parents to let them know. His father, known for being stingy, starts to criticize his son for taking his wife to the hospital using an ambulance because of how expensive it can be. His son answers:

ya:ba: ,   inte   bitfakkir-**li**:   bi-ʔiʒret   l-ambulance ?
dad ,   you   think-**me.D**   of-cost   the-ambulance ?

'Dad, is this the time to think [me] of the cost of the ambulance?!'

From *ha:l l-dunya:* 'this is life' – *baʕdˤ l-ðanni ʔiθm* 'suspicion is sometimes a sin' – 00:03:20 – JOR

3.2 SP-AD representatives as third-person complaints

Third-person complaints take the form of gossip, whereby gossip is defined as a speech event in which a speaker and a hearer engage in a narrative event about an absent third party. The narrative event or story that is the focus of the gossip exchange essentially contains 'codes of conduct and moral rules' that are held in high regard in the community (Sabini and Silver 1982, in Baumeister, Zhang, and Vohs 2004: 112–14; see also Foster 2004: 85). Social actors affirm, redefine, or challenge these codes of conduct and moral rules through gossip, or they introduce and negotiate new ones. Baumeister et al. (2004: 115) maintain that 'gossip serves as a policing device that cultures employ as a low cost method of regulating members' behaviors, especially those that reflect pursuits of selfish interests that come at a cost to the broader community.' See Haddad (2013) and research cited there for an overview of the importance of gossip in the construction of shared values and norms.

Speakers of Levantine Arabic's interest in gossip is evident in examples like (57), where one social actor explicitly invites another social actor to engage with her in stories about other members of the community.

57. Context: Im Bashir visits her neighbor Im Khater. As soon as the two women are about to sit down together, Im Khater says:

ha:ti: ta-ʃu:f ,   hki:-lna: ,   ʃu: ʔaxba:r
give   so-I.see ,   tell-us.D ,   what   news
l-ha:ra   bi-l-tafsˤi:l !
the-neighborhood   in-the-detail !

'Let's hear it! Tell me what's new in the neighborhood, in detail!'

From *ba:b l-ha:ra* 'the neighborhood gate' – Season 1 – Episode 5 – 00:23:30 – SYR

Example (58) is similar, but a bit more interesting for two reasons: first, this time the social actors (Abu Hatem, Abu Marzuq, and Abu Esam) are men rather than women, which goes counter to the misconception that gossip is solely a women's activity; second, the speaker uses a SP-ADC to initiate the gossip event and invite his hearers to engage in it. The SP-AD profiles the speaker as entitled to the knowledge that gossip may bring about by virtue of the relationship he has with the hearers (they are friends) and by virtue of his membership in the community. Entitlement by virtue of community membership is clear in Abu Marzuq's response to Abu Esam's dismissal of the gossip attempt. Abu Marzuq believes that members of the community should be informed about current affairs because it is their responsibility to monitor them.

58. Context: Three shop owners see their neighbor, Abu Qasem, along with two strangers going into the meeting quarters of Mayor Abu Saleh. The three men walk out of their stores, stand together in front of the meeting quarters, and try (unsuccessfully) to figure out who the strangers are.

    Abu Hatem: ʔabu: marzu:ʔ ,   ma: ʕrift-**illi:**   mi:n   ha:do:l
                  Abu Marzuq ,   NEG   you.know-**me.D**   who   these
                  lli: ka:nu: maʕ   ʔabu: Ga:sem ?
                  who   where   with   Abu Qasem   ?
                  'Abu Marzuq, couldn't you find [me] out who these men that came with Abu Qasem are?'

    Abu Marzuq: ʃu: biʕarrif-ni: .   bi-haya:t-i: ma: ʃift-un .
                  what   inform-me .   in-life-my   NEG   saw-them .
                  'How should I know? I've never seen them.'

    Abu Esam: ... kil wa:hed   ʕala: ʃiɣl-o   ...
                  ... everyone   to   work-his   ...
                  'Everyone go back to your work.'

    Abu Marzuq: ʔax-i: ,   ma: bidna: naʕrif   ʃu:
                  Brother-my ,   NEG   we.need   know   what
                  ʕam-bisʕi:r   bi-ha-l-ha:ra ?
                  PROG-happen   in-this-the-neighborhood ?
                  'Brother, don't we need to know what's happening in this neighborhood?'

3.58 From *ba:b l-ha:ra* 'the neighborhood gate' – Season 1 – Episode 6 – 00:40:35 – SYR

When people engage in gossip, they engage in the affirmation, redefinition, or negotiation of social values, beliefs, and norms. For example, in (59) from Syrian Arabic, the neighborhood doctor Abu Esam criticizes a fellow resident's negligence of his sick wife and overtly judges his behavior as unacceptable. By doing this, he affirms the shared value that a husband must take care of his wife, or that people in general must take care of one another. Abu Esam's entitlement to the criticism as profiled by the SP-AD follows from his community membership and his self-assigned role as cultural police. This latter form of authority does not come for free. Abu Esam's reputation as a caring husband and as a charitable community member makes both his criticism and his self-conceptualization as cultural police pass unchallenged.

59. Context: Idaashari's wife is sick, but Idaashari is not doing anything about it. One of Idaashari's sons comes to see Doctor Abu Esam to ask for medication for his mother. Abu Esam asks the young man if his father knows about his wife's illness. When the

son's answer comes back as affirmative, Abu Esam becomes indignant that Idaashari is neglecting his wife. He says:

?alla: yisˤilh-o !   wlek   ta:rek   hirimt-o
God   make.good-him !   INTER   he.leaving   wife-his
daˤfa:ne . . .   bi-l-be:t ,   w-?a:ˤed-**li:**   bi-l-?aha:wi: ?
weak . . .   in-the-house , and-sitting-**me.D**   in-the-coffee shops ?
'May God put some sense into him! He leaves [me] his wife sick at home and sits around in coffee shops?'

From *ba:b l-ḥa:ra* 'the neighborhood gate' – Season 1 – Episode 2 – 00:11:10 – SYR   3.59

The exchange in (60), from the same Syrian show, is a good example of a gossip event about a type of behavior that is frowned upon in the community. By using a SP-AD, the speaker, Abu Khater, instructs the hearer, Abu Esam, to look at the behavior and the individual in question from the perspective of someone acting as cultural police, inviting the hearer to adopt the same attitude that he has.

60. Context: After seeing Abu Satur, an ex-convict, standing on a street corner in the neighborhood, smoking and staring at passers-by, Abu Khater becomes indignant. He stops by Abu Esam's store and gossips about what he saw.

    Abu Khater: wlek   wa:?ef   bi-l-ḥa:ra ,
                 INTER   he.standing   in-the-neighborhood ,
                 w-sa:ned   l-he:tˤ   bi-riʒl-o ,   w-mʃarriˤ-**li:**
                 and-supporting the-wall   with-foot-his ,   and-flauting-**me.D**
                 ha-l-si·ga:ra ,   w-bi-kil   ˤe:n   wi?ha !
                 this-the-cigarette , and-with-all   eye   bold !
                 'He is leaning against a wall in the neighborhood, smoking [me] his cigarette with no shame!'
                 . . .
    Abu Esam: wa:?ef   he:k   bi-nisˤ   l-ḥa:ra ,
                 he.standing   like.this   in-middle   the-neighborhood ,
                 ˤam-byitˤalleˤ   bi-l-ra:yeh   w-l-ʒa:ye ?
                 PROG-looking   at-the-going   and-the-coming ?
                 'Standing in the middle of the neighborhood, staring at passers-by?'
    Abu Khater: ?alla: waki:lak,   ya: ?abu: ˤisˤa:m ,
                 I.swear,   VOC   Abu Esam ,
                 ma: ʃtahe:t   ?illa: ?ixlaˤ-o   kaff ,
                 NEG   I.desired   except   strike-him   slap ,
                 hirril-lo   sna:n-o .
                 shatter-him.D   teeth-his .
                 'Believe me, Abu Esam, all I wanted to do was slap him in the face and knock out his teeth.'
    Abu Esam: . . . l-ˤama: ʃu: ?ali:l   haya:
                 . . . the-blindness   what lacking   modesty

w-ʔali:l   ʔadab !   wlek   mu: ʃa:yef
and-lacking   manner !   INTER   NEG   he.seeing
l-hari:m   bi-ʕyu:n-o   bi-l-ha:ra ?
the-women   with-eyes-his   in-the-neighborhood ?

'May blindness strike him; how lacking in modesty and manners! Can't he see that there are women walking in the neighborhood?'

Abu Khater: ya: ʔax-i: ,   fhimna: ,   ʔabu: l-Na:r
            VOC   brother-my ,   we.understand ,   Abu l-Nar
            ʔaʒʒar-o   l-be:t .   ʔe: yiʔʕod   yindʕirib
            rented-him   the-house . okay   he.sit   be-stricken
            ʕala: ʔalb-o   w-yiʔʕod   bi-be:t-o ,
            on   heart-his   and-sit   in-house-his ,
            mu: yitfattal-**li:**   bi-l-sa ʔa:ye? . . .
            NEG   wander-**me.D**   in-the-alleys . . .

'Brother, we get that he has a rented a house in the neighborhood from Abu l-Nar. But if he has a house, he should stay in it, damn it, and not wander [me] around in the alleys of the neighborhood.'

Abu Esam: lek   ʔax-i: ,   ha:da: wa:ħed   xarri:ʒ hbu:s .
            INTER   brother-my ,   this   one   ex-prisoner .
            ʃu: biddo   yitʕlaʕ   minn-o   yaʕni: ?
            what   should   come   from-him   this.mean ?
            xarri:ʒ hbu:s .
            ex-convict .

'Brother, this guy is an ex-convict. What else should one expect from an ex-convict?'

Abu Khater: bas   ha:ret-na: mu: malfa: li-l-ziʕra:n .
            but   neighborhood-our   NEG   shelter   for-the-bad.guys .
            la:zem   yifham   ha-l-ʃi: .
            he.must   understand   this-the-thing .

'But our neighborhood is not a shelter for bad guys. He must understand this.'

Abu Esam: . . .   raħ   nħitʕ   l-zaʕi:m   bi-l-sʕu:ra ,
            . . .   will   we.put   the-chief   in-the-picture ,
            ʔax-i: ,   w-huwwe   ʃu: byirtiʔi: minsa:wi: .
            brother-my ,   and-he   what   he.suggest   we.do .

'We will inform the mayor, brother, and do what he recommends.'

3.60 From *ba:b l-ha:ra* 'the neighborhood gate' – Season 1 – Episode 18 – 00:21:20 – SYR

The SP-AD complaint in (61) is an additional example. It is interesting for two reasons. First, it shows that gossip may be based on lies. The speaker in this case implies that the subject of his gossip, Abu Esam, is not qualified enough to be a leader and thus he should not pretend to be one. Both he and the hearers know that this characterization of Abu Esam is a lie. The general value motivating the lie still holds, however: one should not pretend to be what one is not. Second, the example confirms Sadiqi's observation that 'gossip cuts across social variables of geographical origin, class,' and so on (2003: 251). The speaker and the hearers are of a low socio-economic status, but their gossip targets an individual of a high socio-economic status. Conversely, in (60) the speaker and hearer are of a high socio-economic status compared to the subject of their gossip. Gossip events like these help in keeping the different social worlds that would otherwise rarely mix informed about each other's news and updates, and about any potential danger that they may pose to one another.

61. Context: Abu Ghaleb, a street vendor, visits his friends Abu l-Nar and Idaashari. Abu Ghaleb updates his friends about *ha:ret l-dˤabeʕ* 'the neighborhood of the hyena,' a community that all three men dislike. He starts by talking about Abu Esam, the neighborhood barber and physician, who had been asked to fill in for the mayor while he and his assistant, Abu Shihab, go out of town. The speaker criticizes Abu Esam for acting as if he were the real mayor while the mayor and Abu Shihab are gone.

    ʔabu: ʕisˤa:m   ma:sik-**li:**   ha-l-ha:ra ,   w-ʕa:mel-**li:**
    Abu Esam   managing-**me.D** this-the-neighborhood , and-making-**me.D**
    la-ha:l-o   ʔi:me w-si:me ,   lek   ma:-nu: msˤaddiʔ
    to-self-him   value and-name ,   INTER   NEG-he   believing
    ha:l-o   bi-ɣya:b   l-zaʕi:m   w-ʔabu: ʃha:b !
    self-him   in-absence   the-chief   and-Abu Shihaab !
    'Abu Esam is managing [me] the neighborhood and acting [me] like a very important person in the absence of the chief and Abu Shihaab!'

From *ha:b l-ha:ra* 'the neighborhood gate' – Season 1 – Episode 9 – 00:12:25 – SYR   3.61

SP-ADCs may be used to criticize a specific individual and a specific behavior as above. They may also be used to criticize a social phenomenon that the speaker finds unacceptable. For example, in (62), from Jordanian Arabic, the speaker Abu Awwad considers it socially unacceptable for salespersons to go from door to door selling merchandise. He goes on to say that there is a security reason behind his objection as well: namely, that vendors who go from door to door may in fact be thieves posing as vendors. Another Jordanian example is shown in (63), in which the speaker criticizes the social phenomenon of hiring housemaids. According to the speaker, some people do so not because they need help at home, but rather as an attempt to show off and pretend that they belong to a certain socio-economic class. In both cases, the speakers put themselves on stage as cultural police, and they instruct their hearers, including the show's viewers, to evaluate their comments from the perspective of community members and citizens who take the higher moral ground.

62. Context: Abu Awwad hears a knock on the door. He opens the door only to find a man going from door to door to sell merchandise. He dislikes the whole idea of door-to-door sales and says:

```
ʔimma:   na:s    ma:    btistiħi:!    galabu:-li:
but      people  NEG    have.shame!   they.converted-me.D
yya:ha:  daka:ki:n  mutanaggile,  ʔi:.
it       stores     mobile,       INTER.
```
'What kind of people are these that have no shame! They have converted [me] conventional storefronts into mobile stores.'

3.62 From *ʔabu: ʕawwa:d* 'Abu Awwad' – Season 1 – Episode 6 – 00:01:00 – JOR

63. Context: Abu Marzuq and Jamil are talking about a new fad in town: hiring housemaids. Abu Marzuq comments:

```
l-ɣi:re       ʕabbet   l-balad,       l-ɣi:re       ʕabbet
the-jealousy  filled   the-country,   the-jealousy  filled
l-balad.      kul      wa:ħed    ga:ʕed   biʒib-li:      bi-binit
the-country.  every    one       keep     bring-me.D     in-girl
w-bihutˤ-ha:   ʕind-o.       miʃa:n   ʔe:ʃ?   miʃa:n
and-put-her   at.place-his.  for      what?   for
yguːlu:       fi:       ʕind-o         xaddaːme!
they.say      there     at.place-his   maid!
```
'People love to make others jealous. Everyone is hiring [me] a maid to work in his house. Why? Just so that people would say that he has a maid and get jealous of him.'

3.63 From *ʔabu: ʕawwa:d* 'Abu Awwad' – Season 1 – Episode 8 – 00:10:15 – JOR

4 Conclusion

This chapter has shown that speakers employ SP-ADs in their utterances in order to assume responsibility for their utterance and for the attitude they attach to it. They also profile themselves as a form of authority in relation to the at-issue content of their utterance, to the hearer, and to the activity they are involved in. In all this, social actors take into account their identities and the identities of their interlocutors, as well as the sociocultural values, beliefs, and norms that members of the community share and take for granted. SP-ADCs may be used in accordance with these identities and sociocultural beliefs and thus affirm and maintain them. Alternatively, they may be used to challenge existing identities and beliefs, redefine them, or even introduce and negotiate new ones.

The next chapter shifts the focus to the hearer and discusses hearer-oriented attitude datives.

Notes

1. https://www.wattpad.com/147685475-aria-a-psych-fanfiction-chapter-12 (accessed on November 25, 2016).
2. The use of *yirdˤa: ʕle:-k* 'may God be pleased with you' makes the order a little milder and ends the conversation on a good note.

3 This is an endearing term that is often – though not exclusively – used by parents or older relatives addressing younger people. It is based on the premise that the young must always outlive the old and not the other way around. As such, it may be translated as 'may you outlive me!'
4 In Islam, a husband may unilaterally divorce his wife by pronouncing her divorced.

4

Hearer-Oriented Attitude Datives in Social Context

1 Introduction

In the previous chapter, we saw that a speaker may choose to profile herself on stage as a form of authority that is entitled to make an utterance (for example, give an order) and to expect any effort or consideration it may require of the hearer. This profile functions as a perspectivizer that instructs the hearer to view the at-issue content of the utterance in a special way. In this chapter, we will examine structures with a different type of dative perspectivizer: namely, hearer-oriented attitude datives (HR-ADs). These utterances contain an optional dative clitic referring to the hearer. Examples (1) through (4) are from Syrian, Lebanese, Jordanian, and Palestinian Arabic respectively. The HR-ADs in boldface in these examples may all be deleted without altering the truth-conditional meaning of the utterances.

1. Context: Abu Ghaleb, a peddler who sells chickpeas in a number of neighborhoods, gossips with his friends about the residents of one neighborhood, *ħa:ret l-dˤabeʕ* 'the neighborhood of the hyena.'
w-ʔabu: di:bo ,   ʕa:mil-**lak**   hafle   mtˤantˤane lyo:m
and-Abu Dibo ,   throwing-**you.D**   party   huge   today
bi-ħa:rt-o ,   ʕa:zem   ʕale:-ha: ʃab:ab   w-rʒa:l
in-neighborhood-his ,   inviting to-it   youth   and-men
ħa:ret   l-dˤabeʕ   killaya:t-un . ʔa:l   ʃu: ,   farħa:n
neighborhood   the-hyena   all-them .   say   what , he.happy
b-raʒʕet   hirimt-o   w-ʔibn-o   ʔil-o .
with-return   wife-his   and-son-his   to-him .
'Abu Dibo is throwing [you] a huge party and he has invited all the men, young and old, of the Neighborhood of the Hyena. All this, he says, is because he is happy that he is back with his wife and kid.'

4.1 From *ba:b l-ħa:ra* 'the neighborhood gate' – Season 1 – Episode 9 – 00:12:30 – SYR

2. Context: Two employees at the presidential palace in Lebanon, a newcomer and an old-timer, are chatting while working. The old-timer is a farmer who, with her husband, takes care of the President's vegetables, milk, eggs, and so on. When the newcomer asks the farmer how long they have worked in the palace, the farmer answers that they have worked there for a year and goes on to explain how she and her husband got the job:

kinna: ʔana: w-raʔi:f ʕe:yʃi:n bi-ha-l-ʒirid ,
we.were I and-Raif living in-this-the-countryside ,
ma: ʕa-be:l-na: be:l . wa-ʔilla:
NEG on-mind-our mind . and-all.of.a.sudden
btiʒi:-**lik** huni:k sayya:ra , ha-l-tˤu:l ,
come-**you.D** there car , this-the-length ,
min hawn la-hawni:k , bitziʔ-na: w-bitʒi:b-na: ,
from here to-there , it.load-us and-bring-us ,
wara:-ha: kamyu:n fi-i kil l-hayawa:ne:t tabaʕ-na: . . .
behind-it truck in-it all the-animals POSS-our . . .

'Raif and I were living in the countryside without a worry in the world. All of a sudden, there came [you] a car, it was this long, from here to there. It brought us [to the palace], followed by a truck that carried all our animals.'

From *l-sayyida l-θa:niya* 'the second lady' – 00:53:50 – LEB   4.2

3. A Jordanian man on Facebook criticizes women whose style of dress and religious behavior are, in his opinion, contradictory.

btilbis-**lak** fi:zo:n w-nisˤ ʒism-a: mbayyan
she.dress-**you.D** tights and-half body-her showing
w-btitˤlaʕ ʔidda:m l-ʕa:lam w-l-na:s
and-she.go.out before the-world and-the-people
bi-l-nha:r . w-bitru:ħ tnazzil post ya: rabb
in-the-daytime . and-she.go upload post VOC Lord
tiʔbal sˤya:m-i: .
accept fasting-my .

'She wears [you] tights, with half of her body showing, and she goes out in front of everyone like this during the day. Then she uploads a post on Facebook saying: O Lord, accept my fasting.'

بتلبسلك فيزون ونص جسمها مبين وبتطلع قدام العالم والناس بالنهار. وبتروح تنزل بوست يا رب تقبل صيامي.

4. Context: A Palestinian man on Facebook criticizes women who complain about thirst during the fasting month of Ramadan.

btiʃrab-**lak** ʔarbaʕa liter mayy ʔabl l-faʒer .
she.drinks-**you.D** four liter water before the-dawn .
bas yʔu:l ʔalla:hu ʔakbar , bithiss bi-l-ʒafa:f .
when he.say God.is.greatest , she.feel of-the-dryness .

subḥa:na lla:h
may.God.be.praised

'She drinks [you] four liters of water before dawn (before fasting begins). Once she hears the call for prayer at dawn (announcing that fasting has begun), she feels thirsty. Praise be to God.'

بتشربلك 4 لتر مي قبل الفجر
بس يقوول الله أكبر بتحس بالجفاف سبحان الله

HR-ADs have two main functions: first, to grab the hearer's attention; and second, to recruit some form of hearer engagement in relation to the speaker, the main message of her utterance, or both. Regarding the second function, a speaker may use a HR to place the hearer on stage in an attempt to recruit his empathy, solicit his assent, and/or invoke shared experience, knowledge, and membership. Section 2 of this chapter provides an overview of the two main functions. Sections 3 and 4 discuss HR-ADs as tools for hearer engagement in more detail, explore how these datives interact with contextual factors, and highlight the different forms that hearer engagement may take. Section 3 deals with HR-ADCs used as commissives, and Section 4 focuses on ADCs as representatives.

2 HR-ADs, attention grabbing, and hearer engagement

One of the main functions of HR-ADs is to grab the attention of the hearer. The speaker uses a HR-AD in order to make sure that the hearer pays attention to her utterance or to the part of her utterance that she thinks is important. Such uses are typical at the beginning of storytelling and personal narratives. Consider (5) and (6), from Syrian and Palestinian Arabic respectively. The speakers in both examples relate a personal experience to an acquaintance. The utterances mark the beginning of the narratives. The speakers use a HR-AD in an attempt to direct the hearers' gaze away from whatever might be distracting them (for example, the howling of the wolves in (5)) and to encourage them to pay attention to the story instead.

5. Context: One night Abdo, a young man who works in the neighborhood public bath, visits the guard of the neighborhood, an older man named Abu Majed. All of a sudden, wolves start howling in the distance. Abdo gets scared, so Abu Majed tells him a story, partly to distract him and partly to show off.

   ʕo:d   la-ʔaḥki:-lak   ha-l-si:re   wlek   ya: ʕabdo: .
   sit   to-tell-you.D   this-the-story   INTER   VOC   Abdo .
   bi-zama:n-i: ʔaʕid-**lak** . . .   la-ḥa:l-i:
   in-past-my   I.was.sitting-**you.D** . . . by-self-my
   bi-ha-l-le:l ,   ma: btismaʕ   so:t   ha: . . .
   in-this-the-night, NEG   you.hear   noise   INTER . . .

   'Sit, Abdo, let me tell you this story. A while ago when I was younger, I was sitting [you] by myself at night. It was so quiet you couldn't hear a noise, I'm telling you.'

4.5 From *ba:b l-ḥa:ra* 'the neighborhood gate' – Season 1 – Episode 7 – 00:13:50 – SYR

6. Context: A man relates to an acquaintance an event that happened to him while driving one day.

kunt-**lak**	maːʃiː-**lak**	bi-l-tˤariːk	l-sˤaħraːwi:	...
I.was-you.D	driving-you.D	in-the-road	the-desert	

   'I was [you] driving [you] on a desert road.'

   From *watˤan ʕa watar* 'a nation on a string' – *dawaːwiːn ʃabaːb* 'young people's anthologies' – 00:02:30 – PAL 4.6

The function of HR-ADs as attention grabbers is not limited to the beginning of narratives. Speakers may use a HR-AD as an attention grabber with any part of their utterance to which they believe their hearer should pay attention. Take (7), for example. The speaker, Abu Qasem, meets with the neighborhood mayor, Abu Saleh, with the intention of telling him about two Palestinian men that he recently met. He plans to ask Abu Saleh if he would be willing to meet with them. The two Palestinians are rebels fighting against the British in Palestine, and they are seeking financial support from different sources. Abu Saleh is an influential leader with connections, and Abu Qasem thinks he may be able to rally support for their cause. Abu Qasem sets the scene by relating the event that led to his encounter with the two Palestinians. He uses a HR-AD in the part of his account to which he wants Abu Saleh to start listening more carefully.

7. Context: Abu Qasem tells Abu Saleh, the neighborhood mayor, about his encounter with two Palestinian men who are seeking help in the form of money and weapons in their fight against the British:

w-ʔanaː	ʔaːʕed	bi-ʔardˤ	l-mleːħa,	maː
while-I	sitting	in-land	the-Mleha,	NEG
ʃift-**illak**	ɣeːr	tneːn	raːkbiːn	ʕalaː faras-un,
see-you.D	except	two	riding	on horses-their,
w-faːytiːn	ʕa-l-ʔardˤ	...		
and-entering	to-the-land	...		

   'I was sitting in the Mleha land, when all of a sudden I see [you] two men coming in on their horses.'

   From *baːb l-ħaːra* 'the neighborhood gate' – Season 1 – Episode 5 – 00:41:50 – SYR 4.7

Attention grabbing is rarely a HR-AD's only function, however. In addition to grabbing the hearer's attention, HR-ADs often anchor the main message of an utterance (the object, or OBJ, in our model), along with any evaluation of it, to the hearer in an attempt to mark or solicit his engagement. As Figure 4.1 schematically illustrates, the speaker places the hearer on stage as an involved actor rather than a passive spectator, and invites him to engage in what is said in some capacity. As I mentioned earlier, a HR-AD is often used as an appeal for the hearer's empathy, assent, and/or shared experience, knowledge, and membership.

The solid lines connecting the hearer to the on-stage entities in Figure 4.1 mark one major difference between HR-ADCs and SP-ADCs. Observe the stancetaking

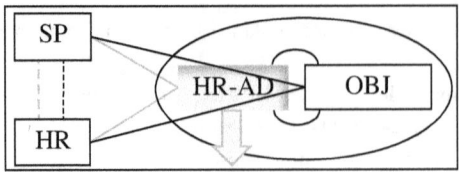

I solicit your engagement.

Figure 4.1 Stancetaking stage model of HR-ADCs

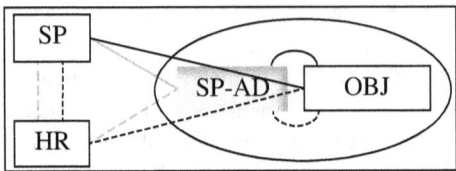

Figure 4.2 – Stancetaking stage model of SP-ADCs

stage model of SP-ADCs in Figure 4.2. The broken lines connecting the hearer to the on-stage entities signify that the speaker has placed these entities and the evaluations anchored to them in the hearer's field, giving him the chance to accept or reject them as part of his dominion or view of reality (see Chapter 2, Section 4.2). In contrast, these lines in Figure 4.1 are solid, signifying that the speaker has already marked the on-stage entities and the evaluations anchored to them as part of the hearer's dominion. This makes it harder for the hearer to align negatively with the speaker because he will first have to reject the engagement she has attributed to him.

Now we turn to attested instances of HR-ADs as markers of hearer engagement. We start with HR-ADs as employed in commissives.

3 HR-ADCs as commissives: recognizing the hearer as an authority

We saw in the previous chapter that a social actor may use a SP-ADC to profile herself on stage as entitled to give a directive (for example, an order) by virtue of a form of authority that she has over the hearer. This authority derives from aspects of the social actors' identities (individual, group, and/or relational) and may be based on hierarchy, reciprocity, or knowledge. When one social actor uses a SP-ADC in this capacity, her interlocutor may respond with a HR-ADC in recognition of her authority and as an appeal for her empathy or assent. Recognizing a social actor's authority or legitimizing it, whether non-verbally by obeying a command or verbally via the use of a HR-AD, is important because authority needs to be accepted to survive; it may not survive without 'some degree of legitimacy' (Dickerson, Flanagan, and O'Neill 2009: 20).

HR-ADCs of the type just described are common in response to hierarchical authority. Consider the following two examples from Chapter 3, which I have included here in more detail as (8) and (9). In both contexts, the exchange starts with a SP-ADC that profiles one social actor as a hierarchical authority in relation to another social actor. By virtue of this authority, the one who utters a SP-ADC considers himself entitled to give orders to the hearer. In (8) the authority figure is a father, and in (9) he is a 'tough guy' at a pub. In these specific cases, the authority figures threaten to inflict physical harm on their hearers if they defy them. When the hearers take the floor and become speakers themselves, they comply with the orders given to them and commit themselves to act on them. In addition, they use a HR-AD to acknowledge the form of authority that their hearers profile for themselves and to solicit their empathy and acceptance.

8. Context: Idaashari has two sons, Sobhi and Maarouf. One night Idaashari comes home drunk and decides that his donkey is cold and needs to be covered. He calls Sobhi and says:

   Idaashari: nitˤtˤ   ʒib-**li:**   lha:f   w-ɣatˤtˤi:-**li:**
                  go   bring-**me.D** blanket   and-cover-me.D
                  ha-l-ʔasˤi:l,   yalla: .
                  this-the-well-bred ,   go.on .
                  'Go bring [me] a blanket and cover this well-bred (normally used for horses). Go on.'

   (Sobhi questions his father's order, so Idaashari gets upset and tries to beat him up. Maarouf steps in in an attempt to resolve the problem):

   Maarouf: halla?   ʔana: bʒib-lo   lha:f
               immediately   I   bring-him.D   blanket
               la-l-ḥma:r ,   w-hɣatˤtˤi:-**lak**   yya·   bi-ʔi·day-i·
               for-the-donkey ,   and-I.cover-**you.D**   it   with-hands-my .
               'I will immediately bring a blanket for the donkey and cover [you] him with my own hands.'

From *ba:b l-ḥa:ra* 'the neighborhood gate' – Season 1 – Episode 17 – 00:22:40 – SYR   4.8

9. Context: During the war in Lebanon, it was common for men with weapons and connections to act tough in public. In this scene, a tough guy in a pub has become upset with one of the waiters. He is about to start a fight when the pub manager tries to calm him down. The customer says with indignation and a patronizing tone:

   Customer: fahhim-**li:**   ʃayyi:l-tak   ʔana   ma: hada:
                explain-**me.D**   workers-your   I   no one
                byitʕa:tˤa: maʕ-i: ʔabadan .   w-ʔana: lli:
                interfere   with-me   ever .   and-I   what
                biddi: yye: bi-l-mahall   biddi: ʔaʕeml-o .
                I.want   it   in-the-store   I.want   do-it .
                'Explain [me] to your employees that they should never mess with me, and that I will do whatever I want in here.'

   Pub manager: . . . halla?   bfahhim-**lak**   ye:h-un   kill-un
                  . . . now   I.explain-**you.D**   them   all-them

        sawa: ,   ʔiste:z
        together , sir
        'I will explain [you] this to all of them right away, Sir.'

4.9 From *bi-l-nisbe la-bukra ʃu:* 'what are the plans for tomorrow' – 00:52:20 – LEB

The HR-ADCs in (8) and (9) are commissives. Citing Austin (1962), Searle (1976: 7) holds that commissives are speech acts, such as promises and pledges, that '"commit the speaker to a certain action."' The use of ADs in examples (8) and (9) are significant because they lead to convergent alignment in a way that the at-issue content alone would not. By using a HR-AD, Maarouf in (8) and the pub manager in (9) commit themselves to acting on the commands of Idaashari and the customer respectively, not because they evaluate the commands as reasonable or fair; in fact, they do not. Rather, they commit because they recognize the sources of the commands as a form of authority; see Dickerson, Flanagan, and O'Neill (2009: 18–20) for a related discussion.

To elaborate, consider Figure 4.3 as a schematic presentation of Maarouf's interaction with his father in (8). Initially, Idaashari uses a SP-ADC to give one of his sons, Sobhi, an order. Sobhi evaluates the order as unreasonable, questions it, and aligns negatively with his father with regard to it. This infuriates Idaashari. Note that Sobhi does not question his father's authority; he only questions the reasonableness of the order (see Figure 3.8). Maarouf, Idaashari's other son, steps in and resolves the issue with a HR-AD commissive. Maarouf, like his brother Sobhi, evaluates Idaashari's order as unreasonable, as the first stage presentation in Figure 4.3 illustrates. That is, under different circumstances, Maarouf would not agree to cover the donkey with a blanket. However, the SP-AD, along with the authority it profiles, serves as a perspectivizer that shapes Maarouf's final decision, resulting in his convergent alignment with his father. This alignment is expressed via a HR-AD commissive. As the viewing arrangement in the second stage presentation in Figure 4.3 illustrates, Maarouf commits himself to covering the donkey with a blanket in recognition of his father as a form of authority and as an attempt to recruit his empathy and assuage his anger. Importantly, he also instructs his father to view the commissive in the same way. The HR-AD commissive makes it clear to the father that the order has been attended to only because he, as an authority figure, gave it. It serves as a reaffirmation of the father's relational identity. Maarouf caters to his father's association rights and to his father's belief that he should be respected and obeyed by his sons, no matter how bizarre his commands may be. This catering is at the expense of Maarouf's equity right that he be 'treated fairly' and 'not duly imposed upon' (Spencer-Oatey 2002: 540). As the second stage presentation in Figure 4.3 shows, Idaashari accepts his son's commissive, and the outcome is positive alignment.

Similar observations may be extended to (9). The pub customer feels that his individual identity as a tough guy, and by association his quality face, which follows from his desire for people to evaluate him positively in terms of this individual identity, are threatened. He uses a SP-AD directive to reaffirm his identity and demand respect. The pub manager recognizes this desire and uses a HR-AD commissive to enhance the customer's quality face, to cater to his association right to be respected,

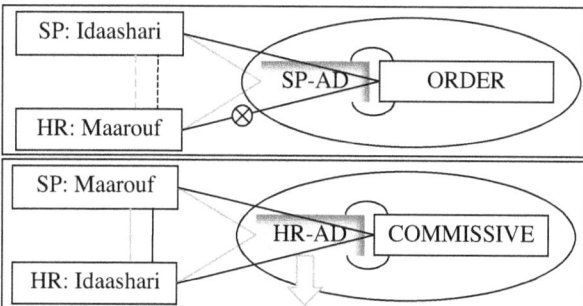

- I commit myself to this action in recognition of your authority and of our corresponding rights and obligations.
- I appeal for your empathy and acceptance.

Figure 4.3 – Stancetaking stage model of (8)

and to assuage his anger. All this is done at the expense of the pub manager's equity right to be treated fairly. Note that the customer's SP-AD directive and the pub manager's HR-AD commissive challenge the latter's identity as a high-ranking employee who is used to giving SP-AD orders and receiving HR-AD commissives rather than the other way around.

A SP-ADC is not a prerequisite for HR-AD commissives. A speaker may extend a promise in the form of a HR-AD commissive to tell the hearer that she is willing to carry out a certain action only if he authorizes it. In this case, the speaker uses a HR-AD to solicit the hearer's assent. To illustrate, consider (10) and (11). The speaker Abu Shihab is second-in-command in the community. He addresses his boss, Mayor Abu Saleh. Abu Shihab recognizes Abu Saleh as the leader of the neighborhood; his authorization is necessary before undertaking any action relevant to the community. By using HR-AD commissives, Abu Shihab not only commits himself to the actions he suggests but also places his hearer on stage as boss, affirming their respective identities in the process. Note that in (10) Abu Brahim would be the primary affectee, should Abu Shihab do what he offers to do. Abu Saleh is placed on stage via the HR-AD as boss and not as affectee.

10. Context: A young man, Brahim, whose father Abu Brahim has been the victim of burglary, was attacked by two men the night before. Abu Brahim complains to Mayor Abu Saleh in the presence of Abu Shihab, the second-in-command in the neighborhood. Abu Brahim believes it was the children of Idaashari, the man whom he has accused of stealing from him, who beat up his son. The conversation unfolds as follows:

Abu Saleh: ... ʔinte   bitʃikk   bi-hada: ?
            ... you   are.suspicious   about-someone ?
            'Do you suspect anyone (of hurting your son)?'

Abu Ibrahim: . . . bʃikk . . . bi-wla:d l-ʔidaʕʃari: . . .
. . . I.am.suspicious . . . about-boys the-Idaashari . . .
hinne l-wahi:di:n lli: ʔilhun masʕlaha yidʕirbu:
they the-only.ones that have benefit beat
bra:hi:m , liʔann-i: ʃtake:t ʕala: ʔabu:-hun l-hara:mi: .
Brahim , because-I told on father-their the-thief .
'I suspect Idaashari's boys. They are the only ones who have a motive to beat up Brahim, since I accused their father of being the thief.'
. . .

Abu Saleh: Abu ʃha:b , ʔo:ltak wla:d l-ʔidaʕʃari: byaʕimluw-a: ?
Abu Shihab , do.you.think boys the-Idaashari do-it ?
'Abu Shihab, do you think Idaashari's boys would do something like this?'

Abu Shihab: kil ʃi: wa:red , zaʕi:m . bithib
everything possible , chief . you.like
niʃhat-**lak** ya:hun , naʕmil-lun badan
drag-**you.D** them , we.give-them.D beating
ʕa-l-naʕem , barki: byiʕtirfu: ?
on-the-gentle , perhaps they.confess?
'Anything is possible, Chief. Would you like us to drag [**you**] them here and give them a beating? Perhaps they'll confess.'

Abu Brahim: la: la: la: ! la: tiʃhatʕ hada: la-ho:n ,
no no no ! NEG drag anyone to-here ,
ʔalla: yirdʕa: ʕle:k , ya: ʔabu: ʃha:b . . .
may.God.be.pleased.with.you , VOC Abu Shihaab . . .
'No, no, no! Don't drag anyone anywhere, I beg you!'

Abu Saleh: bas ʔiza: ma: tʕa:qabu: ʕala ʕamlit-un
but if NEG they.be.punished for action-their
hay , mumkin yittʕa:walu: ʕala: wla:d
this , possible they.go.after children
l-ha:ra !
the-neighborhood !
'But if they aren't punished for what they have done, they may go after others in the neighborhood.'

4.10 From *ba:b l-ha:ra* 'the neighborhood gate' – Season 1 – Episode 5 – 00:16:00 – SYR

11. Context: Abu Saleh, the neighborhood mayor, is upset because Abu l-Nar, a belligerent man from another neighborhood, is causing trouble in the neighborhood. Abu Shihab, who is second-in-command, makes the following suggestion to Abu Saleh:
ʔinte bas ʔaʃʃer , zaʕi:m . w-illi: xalaʔ-ak ,
you only signal , chief . and-who created-you ,
btʕa:liʕ-**lak** yya:h min l-ha:ra
I.remove-**you.D** him from the-neighborhood

ʕam-bidabdeb	ʕala:	ʔi:de-e	w-riʒle-e .
PROG-crawl	on	hands-his	and-legs-his .

'Just say the word, Chief. By God who created you, I will make [you] him leave the neighborhood crawling on all fours.'

From *ba:b l-ha:ra* 'the neighborhood gate' – Season 1 – Episode 10 – 00:48:00 – SYR

4.11

Evidence that the speaker in (10) and (11) treats Abu Saleh as a boss who has the final say comes from such contextualization cues as *bithib* 'would you like' in (10) and *ʔinte bas ʔaffer, zaʕi:m* 'just say the word, Chief' in (11), indicating that no action the speaker suggests will be implemented unless the hearer gives a green light. Additional evidence comes from the last two turns of the dialog in (10). When Abu Brahim pleads with Abu Shihab not to go after Idaashari's children, it is Abu Saleh rather than Abu Shihab who responds. Abu Shihab does not respond because the decision is not his to make.

The four examples above profile the hearer as a form of hierarchical authority. We learned in the previous chapter that two other forms of authority also exist in relation to SP-ADs; these are reciprocal authority and knowledge authority. Consider (12) as an example of a HR-AD commissive used to seek the hearer's assent in recognition of his reciprocal authority. The speaker is the police chief, Abu Jawdat, and the hearer is Idaashari, a suspect in a burglary who has been accused of stealing fifty gold coins. Abu Jawdat is supposed to cross-examine Idaashari. Instead, he tries to strike a deal with him. In a less corrupt world, Abu Jawdat would represent a form of hierarchical authority in relation to the accused. Nevertheless, by trying to strike a deal with Idaashari, he demotes himself to possessing a form of reciprocal authority, and he uses a HR-AD to profile the suspect as an equal. By doing so, he gives Idaashari equal status and equal linguistic freedom. That is, if Idaashari chooses to cooperate, he will be in a mutual debt relation with Abu Jawdat, and he will be able to use SP-AD directives to address him.

12. Context: Idaashari is accused of breaking into a house and stealing fifty Ottoman gold coins. The victim, a textile shop owner named Abu Brahim, files a report with the police to have him arrested. The police chief, Abu Jawdat, is a greedy man. He tries to strike a deal with Idaashari, but the latter denies that he stole the gold in the first place. Here is the part of the conversation where Abu Jawdat tries but eventually fails to draw the suspect in.

ʃu:f,	ya:	ʔidaʕʃari: ,	ʔana:	rah	ʔuwiʕd-ak		
look ,	VOC	Idaashari ,	I	will	promise-you		
waʕed	ʃaraf ,	ʔinn-i:	tʕa:lʕ-ak	min	ha-l-mawdʕu:ʕ		
promise	honor ,	that-I	remove-you	from	this-the-issue		
bari:ʔ ,	w-ʃari:f	kama:n (.)	bas	b-ʃartʕ		wa:ħed (.)	
innocent ,	and-honest	also (.)	but	on-condition		one (.)	
nitʔa:sam	l-dahaba:t (.)	w-la:	mi:n	ʃa:f (.)	wala:	mi:n	diri: (.)
we.divide	the-gold (.)	and-no	one	saw (.)	nor	one	knew (.)
... w-ʔiza:	baddak (.)	ʔihbis-lak		ʔabu: bra:hi:m (.)			
... and-if	you.want (.)	I.imprison-**you.D**		Abu Brahim (.)			

	biħbis-**lak**	yya:h (.)	w-blabs-o	tihme	kama:n .
	I.imprison-you.D	him (.)	and-I.dress-him	accusation	also .

'Listen, Idaashari, I am going to make a solemn promise to get you out of this whole thing innocent and to restore your reputation as well, but on one condition: we divide the gold between us. That will be our secret. If you want that I put [you] Abu Brahim in jail, I will put [you] him in jail and fabricate an accusation for him as well.'

4.12 From *ba:b l-ha:ra* 'the neighborhood gate' – Season 1 – Episode 6 – 00:23:00 – SYR

I have not come across any HR-AD commissive as a response to knowledge authority. In principle, this should be possible. Take the medical advice that a doctor offers his patient in (13), a repetition of (42) in Chapter 3. One might postulate that the patient could say (14) in response.

13. Context: Abu Esam, the neighborhood doctor, prescribes an ointment for the garbage collector and explains how to apply it onto his foot. At one point, Abu Esam says:

ʕind	ʕala:	bukra: ,	bitfikk-**illi:**	ha-l-ʃa:ʃe	...
at	on	morning ,	you.remove-me.D	this-the-dressing	...

'First thing in the morning, you remove [me] the wound dressing.'

4.13 From *ba:b l-ha:ra* 'the neighborhood gate' – Season 1 – Episode 20 – 00:46:30 – SYR

14.	bi-ʔamr-ak	haki:m .| ʕala:	bukra: ,	bifikk-**illak**	yya:ha: .
at-order-your	doctor .	on	morning ,	I.remove-you.D	it .

'Okay, Doctor, tomorrow morning I shall remove [you] it.'

Native speakers find (14) slightly awkward in this context. This is because knowledge authority does not require the same type of legitimization or validation that hierarchical or reciprocal authority requires. The latter types of authority are inherently relational and dyadic; a social actor may not be considered a mother, a boss, or a sister if she does not have a child, an employee, or a sibling. When a mother, a boss, or a sister exercises hierarchical or reciprocal authority via a directive, the social actor on the receiving end of this directive may use a HR-AD commissive to acknowledge this relational form of authority and to solicit empathy and/or assent. Knowledge authority, on the other hand, is not inherently dyadic. A social actor may be considered a physician in her own right, whether she has patients or not. The legitimacy of a social actor's role as a knowledge authority is not contingent on the respect and obedience that she may receive from other social actors; rather, it is based on diplomas, skills, expertise, record, and so on. In this sense, knowledge authority does not need the same type of validation via a HR-AD as the other two types of authority.

HR-ADs in commissives of the type we have just examined may be viewed as self-excluding datives. The speaker in such commissives tells the hearer that the ball is in his court, so to speak, and that any action she takes will depend on him. Now we turn to another type of HR-ADC used as representatives. As we will see, unlike in HR-AD commissives, which reference only the hearer, HR-ADs in representatives are self-including datives. That is, although they take the hearer as a referent, the involvement of the hearer is profiled in terms of his membership to a group that the speaker also belongs to.

4 HR-ADCs as representatives

HR-ADCs may also be used as representatives. As we saw in the previous chapter, these are speech acts that 'commit the speaker (in varying degrees) to something's being the case, to the truth of the expressed proposition,' and their content may be assessed as true or false (Searle 1976: 10). A speaker may use a HR-AD representative to praise herself, which often takes the form of bragging. She may also use a HR-AD representative to praise or criticize a third party, a behavior, or a state of affairs. This latter kind of representative is typical of gossip events, in which case HR-ADCs may focus on specific incidents or take the form of truisms. In all this, the function of the HR-AD is to mark the hearer's engagement in the profiled praise or criticism, appealing to shared experience, knowledge, and membership. The HR-AD places the hearer on stage as actively involved rather than passively observing. It instructs him to view the at-issue content of the speaker's utterance from the perspective of an involved individual who shares the speaker's affective stance toward what is being said (for example, interest, amazement, indignation) and her evaluation of the profiled individual, behavior, or state of affairs as acceptable, praiseworthy, revolting, unethical, and so on.

I start with representatives used to brag about one's accomplishments before I turn to gossip events and third-person praise and criticism.

4.1 HR-AD representatives as first-person bragging

Speakers may use HR-AD representatives to talk about specific events. These normally take the form of narratives. When the narrative is about the speaker herself and her personal experience, a HR-AD representative usually takes the form of self-praise, self-promotion, or even bragging.

When a speaker is involved in self-praise or self-promotion, she normally focuses on her affective stance toward her personal experience and tries to communicate value-laden and emotionally charged feelings about certain aspects of it. The affective stance corresponds to what Martin and White (2005) label as affect; it constitutes only one of three types of evaluation, the other two being judgment and appreciation. Culpeper and Haugh (2014), drawing on Edwards (1999: 273), label affect as interpersonal emotions that they define as 'feelings or states of mind often characterized by participants as "irrational and subjective, unconscious rather than deliberate [and] genuine rather than artificial"' (197). As for judgment and appreciation, Martin and White define them as 'institutionalized feelings' that focus on 'shared community values' rather than emotions (2005: 45). Judgment and appreciation may be (and often are) present in exchanges about personal experiences; however, their role is usually subservient to affect and how the event makes the speaker feel about herself and her achievement (for example, excited, impressed).

Self-praise and self-promotion are most effective if the speaker is able to solicit the hearer's emotional engagement and positive alignment. If she succeeds in making another person feel the same about the main content of her utterance, she validates her own feelings. To increase her chances of success, the speaker uses a HR-AD to anchor her narrative to the hearer and to characterize the feelings it invokes as feelings that the hearer would experience if he were in the same situation. The HR-ADs are often attached to the evaluative parts of the narrative or the parts that the speaker thinks are most exciting; see Labov and Waletzky (1967), Labov (1972), and O'Connor (1994). They have an effect similar to that of English utterances like *And get this!* in (15) or *and I kid you not* in the Yelp review in (16).

15. Anyway, this guy says he'll have my job and my pension if I fall asleep again. Just like that! No, sir! You don't mess with a guy like that. **And get this,** he takes the key and locks me in here.

From George C. Chesbro's *Strange Prey and Other Tales of the Hunt* (2004: 41)

16. 'Like I said, **and I kid you not**, $0.01 for a side of jalapeños. Never seen that before, lol.'

From https://www.yelp.com/biz_photos/flights-craft-beer-sports-grill-hawthorne?reviewid=gto74VLHdKrUUO0nyO7G3w&select=89IzNxFkWaknmExrbSF6kw (accessed December 20, 2016)

When a speaker of English uses expressions like these in relation to an evaluative part of her narrative, she tries to accomplish two things: she tries to direct the hearer's gaze to the part she thinks is important, while also anchoring her evaluation and the feelings it invokes in her to the hearer in an attempt to solicit his emotional engagement. This is exactly what the HR-ADs do in the narratives in (17) and (18), parts of which were presented in (5) and (6) in the introduction to this chapter.

17. Context: One night Abdo, a young man who works in the neighborhood public bath, visits the guard of the neighborhood, an older man named Abu Majed. All of a sudden, wolves start howling in the distance. Abdo gets scared, so Abu Majed tells him a story, partly to distract him and partly to show off.

ʕo:d la-ʔaħki:-lak ha-l-si:re , wlek ya: ʕabdo: .
sit to-tell-you.D this-the-story , INTER VOC Abdo .
bi-zama:n-i: ʔaʕid-lak . . . la-ha:l-i:
in-past-my I.was.sitting-you.D . . . by-self-my
bi-ha-l-le:l (.) ma: btismaʕ so:t ha: !
in-this-the-night (.) NEG you.hear noise INTER !
ma: bismaʕ-lak ɣe:r xarbaʃe ʕa-l-ba:b . . .
NEG I.hear-you.D except scratching on-the-door . . .
fazze:t diɣri: ʕa-l-ba:b w-fataħet . . .
I.jumped directly to-the-door and-opened . . .

HEARER-ORIENTED ATTITUDE DATIVES IN SOCIAL CONTEXT

l?i:t-**illak** dˤabeʕ, t?u:l ħma:r ...
I.found-**you.D** hyena, you.say donkey ...
stnawalt-**illak** ha-l-ʕasˤa:ye diɣri: ...
I.grabbed-**you.D** this-the-stick directly ...

'Sit, Abdo, let me tell you this story. A while ago when I was younger, I was sitting [you] by myself at night; it was so quiet you couldn't hear a noise, I'm telling you. All of a sudden, I hear [you] scratching on the door. I saw [you] standing in front of me a hyena so big you would say it was a donkey. I immediately grabbed [you] a stick.'

From *ba:b l-ħa:ra* 'the neighborhood gate' – Season 1 – Episode 7 – 00:13:50 – SYR 4.17

18. Context: A man tries to impress an acquaintance with the outlandish story that he replaced a flat tire on his car with his child's bicycle wheel. This excerpt comes from a YouTube show making fun of individuals like the speaker who think others are too naïve to see through their obvious lies.

kunt-**lak** ma:ʃi:-**lak** bi-l-tˤari:k l-sˤaħra:wi: ...
I.was-**you.D** driving-**you.D** in-the-road the-desert ...
hop ?illa: l-ʕaʒal mbanʃar. ʃu:
oops all.of.a.sudden the-tire flat. what
biddi: ʕmel? fatiħt-**lak** l-sayya:ra min
I.need do? I.opened-**you.D** the-car from
wara:, la?e:t baskale:tit ?ibni: ...
behind, I.found bicycle son-my ...

'I was [you] driving [you] on a desert road, when all of a sudden I had a flat tire. What did I do then? I opened [you] the trunk of the car and found my son's bicycle.'

From *watˤan ʕa watar* 'a nation on a string' – *dawa:wi:n ʃaba:b* 'young people's anthologies' 4.18
– 00:02:30 – PAL

The speaker in (17), Abu Majed, is a guard. Crucial elements of his identity as a guard are his bravery and resourcefulness in times of crisis. He uses the narrative in (17) to promote himself as brave and resourceful. By using HR-ADs, Abu Majed draws the hearer's attention to the important parts of his narrative. As the schematic presentation in Figure 4.4 shows, he also anchors his experience and emotions (for

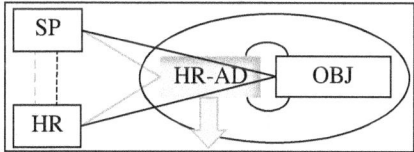

- I instruct you to pay attention to this part.
- I solicit your emotional engagement:
  I find this impressive/amazing/etc., and
  I am sure you will too.

Figure 4.4 Stancetaking stage model of (17)

example, excitement, fear) to the hearer and invites him to accept them as his own. In this sense, the HR-AD resembles an 'involving' *you* as described in O'Connor (1994), which 'draws the interlocutor in' and assigns him the role of agent alongside the speaker (59).

The speaker in (17) may have an additional purpose. He may be using the narrative not only to tell the hearer how brave he is but also to instill bravery as a cultural value in his hearer. However, such purposes are not a necessary driving force behind the use of HR-AD representatives of this type. That is, HR-ADCs that involve self-praise and self-promotion may take the form of pure bragging. This is the case in (18) above and also in (19) and (20) below.

19. Context: Abu Khidir, a relative of Abu Awwad's, comes for a visit. The two have not seen each other for a long time. In this scene, Abu Khidir brags about the multiple cars he owns.

    lda:ʕi: ʕindo   sayya:ra ,   w-ʔixt-ak   ʔim xidʕir
    yours.truly have   car ,   and-sister-your   Im Khidir
    ʕinda: sayya:ra ,   w-xidʕir   ʕindo   sayya:ra   ...
    have   car ,   and-Khidir has   car   ...
    bi-ʔa:xer l-nha:r ,   basʕif-**lak**   yya:hun
    in-end   the-day ,   I.park-**you.D** them
    he:k   bi-ba:b   l-da:r   miθl   l-zi:ne .
    like.this in-door   the-house like   the-ornament .
    'Yours Truly has a car, your sister (my wife) Im Khidir has a car, Khidir has a car ... At the end of the day, I park [you] them like this in front of the house like a decoration.'

4.19 From *ʔabu: ʕawwa:d* 'Abu Awwad' – Season 1 – Episode 1 – 00:02:40 – JOR

20. Context: Nuri, a police officer, brags to his superior, Abu Jawdat, about splashing a suspect with water while the suspect was sleeping as a technique to make him confess to a robbery.

    Nuri: w-safaħt-**illak**   ʕle-e   satʕel   mayy   ba:rde ,
               and-I.splashed-**you.D**   on-him   bucket   water cold ,
               baʕed   ma: ka:n   ɣa:tʕetʕ   bi-l-no:me ...
               after   that he.was   deep   in-the-sleep ...
               'And I splashed [you] him with a bucket of water while he was fast asleep.'
               ((Both Nuri and Abu Jawdat laugh.))

    Abu Jawdat: ʕazʕi:m   ya: Nu:ri: ʕazʕi:m ,
                excellent   VOC   Nuri   excellent ,
                barkatan   byisʕha: w-biɣayyer   raʔy-o .
                perhaps   he.wake.up   and-change   mind-his .
                bas   ʔill-i: ,   inte   mne:n   ʕam-bitʒi:b
                but   tell-me ,   you   from.where   PROG-bring
                ha-l-ʔasa:li:b   ha:y   ha: ?
                these-the-techniques these   INTER ?

'Excellent work, Nuri, excellent work! Perhaps this way he will wake up and change his mind (and confess). Tell me though, where have you learned these techniques?'

From *ba:b l-ha:ra* 'the neighborhood gate' – Season 1 – Episode 4 – 00:41:30 – SYR

In (19), the speaker does little more than directly brag about his cars. In (20), the speaker brags to his superior about what he considers a personal accomplishment or skill. The speaker evaluates his skill positively and feels good about himself for having acquired it.

Drawing on Bolinger (1979) and Stirling and Manderson (2011: 1585), we may characterize the type of *you* in the HR-ADs in the above examples as both personal and general. It is personal in that it allows the speakers to invite their hearers to share the profiled experience and feelings as their own. By involving the hearer, the speakers hope to increase the chances of success in recruiting the hearers' acceptance of the narrative as credible and in achieving positive alignment (Stirling and Manderson 2011: 1597).

At the same time, this type of self-promoting *you* is general in that it goes beyond the speaker and hearer, and profiles any member of their group as a potential experiencer of the same emotions. In this sense, a HR-AD does what Kitagawa and Lehrer, citing Laberge and Sankoff (1979: 281), ascribe to a general *you*: 'By using *you*, the speaker "assimilates himself" . . . "to a much wider class of people, downgrading his own experience to incidental status in the discourse, phrasing it as something that could or would be anybody's"' (1990: 749).

Group membership and a shared identity are important for achieving alignment. Consider (19) and (20) again. By using a HR-AD, the speakers in these examples attribute their attitudes to their hearers in an attempt to solicit positive alignment. The speaker in (19), Abu Khidir, fails. This is so because he and his hearer, Abu Awwad, belong to two different socio-economic groups. Abu Khidir is a well-off man who can afford to purchase several cars, while Abu Awwad is of a lower middle class and can hardly afford one. This is why Abu Khidir's appeal to shared experience and membership via the use of a HR-AD only generates resentment in Abu Awwad; the HR-AD attributes to Abu Awwad a membership that he does not have. The situation is different in (20). In this case, the speaker, Nuri, is a police officer relating his skill to a like-minded superior. They both believe that interrogation techniques involving torture are permissible, and as such they share a group membership. If Nuri tries to relate the same event to the suspect's family or to a hearer who does not believe in these techniques, he will have to do so without the use of a HR-AD.

4.2 HR-AD representatives as third-person praise and criticism

HR-AD representatives may be used to praise or criticize a third party, a behavior, or a state of affairs. In this case, the representatives are typical of what is normally characterized as gossip. They may take the form of a narrative about a specific event that the speaker has heard about or has had the chance to experience. They may also take the form of generalizations or truisms. I discuss these separately. First, however, I start with HR-AD representatives that are used in private conversation to recruit gossip accomplices.

4.2.1 HR-AD representatives: recruiting gossip accomplices

'Without gossip, there would be no society,' holds anthropologist and evolutionary psychologist Robin Dunbar. To him, 'gossip is what makes human society as we know it possible' (2004: 100). This is so, he maintains, because it allows social actors to stay informed about what is going on in their social networks. It promotes social bonds among the members of the society, and it helps them protect themselves and each other from those who plan to cause harm. News updates in social networks take the form of stories about individuals and behaviors. Some of these stories may be true, while others may be pure lies. Importantly, however, speakers use these gossip events to evaluate individuals and behaviors, and by doing so have the chance to define, redefine, challenge, or negotiate the social values, beliefs, and norms that are behind the stories they share.

For all this to be successful, a gossiper cannot work alone; she needs an accomplice who legitimizes her role by participating in the gossip event as both a recipient and a contributor. Social actors who are interested in gossip try to recruit accomplices via different means. For example, a gossip initiator may lean forward toward a potential gossip accomplice and begin whispering a gossip story. She may also use the hand scoop gesture, emphasize the seriousness of the information, or urge the hearer to keep it a secret. These strategies make the recruit feel that he has been handpicked for receiving the gossip story and thus give him a sense of importance.

In addition to the above strategies, Levantine Arabic speakers/gossipers may use HR-ADCs to recruit gossip accomplices. These often start with verbs of perception like *smiʕit* 'I heard' and *ʃifit* 'I saw' plus a HR-AD. The gossip initiator often sees herself as a community member who is entitled to knowing about going-ons in the community by virtue of her personal, social, and/or relational identity. The HR-AD places the hearer on stage as entitled to the same knowledge. The community may be small (for example, an apartment complex) or large (for example, a village). Gossip membership often constitutes a subpart of the community and is determined by such factors as common socio-economic status, common gender, or even a common enemy. By using a HR-AD, the gossip initiator bestows on the hearer a gossip membership in an attempt to recruit him as a gossip accomplice. As Stirling and Manderson would put it, by using a HR-AD, 'the speaker implicates the addressee as at least a potential member of the group, hence the "involving" effects' (Stirling and Manderson 2011: 1599).

The excerpts in (21) and (22) are examples from Syrian Arabic. In (21), the speaker is a street vendor named Abu Ghaleb. He tries to recruit the hearer, a garbage collector named Abu Ahmad, as a gossip accomplice. To be more effective in his attempt, Abu Ghaleb uses multiple means: he takes Abu Ahmad aside and addresses him in such a way that no one else could hear, he uses a rising tone that shows a high level of enthusiasm in an attempt to get the hearer excited about the gossip story, and, importantly, he uses a HR-AD to place his hearer on stage as an accomplice. Abu Ghaleb also uses a subject-oriented attitude dative, or SUBJ-AD (in italics); there is more on this type of dative in the next chapter. The expression *le:ra tˤintˤah le:ra* 'one pound pokes another' in (21) is used in reference to what the speaker believes is a large amount of money. See further discussion of the same example in Chapter 5, repeated there as (15).

21. Context: Abu Ghaleb is a street vendor who is interested in gossip, often maliciously in order to cause trouble. He tries to involve Abu Ahmad, a garbage collector, in a gossip situation about recent events in a rich neighborhood where they work.

Abu Ghaleb: mazbu:tˤ   mitil   ma: smiʕit,   ʔabu: ʔahmad?
true   like   that   I.heard,   Abu   Ahmad?
'Is it true what I heard, Abu Ahmad?'

Abu Ahmad: w-ʃu: smiʕit,   ta:ʒ   ra:s-i:?
and-what   you.hear,   crown   head-my?
'What did you hear, my man?'

Abu Ghaleb: smiʕt-**illak**   ʔinno   l-ha:ra   ʔa:yme   ʔa:ʕde ...
I.heard-**you.D**   that   the-neighborhood   upside   down ...
w-ʕam-biʔu:lu: kama:n   ʔinno   ʔabu: Samʕo
and-PROG-they.say   also   that   Abu Samo
sˤar-*lo*   mixtifi: yawme:n   tla:te,   mu:
happen-*him.D*   unfound   two.days three,   NEG
mbayyen,   w-ʕam-biʔu:lu: kama:n   ʔinno
showing,   and-PROG-they.say also   that
ha:fif-*lo*   mi:te:n   le:ra   dahab,   le:ra
he.stole-*him.D*   two.hundred liras   gold,   lira
tˤintˤah   le:ra!
poking   lira!
'I heard [you] that the neighborhood is in turmoil, and they're saying that Abu Samo has been gone for two or three days and no one knows where he is, and they are saying that he stole [him] two hundred gold coins, a king's ransom.'
...

Abu Ahmad: ʔabu: ɣa:leb,   ʔana: ʔili: ʕaʃr   sni:n   zabba:l
Abu Ghaleb,   I   have   ten   years   garbage.collector
bi-ha-l-ha:ra.   bi-haya:t-i: ma: ʒibit   si:ret
in-this-the-neighborhood.   in-life-my   NEG   bring   topic
hada: ʕala: lsa:n-i:,   liʔanno   l-na:s
person on   tongue-my, because   the-people
ʔammanu:-ni: ʕala: byu:t-un   w-ʔaʕra:dˤ-un.
entrusted-me   with   houses-their   and-honor-their.
binsˤah-ak   ...   ma: tʒi:b   si:ret   hada: ...
I.advise-you   ...   NEG   bring   topic   person ...

ʕala: lsa:n-ak   bi-l-ʕa:tˤel .
on   tongue-your in-the-bad .

'Abu Ghaleb, I have been a garbage collector in this neighborhood for ten years. I have never gossiped about anyone because the residents entrust their houses and honor to me. I advise you not to tell bad stories about anyone either.'

4.21 From *ba:b l-ḥa:ra* 'the neighborhood gate' – Season 1 – Episode 2 – 00:37:00 – SYR

In (21), Abu Ghaleb's attempt to interest Abu Ahmad in the gossip story and to recruit him as an accomplice is triggered by a shared membership that is assumed by the speaker, based on their shared group identities. Both social actors belong to the same socio-economic group. They are both poor outsiders who come to this rich neighborhood only in order to work and make a living. Abu Ghaleb tries to appeal to this shared membership but he fails. As Abu Ahmad's answer indicates, the two are different in terms of their individual identities and in terms of how they perceive their job and relation with their workplace, the neighborhood. Abu Ahmad uses his history and reputation to present himself as an honest man who respects the privacy of those he works for. He views Abu Ghaleb as exactly the opposite. To Abu Ahmad, these differences are enough for him to turn down Abu Ghaleb's invitation and reject the shared membership. As Figure 4.5 shows, Abu Ahmad does not question the validity of the story and does not indicate whether he aligns with Abu Ghaleb positively or negatively with regard to it. Rather, he rejects Abu Ghaleb's profile of him as a gossip accomplice and the anchoring of the story to him as one.

While (21) involves a negotiation of a shared membership, (22) is an appeal to an existing one. The speaker, a midwife named Im Ziki, uses a HR-AD to place her friend Firyal overtly on stage and profile her involvement in the gossip. Im Ziki relates a gossip event to Firyal about a woman named Im Esam, whom Firyal abhors. Im Ziki knows that Firyal is interested in any mishap that may happen to Im Esam and her family, and the HR-AD overtly anchors the mishap to Firyal, who then immediately embraces it.

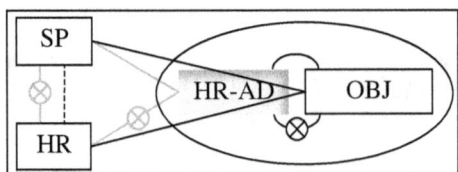

Figure 4.5 Stancetaking stage model of (21)

22. Context: Im Ziki, the neighborhood midwife, relates a story to her friend Firyal about Buran, the daughter of Firyal's archenemy, Im Esam. During her last visit to Im Esam's house, Im Ziki inferred – although she was not entirely certain – that Buran and her husband had had a falling out.

Im Ziki: ʕala: hawa: ma: fhimt-**illik** min l-ʒaww ,
according to what I.understood-**you.D** from the-ambience ,
ʔinno bu:ra:n , ʔalla:hu ʔaʕlam , ʔalla:hu ʔaʕlam
that Buran , God.knows , God.knows
ha: , mitxa:nʔa hiyye w-ʒawz-a:
INTER , had.a.falling.out she and-husband-her
l-hme:ma:ti: .
the-pigeon.keeper .
'As I understood [you], Buran and her husband, the pigeon keeper, had a falling out. This is what I understood from the general ambience (in their house).'

Firyal: ʃu: ʕarraf-ik ? haku: ʃi:
what informed-you ? they.said anything
ʔidda:m-ik ?
in.front.of-you ?
'How do you know? Did they say anything in front of you?'

Im Ziki: . . . laʔa: ma: haku: ʃi: . . . bas lli:
. . . no NEG they.said anything . . . but what
fhimt-o , ʔinno ʒa:ye tna:m ʕind-un
I.understood-it , that she.came sleep at.place-their
hiyye w-wla:d-a: .
she and-children-her .
. . .
bas ʔalla:h yxalli:ki . . . ʔu:ʕa tiħki: walla: tʔu:li:
but may.God.save.you . . . don't.you say or talk
ʔinno ʔim ziki: haket ʃi: walla: ʔa:let ʃi: .
that Im Ziki said anything or talked anything .
ħa:kem l-ʒama:ʕa mʔamni:n-ni: ʕala: ʔasra:r-un . . .
because the-people entrusted-me with secrets-their . . .
'No, they didn't say anything, but as I understood, she came with her kids to sleep at their (her parents') house. But don't say anything, I beg of you, or tell anyone that I told you this. The people have trusted me with their secrets.'

Firyal: ((laugh)) mʔamni:n-ek ʕala: ʔasra:r-un ?
entrusted-you with secrets-their ?
ʔe la: , ya: tiʔibʃi: albi: , ma:-nun
INTER no , VOC sweetheart , NEG-they
mʔamni:n-ek ʕala: ʔasra:r-un . law ka:nu:
entrusted-you with secrets-their . if they.were
mʔamni:n-ek , ka:nu: ħaku: kil ʃi:
entrusted-you , they.were said every.thing
ʔidda:m-ek .
in.front.of-you .

'Trusted you with their secrets? No, sweetheart, they did not trust you with their secrets. Had they trusted you, they would have said everything in front of you.'

4.22 From *ba:b l-ha:ra* 'the neighborhood gate' – Season 1 – Episode 11 – 00:04:00 – SYR

Im Ziki's use of a HR-ADC in (22) is less risky than Abu Ghaleb's in (21). Abu Ghaleb does not know his hearer very well; he approaches him with the purpose of recruiting him, based on a shared socio-economic identity, without knowing that his hearer's identity differs from his in other ways. Im Ziki in (22), on the other hand, knows her hearer well, and she approaches her with confidence, based on their history as friends. She uses the HR-AD as an invoker of their shared membership as community women who are entitled to knowing the news of the community. Not only does Firyal embrace this shared membership and align positively with Im Ziki with respect to it but also she tries to drive a wedge between Im Ziki and the family they are gossiping about. She does this in an attempt to draw Im Ziki closer to her and farther from Im Esam and her family.

Gossiping and recruiting gossip accomplices are a risky business. We saw in (21) that it may lead to confrontation. This may explain why speakers or gossip initiators often use verbs of perception like 'heard' and 'understood' in relating gossip events. If the potential gossip recruit refuses to cooperate and turns down the invitation, he may also question the credibility of the gossip story. When this happens, verbs of perception allow the speaker to serve as 'author' but deny her involvement as 'principle': that is, the speaker poses as the person who has composed the utterance without necessarily taking a definitive stance or even responsibility toward its content (Goffman 1981).

Another verb that is often used in the same capacity is *ʃa:yfe/ʃa:yef*, the feminine/masculine active participial form of verb 'see,' roughly the equivalent of the English *It seems to me that*. Consider the exchange in (23), which contains the verb *ʃa:yef* plus a HR-AD. The verb *ʃa:yef* allows the speaker to entertain the proposition rather than assert it, as Martin and White (2005) would put it. That is, it allows the speaker to present a proposition as a possibility rather than a certainty. By presenting a proposition as only one possibility, the speaker indicates that there are other possibilities worth entertaining. And by using a HR-AD, the speaker invokes the hearer's knowledge engagement, inviting him either to provide an alternative or to corroborate the presented possibility. Of course, the hearer's corroboration is in the best interest of the speaker. At the same, any additional gossip information that the hearer may provide in response means that he has accepted his role as an accomplice. The HR-AD helps make this happen. The hearer in (23), Abu Esam, responds by saying that he has no idea. This may be an authentic admission of ignorance or a refusal to share his opinion and take part in the gossip event.

23. Context: A resident of the neighborhood, Abu Samir, who owns a fava bean and chickpea restaurant, expresses his opinion to Abu Esam, the neighborhood doctor, about a recent event.

Abu Samir:	ʃa:yef-**lak**		l-ʔidaʕʃari:		nzalam .
	I.see-**you.D**		Idaashari		wrongly.accused .
	walla:	ʃu:	raʔy-ak ,		ħaki:m ?
	or	what	opinion-your ,		doctor ?
	'I think [you] Idaashari has been wrongly accused. What do you think, Doctor?'				
Abu Esam:	walla:	ma:	baʕref .	ʃi:	biħayyer !
	by.God	NEG	I.know .	something	confusing !
	'I have no idea. This is confusing!'				

From *ba:b l-ħa:ra* 'the neighborhood gate' – Season 1 – Episode 8 – 00:19:45 – SYR   **4.23**

4.2.2 HR-AD representatives about specific events

When a speaker engages a hearer in a gossip event about a third party or a state of affairs, her purpose is often to share either her excitement or her indignation about an individual, a situation, or a behavior that she evaluates as good or bad. And just as the use of a SP-AD places the speaker on stage as cultural police, as we saw in the previous chapter, the use of a HR-AD assigns the role of cultural police to the hearer as well. In this respect, the HR-AD functions as a self-including *you*, under which both the speaker and the hearer are subsumed (Stirling and Manderson 2011: 1592). By using a HR-AD, the speaker places the hearer on stage in an attempt to recruit his emotional engagement.

The HR-AD fulfills another role: it invokes shared membership and shared cultural understanding. As such, it makes the gossip story more credible by tying 'the content being presented to the interlocutor's knowledge and experience' (Stirling and Manderson 2011: 1597). The HR-AD and the anchoring it accomplishes make it hard for the hearer to challenge the credibility of the story or his membership unless he unanchors himself first.

Consider (24), from Syrian Arabic. It features an exchange between two women, Im Ziki and Im Khater. Im Ziki is impressed with another woman in the neighborhood, Im Samir, and her skill in making *makdu:s*, oil-pickled eggplants that are traditionally prepared as a type of winter provision. She describes the *makdu:s* as *bya:xdu: l-ʕaʔel* 'they blow your mind.' She uses a HR-AD to recruit Im Khater's emotional engagement. Based on their shared membership, Im Ziki believes that Im Khater would be equally impressed if she tasted Im Samir's *makdu:s*. Im Khater takes Im Ziki's comment to mean that Im Samir's skills as a housewife are a rarity that should impress her and her cohort, and she takes offense at that statement. Im Khater believes that she too is a skilled housewife who makes good *makdu:s*, among other things. Im Ziki's attempt to recruit Im Khater's emotional engagement fails because the profile of Im Samir as a model housewife clashes with Im Khater's identity and her view of herself as an excellent housewife. This is why she refuses to be impressed and thus rejects the anchoring of the main message of Im Ziki's utterance to her person, as profiled via the HR-AD. Im Khater does not stop there. She goes on to discredit Im Samir completely. The result is divergent alignment between the two social actors, as Figure 4.6 shows.

24. Context: Im Ziki, the neighborhood midwife, pays a visit to Im Khater, the coppersmith's wife. When Im Khater invites Im Ziki to eat with her, Im Ziki declines and explains that she had stopped by Im Samir's house earlier and ate there. She then goes on to praise Im Samir for her *makdu:s* (small eggplants stuffed with walnuts and preserved in olive oil).

Im Ziki: ʔamma: ʃu: btaʕmil-**lik**   makdu:sa:t
but   what   she.makes-**you.D**   oil.pickled.eggplants
ha-l-maʔsˤu:fet l-raʔabe,   bya:xdu: l-ʕaʔel !
this.woman,   they.take the-mind !
'This woman prepares [you] oil-pickled eggplants that are mind-blowing.'

Im Khater: yaʕni: ʃu: makdu:sa:t-a: ʔatˤyab   min
this.mean what eggplants-her   tastier   than
makdu:sa:t-i: ?
eggplants-my ?
'Do you mean that her oil-pickled eggplants are more delicious than mine?'

Im Ziki: la: ,   w-makdu:sa:t-ik   kama:n   tˤaybi:n .
No , and-eggplants-your   also   delicious .
'No, your oil-pickled eggplants are also delicious.'

Im Khater: ʔe daxi:lek ,   ʔim sami:r   ma: btaʕmil   ʔay ʃi:
INTER come.on , Im Samir   NEG   make   any thing
ʕala: ʔi:d-a: .   kill-o ʃiɣil   hama:t-a: .
by   hand-her .   all-it work   mother-in-law-her .
'Come on, Im Samir doesn't make anything herself. It is all made by her mother-in-law.'

4.24 From *ba:b l-ḥa:ra* 'the neighborhood gate' – Season 1 – Episode 11 – 00:45:30 – SYR

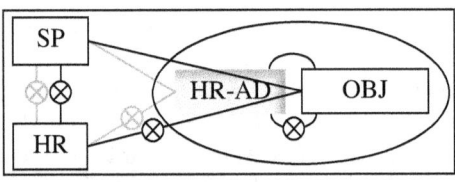

Figure 4.6 Stancetaking stage model of (24)

Despite the negative alignment at the emotional level, the social actors in (24) agree on one thing: being a good housewife who is skilled at preparing winter provisions is a welcome value. In this respect, the dialog is an affirmation of a shared cultural understanding. In fact, while many HR-ADCs that are employed in personal narratives are used to recruit the hearers' emotional involvement and to encourage them to embrace the speaker's feelings and experience as their own, there is often another tier on which a broader shared cultural value is tacitly presented. In the process, the value is affirmed, redefined, negotiated, or challenged. For example, the conversation in (24) would take a different direction if the hearer were a professional woman in a contemporary urban center. The hearer may be impressed with Im Samir's skills as a housewife but may go on to question the cultural value of being only a housewife. She may argue that a woman must be active outside the house instead or as well.

The excerpts in (25) and (26) are from the same Syrian show. The speakers each praise an individual for a specific feat. Contextualization cues, such as a rising tone of voice and specific descriptive details, express how impressed and grateful the speakers are. By using a HR-AD, they place the hearers on stage and recruit their emotional engagement. They also characterize the experience as shared: that is, as something that the hearers as individuals or as representatives of a specific group (as Damascene, Arab, male, and so on) would also experience under similar circumstances. As such, the speakers emphasize in-group membership and affirm the hearers' group identity.

25. Context: Abu Esam and Abu Shihaab, two men with leading roles in the community, have just come back from a tour of surrounding neighborhoods to collect money in support of the rebels against the British occupation of Palestine. In a meeting with the neighborhood committee, the sheikh inquires about the tour and whether it has paid off. Abu Esam answers:

    Abu Esam: ... ma: fi: riʒʒa:l   bi-kil   l-ʃa:m ...   ma:
              ... NEG   there   man   in-all   the-Damascus...   NEG
              ntaxa: w-dafaʕ   min   xa:tˤr-o ...   bi-ba:b   tu:ma
              acted   and-pay   from   will-his ...   in-Bab   Tuma
              ...   fat-**lak**   waːhed,   ʔalla:h   yku:n
              ...   enter-**you.D**   one,   God   be
              bi-ʕo:n-u,   byiʃtiɣel   ʕata:l,   ʃe:x-i:.   walla:h
              in-help-his, he.work   carrier,   sheikh-my.   by.God
              l-ʕazˤi:m   kil   nha:r-o   biʔadˤi: ʔarbaʕ
              the-almighty   all   day-his   he.pass   four
              xams   ʔru:ʃ   ytˤaliʕ-hum.   hatˤtˤ-un
              five   pennies   he.earn-them.   he.put-them
              mitil   ma: hinne   ʕa-l-tˤa:wle   w-ra:ħ!
              like   that   they   on-the-table   and-left!

    'There was no man in Damascus who didn't man up and pay of his own will. In the neighborhood of Bab Tuma, there entered [you] a man, God help him, who works as a carrier. I swear he works all day to earn four or five pennies. He placed his whole earnings on the table and left.'

    The Sheikh: ʔalla: yʕawwidˤ-hun   ʕale-e   w-ʕala:
                God   replace-them   for-him   and-for
                kil   mi:n   biʔa:ʒir   bi-ʔirʃ   walla: bi-nigli.
                every   who   contribute   with-penny   or   with-dime.

    'May God reward him and anyone like him who has made a donation, no matter how small.'

Everyone: ʔa:mi:n ...
'Amen.'

4.25 From *ba:b l-ha:ra* 'the neighborhood gate' – Season 1 – Episode 15 – 00:46:00 – SYR

26. Context: Abu Shihab has just found out that Idaashari, who has been working as a night guard in Abu Shihab's barn, heroically stopped an intruder from burning down the store. In a meeting with the neighborhood committee, Abu Shihab reports what happened.

Abu Shihab: ʔiʒi:t   ʔala: ha-l-ba:yke ,   lʕi:t-**illak**
            I.came   to   this-the-barn, I.found-**you.D**
            l-ʔidaʕʕari: mrabtˁ-o   la-ʔabu: sa:tˁu:r ,
            the-Idaashari   having.tied.up-him   for-Abu Satur ,
            w-ha:tˁitˁ-lo   ki:s xe:ʃ   bi-ra:s-o ...
            and-having.put-him.D   bag   in-head-his ...
            law-la: ,   ka:net   ra:het   l-ba:yke
            if.not-him ,   was   gone   the-barn
            bi-l-rizʔ   lli: fiyy-a: ...
            with-the-produce that   in-it   ...
            'I arrived at the barn only to find [you] Idaashari having tied up Abu Satur and put a bag in his head. Had it not been for him, I would have lost the barn and all that is in it.'

Abu Esam: walla: ʔana: kil   ʕimr-i: bʔu:l
            by.God   I   all   life-my   say
            ʔann-o   hada   riʒʒa:l   zkirt ...
            that-he   this   man   manly ...
            'I swear I always say that this man is all a man should be.'

4.26 From *ba:b l-ha:ra* 'the neighborhood gate' – Season 1 – Episode 29 – 00:27:30 – SYR

The evaluations in (25) and (26) go beyond affect and take the form of judgment and appreciation as well. The speakers evaluate the feats they describe and the agents responsible for them as exemplary, as far as charity (25) and valor (26) are concerned. The general message is that charity and valor are laudable cultural values. The reactions of the hearers in both examples are evidence of positive alignment with the speakers with respect to both the at-issue content of the utterances and the evaluations attached to them. The outcome is an affirmation of shared cultural understanding.

The examples so far have featured speakers with positive, elevated emotions using HR-ADCs to invite their hearers to adopt the same attitude. This is not always the case, however. The speakers in (27) and (28), for example, position themselves negatively with respect to the profiled events. They use HR-ADs to anchor the same attitude to the hearers and to solicit their emotional involvement and their positive alignment. In (27), the speaker talks about a garbage crisis in Lebanon. He explains how this crisis and the government's inaction have affected his life negatively. He also expresses how disgusted he feels by the overwhelming amount of garbage at the abandoned dumpsters. By using a HR-AD, he presents his experience as shared and invites the hearer – and probably all TV viewers – to share the emotion and to validate his feelings.

27. Context: Lebanon experienced a long garbage crisis that resulted in an unbearable amount of garbage on the streets. In an interview with Lebanese citizens, a man makes the following comment:
bru:h ʔana: ta-kibb l-zbe:le , ble:ʔi:-**lik**
I.go I to-throw the-trash , I.find-**you.D**
l-dibbe:n mʕafʕaf w-ʔiʃya: w-kaza: .
the-flies be.all.over and-things and-so.on .
yaʕni: biʔraf , bzit min l-sayya:ra w-bimʃi: .
this.mean I.get.disgusted , I.toss from the-car and-leave .
'When I go to throw away the trash, I find [you] flies and things all over the place. I get grossed out, so I toss the trash out of the car and leave.'
https://www.youtube.com/watch?v=elaUQyA8-0M (accessed October 25, 2016) – 00:04:05 – LEB
4.27

In (28), from a Lebanese play, the speaker and hearer are playing backgammon and chatting. The speaker relates to the hearer his experience with the Lebanese government and its decision to ban hashish plantations in the Beqaa Valley in eastern Lebanon. He describes how that decision has affected his source of income. In order to attract the hearer's attention, the speaker uses a HR-AD, placing him on stage and directing his gaze temporarily away from the game and to the on-stage region. Importantly, the speaker is dissatisfied with the government; by using a HR-AD, he invites his hearer to feel the same. He also affirms his and the hearer's group identity and their in-group membership as supporters of hashish plantations. If the hearer were a government official, the speaker could still perform the same complaint. However, the use of a HR-AD would create a sense of awkwardness due to a mismatch between what the dative tries to invoke and what the reality is. The HR-AD would profile an out-group as an in-group; it would invoke his empathy and shared understanding when, in fact, he is the one causing the damage.

28. Context: One man explains to another how the government has banned hashish plantations and how that has affected his life.
baʔa , ya si:d-na: l-kari:m (.) tˤilʕit-**lak** ha-l-dawle
so , VOC good sir (.) go.up-**you.D** this-the-government
ʕa-l-sahel (.) w-ʔe:l mamnu:ʕ zarʕ l-haʃi:ʃe (.)
to-the-plain (.) and-said forbidden planting the-hashish (.)
smaʕu: ʔʃaʕu: , ya: ʒame:ʕa (.) nihna: ʕe:yʃi:n
listen look , VOC people (.) we living
ʕa-ha-l-ʃatle (.) le: , ma: fi: (.) ki:f ma: fi: .
on-this-the-plant (.) why , no.answer (.) how no.answer .
l-has'l-o bi-l-nihe:ye , ʕidna: zraʕna: dara .
the-conclusion-it in-the-end , we.went.ahead planted corn .

'So, my good sir, government officials went to the plains of the Beqaa Valley and forbade the planting of hashish. We tried to explain to them that this plant is our livelihood, but in vain. So eventually we ended up planting corn.'

4.28 From *Nazl l-suru:r* 'the Surour Inn' – 02:03:20 – LEB

The HR-ADs used in representatives about specific events may be characterized as a form of generalized *you*. Unlike HR-ADs that are used in commissives in recognition of the hearer's authority (Section 3) or even in representatives for the purpose of recruiting gossip accomplices (Section 4.2.1), the HR-ADs in the representatives discussed in this subsection make reference to the hearers not only as individuals but also as representatives of all members in their group. This form of *you* may be replaced with *I* or *we*, as Stirling and Manderson (2011) and Kitagawa and Lehrer (1990) observe. We saw in the previous chapter that representatives about culturally unacceptable or reprehensible individuals, situations, or behaviors may also be expressed via SP-ADCs. All the HR-ADs in the examples in this subsection may be replaced by a SP-AD with minimal change in their pragmatic effect. Both SP-ADs and HR-ADs profile their referent as cultural police who monitors individuals and behaviors in terms of their adherence to cultural values, beliefs, and norms. The difference is that the HR-AD places the hearer on stage as a member of a category shared by the speaker, attributing the knowledge entitlement and authority of the speaker to the hearer as well. Both types of AD solicit the hearer's assent, but a HR-AD does so more aggressively. As Kitagawa and Lehrer (1990) put it, a HR-AD invokes camaraderie between the speaker and hearer, and this makes it harder on the hearer to challenge the speaker. By using a HR-AD, Kitagawa and Lehrer hold, the speaker invites the hearer into her world, 'implying that the hearer also shares the same perspective'; this, Kitagawa and Lehrer maintain, 'can be considered as an act of camaraderie' (1990: 752).

Interestingly, my data show that criticisms targeting specific events and individuals are more common as SP-ADCs, while praise of specific events and the individuals or behavior they feature are more common as HR-ADCs. Frequency of this type normally leads to preferred readings. To test this observation, I presented native speakers of Lebanese Arabic with structures like (a) and (b) in (29) in written form and asked them to act out the statements as they would imagine they should sound. My consultants tended to read the (a) example with a dismissive tone, while they read the (b) example with a rising tone of excitement.

29. a. kari:m ʃtare:-**li:** sayya:ra bi-ʕiʃri:n ʔalef do:la:r
    Karim bought-**me.D** car for-twenty.thousand.dollars
    'Karim bought [me] a car for twenty thousand dollars.'
   b. kari:m ʃtare:-**lak** sayya:ra bi-ʕiʃri:n ʔalef do:la:r
    Karim bought-**you.D** car for-twenty.thousand.dollars
    'Karim bought [you] a car for twenty thousand dollars.'

Although both (a) and (b) may be linked to positive or negative evaluations, the speakers assumed that the writer of (a) evaluated Karim's behavior as negative (that is, what Karim did is bad/outrageous; he should not have bought an expensive car), but they visualized the writer of (b) as excited about Karim's purchase. All this seems to suggest that frequency affects what kind of interpretation speakers consider as the default; see Ochs (1996: 430).

One explanation of the preferences and default readings associated with HR-AD and SP-AD representatives about specific events is offered in Haddad (2013). When it comes to value judgments of cultural behavior, HR-ADCs are not as common as SP-ADCs because they are riskier; they are an aggressive way to solicit the hearer's alignment because they explicitly attribute the speaker's feelings and evaluation to the hearer. When faced with the decision of communicating these feelings and evaluations, speakers seem to be more willing to anchor positive ones to the hearer via HR-ADCs, but they are more inclined to anchor negative ones to themselves via SP-ADCs, giving the hearer more freedom to accept or reject them as part of his dominion.

4.2.3 HR-AD representatives as truisms

Things become a little less restrictive when speakers use representatives as general observations or truisms. These are characterized as 'commonplaces' (Myers and Lampropoulou 2012) or 'general truths about the world' (Stirling and Manderson 2011: 1586), rather than statements about specific events and individuals. When stating truisms and general observations, social actors seem to be more willing to use a HR-AD representative to evaluate a general phenomenon negatively. I have not come across such HR-AD representatives in the shows and plays I analyzed, but plenty of examples are available on social media (for example, Facebook) in the form of written colloquial Arabic. The medium seems to make contributors more willing to take the risk of attributing a negative evaluation to other social actors – in this case, other social-media users.

There are a couple of reasons why social media are more conducive than face-to-face conversations when it comes to the use of HR-ADs in association with negatively evaluated content. First, in the absence of a present social actor (that is, a social actor that is physically present and that may be directly addressed), the specific referential use of a HR-AD becomes less obvious and its generalized use becomes more pronounced. In other words, a HR-AD on social media is more readily understood as referring to people in general or to a contextually determined group (for example, Jordanian men), including the writer and the reader. As such, it anchors the writer's evaluation to and solicits agreement from an unknown or unidentified social actor; see Myers and Lampropoulou (2012) and work cited within for a similar observation about generalized *you*. The HR-AD still draws the reader in and, as Myers and Lampropoulou (2012: 1206) put it, presents 'perceptions as shared, not merely individual'; however, it does this with less risk than that involved in face-to-face confrontation where the specific referential use of the HR-AD is also invoked. In addition, the situation of a social-media user may be described as 'ineffable solitude,' to use Freadman's (1999) term. Freadman adds, 'The condition of the isolated *I* is intolerable'; using a HR-AD may help get social-media users out of this solitary situation. See also Stirling and Manderson (2011).

Before providing some examples, it is worth noting that social-media HR-ADCs may still be characterized as dialogic in that writers, just like speakers in face-to-face conversations, anticipate responses from potential contributors on social media (see Martin and White 2005: 92).[1] By using a HR-AD, contributors on social media '"write the reader into the text,"' to borrow an expression from Martin and White (2005: 96). By doing so, the contributors seem to assume that readers share their perspective, or that the HR-AD would put some pressure on them so that they adopt the perspective.

The range of behaviors and objects that may be targeted on social media, along with the implicated social values and norms that underlie them, is vast. Some comments may be considered trivial, while others are more serious. Some target current political events (for example, the civil war in Syria, which unfortunately was still current at the time of writing this book), while others may address social issues (for example, gender-related issues). Regardless of how one may judge or describe them, these comments still speak to what the contributors consider important and how they use HR-ADCs to invite others to agree with them.

Here are a few examples. The contributor of (30) criticizes Jordanian smokers for smelling like cigarettes and pretending that they do not. Similarly, the contributor in (31) criticizes men who pretend to be pious supporters of the Islamic caliphate while their lifestyle tells a different story. The contributors do not seem to be criticizing the behavior per se (that is, smoking, wearing jeans); rather, they criticize those who carry out the behavior for having the audacity to pretend that despite smoking they still smell fine, or despite their lifestyle they are still religious. The contributors consider such hypocrisy as culturally unacceptable.

30. Context: A Facebook user comments on Jordanian smokers.

l-ʔurduni: bidaxxin-**lak**   tnaʕʕar   si:ga:ra ,
the-Jordanian.man   smoke-**you.D**   twelve   cigarettes ,
baʕde:n   ga:l   biʒi: bisʔal-ak ,
then   say.what   he.come   he.ask-you ,
balla: ri:ht-i: duxxa:n   ʃi: ?
by.God   smell-my   smoke   Q ?
la: ,   ya: habib-i: ,   ri:ht-ak   lotion   ʕala: fara:wla !
no ,   VOC   dear-my ,   smell-you   lotion   on   strawberries !

'The Jordanian man smokes [you] a dozen cigarettes, only then to come and ask you, 'Do I smell like cigarettes? No, darling, you smell like strawberry lotion!'

الاردني بدخنلك 12 سيجاره
بعدين قال بيجي يسالك
بالله ريحتني دخان شي
>
دلا يا حبيبي ريحتك لوشن علي فراوله

31. Context: A Facebook user comments on men who pretend to be pious, bragging about the Islamic caliphate and preaching to everyone about Islam while doing things that do not align with what they preach.

ʔaħla:	ʃi: ,	bitʃu:f	wa:ħed	byiħki:	ʕan	l-xila:fe
nicest	thing ,	you.see	one	speak	about	the-caliphate
l-ʔisla:miyye ,		w-ʕa:mil-**lak**		like	ʕala:	sˤafaħa:t ħubb
the-Islamic ,		and-making-**you.D**		like	on	pages love
w-ʕiʃiq ,		w-msˤa:ħeb	ma:	baʕref	kam	binit ,
and-passion ,		and-dating	NEG	I.know	how.many	girl ,
w-biʃu:f		Arab Idol ,	w-byilbis-**lak**		jeans	la-taħt
and-he.watch		Arab Idol ,	and-he.dress-**you.D**		jeans	to-below
l-dˤahar ,		w-byismaʕ	ʔaɣa:ni:	w-mu:si:ʔa .	ħabi:b-i: ,	law
the-back ,		and-he.listen	songs	and-music .	dear-my ,	if
biddak		ttˤabbiʔ	l-xila:fe ,		fa-balliʃ	min
you.want		apply	the-caliphate ,		so-start	with
ħa:l-ak		bi-l-ʔawwal	w-baʕde:n	tʃa:tˤar	ʕa-l-na:s .	
self-your		at-the-first	and-then	be.smart	with-the-people .	

'The most interesting thing is when you see a man talk about the Islamic caliphate while at the same time he 'likes' [you] Facebook pages on love and passion, and you see him dating God knows how many girls, and he watches Arab Idol and wears [you] his jeans low and listens to songs and music. Please, if you want to promote the caliphate, you should start with yourself first before you try to convert others.'

احلى شي بتشوف واحد بيحكي عن الخلافة الأسلامية و عاملك لايك على صفحات حب و عشق و مصاحب ما بعرف كم بنت و بيشوف أراب آيدول و بيلبسلك جينز لتحت الظهر و بيسمع أغاني و موسيقا ..... حبيبي لو بدك تطبق الخلافة فـ بلش من حالك بالأول بعدين تشاطر عالناس !!

In (32), a Facebook user criticizes Lebanese women for being able to tolerate all the walking that needs to be done during shopping, only to complain about how far away the car is when they get to the parking lot. Similar to the two previous examples, it is mainly women's willingness to tolerate walking long distances only when it is convenient that the contributor criticizes.

32. Context: A Facebook user comments on Lebanese women when they go shopping.

l-ħilo	bi-l-bint	l-libne:niyye	ʔinno	btinzal-**lak**		
the-nice.thing	with-the-girl	the-Lebanese	that	she.go-**you.D**		
ʕa-l-su:ʔ ,	w-btibrum	l-mall	sabʕi:n	marra		
to-the-mall ,	and-go.around	the-mall	seventy	time		
w-ʃi:	ʕaʃr	tˤwa:biʔ	w-mi:t		ki:lomitir	
and-some	ten	floors	and-a.hundred		kilometer	
bidu:n	ma:	titʕab .	bas	lamma:	tixlasˤ	
without	that	get.tired .	but	when	be.done	
w-titˤlaʕ ,	bitʔil-**lak**	ʔu:f	le:ʃ	sˤa:fif		
and-get.out ,	she.say-**you.D**	ʔu:f	why	parking		

l-sayya:ra   bʕi:d ?
the-car   far ?

'The interesting thing about Lebanese women is that they go [you] shopping, they walk around the mall seventy times – a mall of about ten floors and a hundred kilometers – without getting tired. However, when they are done and they step outside the mall, they complain about how far away you parked your car.'

الحلو بالبنت اللبنانية انو بتنزلك عالسوق و بتبرم ال"mall" سبعين مرة و شي ١٠ طوابق و ١٠٠ كلم بدون ما تتعب ... بس لما تخلص و تطلع بتقلك : " اووووف ليش صافف السيارة بعيد ..!!!!"

In all of the three examples above, the contributors resort to mockery in order to pass their judgments about the profiled behaviors. They use HR-ADs to draw the readers in and to anchor the judgments to them in an attempt to validate these judgments. The replies that the contributions receive on Facebook are usually nods of agreement (for example, lol 'laughing out loud', hahahaha) posted by what seem to be like-minded individuals.

HR-ADCs about shared cultural understandings like the ones we have just seen have a couple of characteristics in common: first, 'the provision of vivid detail, to sustain the category entitlement of "witness"' (Stirling and Manderson 2011: 1597, citing Potter 1996); and second, the use of the present tense, which gives the comment the form of 'structural knowledge description' and the contributor the identity of an 'acknowledged insider' (Kitagawa and Lehrer 1999, drawing on Goldsmith and Woisetschlaeger 1982; see also Bolinger 1979; Stirling and Manderson 2011). Citing Laberge and Sankoff (1979), Myers and Lampropoulou (2012: 1207) maintain that 'often the generality of a truism is signaled by a change from the past tense of narrative to the present tense of knowledge statements,' and this is evident in the Facebook posts presented above.

Let us look at one more example before we conclude. The Facebook post in (33) is interesting for a couple of reasons. According to the contributor, women choose fashion over practicality when it comes to clothes. Men are the opposite: they go for practical choices and do not care for fashion. As a native speaker of Lebanese Arabic, I had a hard time determining whether the statement was a criticism of the profiled women or men, or both, and thus I was not sure what kind of evaluation was anchored to me as a reader who is placed on stage via the use of a HR-AD. The contextualization cues in the form of lexical choices were not clear; there is some mockery in the description of both women and men. And since this is a written comment, intonation and facial expressions are not involved. The contribution does not receive many meaningful replies, but one reply posted by a woman is helpful. The reply is included in (33). The woman assumes that the evaluation anchored to her as a reader via the use of the HR-AD is in favor of practicality. She agrees with the evaluation that practicality is important, but she aligns negatively with the judgment that women are not practical in their choice of clothes.

33. Context: A Facebook user compares how women and men decide on their outfits. This could be a criticism of how women care too much about fashion or of how men care

too little. From the replies, it seems to be the former. Most women reply that they have clothes that are both fashionable and warm. One woman comments that she does not care about fashion; she cares about warmth.

Original post: miski:ne l-binit , btitħammal l-bard l-qa:risˤ ,
poor the-girl , she.endure the-cold the-severe ,
l-muhimm tilbos ʕala: l-muːdˤa .
the-important.thing she.dress to the-fashion .
ʔamma: l-ʃabb , biyilbis-**lak** kabbu:d
as.to the-young.man , he.dress-**you.D** coat
ʔab-u: l-zayti: w-boːtˤ ʕaskari:
father-his the-olive.green and-boots military
ʔayya:m l-ʒeːʃ , w-byitˤlaʕ ʃibih briːʔ ʃa:y
days the-army , and-come.out semi kettle tea
ʔasˤli: . l-muhimm l-dafa: , ya: ʕamm-i: .
original . the-important.thing the-warmth , VOC uncle-my .
ʔahamm ʃi: l-siħħa .
the.most.important thing the-health .

'Poor women; they endure the severe cold weather as long as they are dressed à la mode. Men, on the other hand, would wear **[you]** their father's olive-green coat and military boots that he had when he was in the army. They could look like a tea kettle and they wouldn't mind as long as they are warm and healthy.'

Reply: ʔe: w-niħna: kama:n mniʃtiri:
yeah and-we too buy
ʒa:keta:t ħilwi:n w-ʕa-l-muːdˤa w-bidaffu: .
coats pretty and-on-the-fashion and-warm .

'Yeah? Well we also buy pretty and fashionable coats that are warm.'

مسكينه البنت !!
بتتحمل البرد القارص ۱۸۸
المهم تلبس على الموضه
اما الشب بيلبسلك كبود ابوووه الزيتي |:
وبوطططط عسكري ايام الجيش ..
وبيطلع شبه ابريق الشآي ۱۸۸
اصلي
المهم الدفى ياااا عمي ..
اهم اشي الصحة !!

Shereen

اي ونحنا كمان منشري جاكيتات حلوين وعلموضى وبيدفو

5 Conclusion

This chapter has shown that speakers use HR-ADs to place their hearer on stage in an attempt to grab his attention and to mark his engagement. Hearer engagement may involve recruiting the hearer's empathy, soliciting his assent, or appealing to shared membership, knowledge, and experience. To illustrate these social functions and pragmatic contributions of HR-ADs, the chapter has presented examples from four different varieties of Levantine Arabic. The next chapter deals with the fourth and last type of dative that this study is concerned with: subject-oriented attitude datives.

Note

1. The definition of dialogism is more complex. Drawing on Bakhtin (1981) and Voloshinov (1995), Martin and White hold that

    all verbal communication, whether written or spoken, is 'dialogic' in that to speak or write is always to reveal the influence of, refer to, or to take up in some way, what has been said/written before, and simultaneously to anticipate the responses of actual, potential or imagined readers/listeners. (2005: 92)

5

Subject-Oriented Attitude Datives in Social Context

1 Introduction

The focus of this chapter is on attitude datives that take the subject of the predicate they attach to as a referent. We referred to these as subject-oriented attitude datives, or SUBJ-ADs. The utterances in (1) through (4) are examples from the four Levantine Arabic varieties involved in this study.

1. Context: The chief of the police district, Abu Jawdat, and his subordinate, Nuri, are doing a patrol tour in one of the neighborhoods. When they arrive at the mayor's office, Abu Jawdat decides to drop by to schmooze for a few minutes. He does not want Nuri to join him, so he gives him the following instructions:
    ʕmil-**lak**   fatle   bi-l-ha:ra ,   w-mnilta?a
    make-**you.D** round   in-the-neighborhood , and-we.meet
    baʕed   ʕaʃer   daʔa:yi?   ho:n .
    after   ten   minutes   here .
    'Make [you] a tour in the neighborhood and we'll meet here in ten minutes.'
From *ba:b l-ha:ra* 'the neighborhood gate' – Season 1 – Episode 17 – 00:09:10 – SYR   5.1

2. Context: In an interview with poor citizens in Lebanon, a very poor woman describes her plight and the plight of her husband and children. She does not have a steady job, but she is occasionally hired as a temporary worker. She says:
    ʔana: masalan   kinit   ʔiʃtiɣil ,   bas   halla?
    I   for.example   was   work ,   but   now
    ma: ʕam-biʃtiɣil (.)   yaʕni: bisnud   ʃway
    NEG   PROG-work (.)   this.mean   I.support   a.little
    ʒawz-i: bas   yku:n   ʔa:ʕid bi-l-be:t .   ʔana: bru:h
    husband-my   when   he.is   staying in-the-house .   I   go

biʃtiɣil-**li:**   ʃaɣli   hoːn ,   biʃtiɣil-**li:**
I.work-**me.D**   job   here ,   I.work-**me.D**
hoːn ʃaɣli ,   laħatta: tˤaʕmi: wleːd-iː .
here   job ,   in.order.to   feed   children-my .

'I, for instance, used to have a job, but I do not have a job now. I support my husband when he stays at home. I find [**me**] a job here, I find [**me**] a job there, in order to feed my family.'

5.2   From *taħqiːq* 'investigations' – *28% of the Lebanese Live Below Poverty Line* – 00:31:00 – LEB

   3. Context: A man explains to his brother his situation with his new fiancée and her mother.

haːy   hamaːt-iː   bidda: tifruʃ   l-villa ,   w-taʕmil-la:
this   mother-in-law-my   want   furnish   the-villa ,   and-do-it.**D**
dekoːraːt .   yaʕni: haːda: l-mawdˤuːʕ   bikallif-**lo**
decorations . this.mean   this   the-project   cost-**it.D**
hawaːli: ʕiʃriːn   ʔalef dinaːr .   w-ʔana: zalame   maː
about   twenty   thousand dinars . and-I   man   NEG
bagdar .   ʔana: bagdar   ʔastaʔʒer   beːt   ʕala: gadd-iː .
can .   I   can   rent   house   up.to   ability-my .

'My mother-in-law wants to have new furniture and new decorations for her villa. This project costs [**it**] some twenty thousand dinars, and I cannot afford that. I can afford renting a house that matches my budget.'

5.3   From *haːl l-dunya:* 'this is life' – *farsˤa w-xarsa:* 'Farsa and Kharsa' – 00:15:25 – JOR

   4. Context: A young man complains about taxi drivers.

haːy   ʃuːfeːriyyet   l-takaːsi: ktiːr   ʕam-bizawdu-ha:
these   drivers   the-cabs   a.lot   PROG-acting.up-it
ha-l-ʔayyaːm .   sˤaːru: ʔiza   byimʃuː-**lun**
these-the-days . they.became   if   they.go-**them.D**
ʔakammin   kiːlo ,   yitˤʕilbu: xamestaʕaʃ .
a.few   kilometers , they.charge   fifteen .

'These cab drivers are out of line these days. It has become the case that if they drive [**them**] a few kilometers, they charge fifteen (shekels).'

5.4   From *maʃruːʕ tawfiːr* 'a saving project' – Episode 1 – 00:05:30 – PAL

As I mentioned in Chapter 1, once an AD refers to the subject, it is a SUBJ-AD. It may not be interpreted as a TOP/AFF-, SP-, or HR-AD. This is true in cases when the subject refers to the hearer as in (1) or the speaker as in (2). Once an entity is a subject, no matter what other role it plays in discourse (topic, speaker, hearer), the AD referring to it may be interpreted only as a SUBJ-AD. This implies that subjects are linguistically/cartographically different from other elements in the left periphery or that SUBJ-ADs are structurally different from the three other types of AD, a topic that I leave for another occasion.

The first extensive analysis of SUBJ-ADs in Arabic was put forth by Al-Zahre and Boneh (2010), with a follow-up in Al-Zahre and Boneh (2016); see also Haddad

(2014, to appear). Al-Zahre and Boneh's work focuses on Syrian Arabic and labels constructions with such datives as coreferential dative constructions.

In general terms, when a speaker uses a SUBJ-AD, she expresses an evaluative attitude toward an event as either unimportant/trivial/not a big deal or unexpected/surprising/a big deal, based on her familiarity with the subject and her expectations of her or him. The former type of attitude is more frequent, as we will see shortly. Section 2 deals with SUBJ-ADCs as used in representatives; these are statements that speakers make about themselves, their hearers, or a third party. Section 3 moves to SUBJ-AD directives which may take the form of requests, suggestions, or challenges.

2 SUBJ-ADCs as representatives

SUBJ-ADCs may be used in representatives: that is, in statements that may be assessed as true or false. Speakers employ a SUBJ-AD in representatives to evaluate an event as insignificant or as not unexpected, based on their familiarity with the subject's individual, group, or relational identities and their expectations of the subject with respect to these identities. Alternatively, they may use a SUBJ-AD to emphasize how surprising and how big of a deal an event is based on their familiarity with and expectations of the subject. In either case, they instruct the hearer to view the event from their perspective and to embrace the evaluation anchored to it. Context and common ground – that is, shared knowledge, including cultural knowledge and beliefs – are usually sufficient to help the hearer tell whether the speaker evaluates an event or a behavior as falling short of expectations or exceeding them. Often, however, speakers use SUBJ-ADCs in tandem with two types of intonation to express their attitude toward a given event or behavior: first, a falling intonation with a dismissive tone, implying that the event is insignificant/not worth mentioning; and second, a rising intonation with a surprised tone, implying that the event is surprising/unexpected. Tone, context, and common ground provide the measure. The SUBJ-AD, on the other hand, provides the measuring stick, as Figure 5.1 schematically illustrates.

In the following subsections, I present and discuss examples of the two options presented in Figure 5.1.

2.1 SUBJ-AD representatives about insignificant events

SUBJ-ADs are commonly used to evaluate an event or a behavior as insignificant, unsurprising, or non-consequential. The speaker presents this evaluation based on her familiarity with a certain aspect or aspects of the subject's identity and any rights and obligations associated with this identity. She also instructs the hearer to view the event or behavior, along with her evaluation, from the same perspective.

Consider (5), for example. The speaker, Abu Esam, is a business owner. His store, like most stores in the Syrian show about a neighborhood in early twentieth-century Damascus, is within walking distance of home. He and one of his sons, who is also his

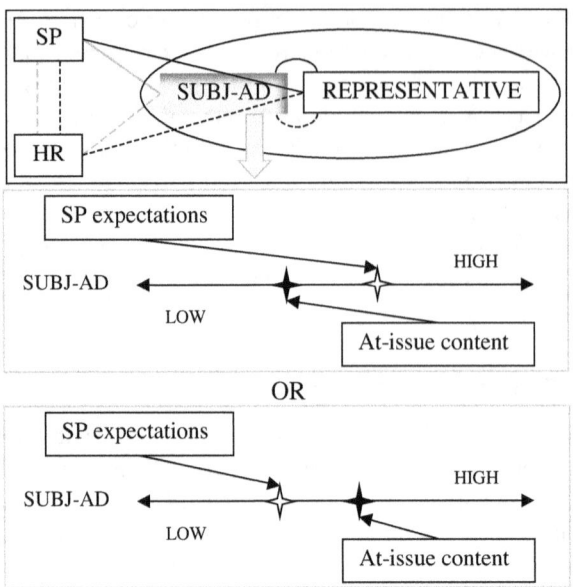

Figure 5.1 Stancetaking stage model of SUBJ-AD representatives

employee, normally close the store at noon and have lunch with the whole family at home. The utterance in (5) takes place after lunch. The speaker tells his wife that he is going to take a nap, and he asks her to wake him up in an hour before the time for prayer. The SUBJ-AD suggests that the siesta he is going to take is insignificant in terms of its duration. This evaluation, however, is contingent on his individual identity as a business owner and as his own boss, as well as the rights and obligations linked to this identity. If his son/employee says something similar after lunch, Abu Esam is likely to scold him and order him to go to the store. His son's identity as an employee does not qualify him for the right to an afternoon nap. Evidence comes from the fact that on at least one occasion in the show, while the whole family is having lunch, Abu Esam asks his son to finish eating before the others and go open the store.

5. Context: Abu Esam is the neighborhood doctor and barber. He comes home for lunch. After lunch, he tells his wife:

ʔana: tˤa:leʕ   ʔitsatˤtˤah-**li:**   sa:ʕet   zama:n ,
I   going.up   lie.down-**me.D**   hour   time ,
suʕa:d .   ʔalla: yirdˤa: ʕle:ki ,   bas   yʔadden
Suaad .   may.God.be.pleased.with.you ,   when   call
l-miɣrib ,   fayʔi:-ni: diɣri: ha: .
the-Maghrib.prayer ,   wake.up-me   immediately   huh .

'Suaad, I am going upstairs to lie [me] down for an hour. When the call for Maghrib prayer (or sunset prayer) comes on, wake me up right away.'

5.5 From *ba:b l-ḥa:ra* 'the neighborhood gate' – Season 1 – Episode 13 – 00:32:30 – SYR

The utterances in (6) and (7) are additional examples from Lebanese and Jordanian Arabic respectively. In both cases, the speakers evaluate the profiled events as potentially insignificant, based on the subjects' individual identities. In (6), the speaker implies that buying two additional houses would not be a burden to the subject, Mr. Adnan. Mr. Adnan is a wealthy individual who seems to buy houses generously for people he knows. The same sentence would be infelicitous if Mr. Adnan were not rich or if he were not known to be generous. In (7), the speaker is also the subject; he considers buying two or three pieces of land as normal and attainable, based on his identity as a rich person.

6. Context: Two men are gossiping about a rich acquaintance, Mr. Adnan, who keeps on buying houses for women he intends to seduce. Eventually, one of the interlocutors says:
law   byiftah-**lo**   ʃi: be:t   laʔil-i: w-laʔil-ak ,
if.only   he.open-**him.D** some   house   for-me   and-for-you ,
ʃu: ke:n   ʕa-be:l-na ?
what   was   on-mind-our ?
'If only he bought [him] a house for me and a house for you, that would be wonderful.'
From *bi-l-nisbe la-bukra ʃu:* 'what are the plans for tomorrow' – 00:15:30 – LEB   5.6

7. Context: Abu Awwad's cousin, Abu Khidir, explains to him that he is considering buying some land (bragging about how much money he has).
walla: ,   ya: ʔibn ʕamm-i: ʔabu: ʕawwa:d ,
by.God ,   VOC   son uncle-my   Abu Awwad ,
mfakkir   yaʕni: ʔiʃtri:-**li:**   gitʕiʕt-e:n ,
I.thinking   this.mean   I.buy-**me.D**   piece-two ,
gu:l   θala:θ   ʔaraːdʕi: .
say   three   land .
'To tell you the truth, cousin Abu Awwad, I am considering buying [me] two or maybe three pieces of land.'
From *ʔabu: ʕawwa:d* 'Abu Awwad' – Season 1 – Episode 1 – 00:11:30 – JOR   5.7

The pragmatic ability of SUBJ-ADs to dismiss a behavior as insignificant makes them a perfect tool that a speaker may use to defend the AD referent for behaving in a certain way that the hearer does not approve of. In this case, the speaker uses a SUBJ-AD in order to diminish the seriousness of the behavior by profiling it as insignificant compared to the types of vice or bad behavior that the subject or any member of her or his cohort may get involved in. In a way, the speaker expresses the attitude that the subject, based on some aspect of her or his identity, is entitled to some vice.

The utterance in (8) is an example. In this case, the speaker, Abu l-Nar, is also the subject. When confronted by the mayor, Abu Saleh, regarding a behavior that is considered sinful in Islam and in the community – namely, consuming alcohol – he admits wrongdoing. At the same time, however, he uses a SUBJ-AD in reference to himself to imply, untruthfully, that he is not a full-fledged alcoholic and that the two glasses of alcohol he drinks are insignificant or negligible compared to the amount of alcohol that a man like him could consume. Notice that Abu l-Nar says that he has his two drinks *maʕ l-rʒa:l* 'with the men' to say that all men drink a little and that his evaluation of this behavior is based on his identity as a man. To this, the mayor answers *ʔilt-illi rʒa:l* 'men, you say!' before he moves on to a different topic. The mayor's answer implies that he and Abu l-Nar attribute different identities, and thus different rights and obligations, to 'men.' To Mayor Abu Saleh, 'men' are righteous and pious and should be held up to high standards, whereas to Abu l-Nar 'men' should be cut some slack, so to speak. The outcome, of course, is negative alignment.

8. Context: Mayor Abu Saleh learns that Abu l-Nar, a troublemaker from another community, is spending time in the neighborhood at his deceased aunt's house, partying and drinking alcohol with his friends. When the mayor asks him if this is true, Abu l-Nar does not deny it, but says:

   ʔana: (.)   yaʕni: he:k   bitsalla:-**li**   bi-ʔadah
   I (.)   this.mean   like.this   I.pass.time-**me.D** with-glass
   ʔadah-e:n (.)   he:k   tisla:ye   maʕ   l-rʒa:l .
   glass-DUAL (.)   like.this   pastime   with   the-men .

   'Me, I have [**me**] a glass or two (of alcohol) just for fun with the men.'

5.8 From *ba:b l-ha:ra* 'the neighborhood gate' – Season 1 – Episode 13 – 00:17:30 – SYR

The view that men, but certainly not women, should be 'cut some slack' is shared by the speakers in (9) and especially (10). In (9), a wife uses a SUBJ-AD in an attempt to diminish the seriousness of her husband's embarrassing obsession with raising pigeons. When confronted by her mother about it, she justifies her husband's behavior by implying that his current obsession is not as bad as it used to be and that, as a man, he is entitled to a hobby. The speaker would not use a SUBJ-AD in the same dismissive manner in reference to herself if she were the one raising pigeons. This sort of hobby would not even be an option for women in the context of the show.

9. Context: Buran's mother, Suaad, asks her if her husband has really given up his obsession with raising pigeons, an activity that involves competing with other pigeon keepers and is frowned upon in the community. Buran, defending her husband, explains that he has, adding that he has gotten rid of all of the pigeons except for two or three which he keeps as a hobby during his free time.

   Suaad: yaʕni: xalasˤ ,   su:set   l-hama:m
           this.mean   that's.it ,   obsession   the-pigeons
           batˤtˤal-a: ?
           he.gave.up-it ?
           'Do you mean that's it? He has given up his obsession with pigeon raising?'

Buran:	ʔe:	ʔe:	batˤtˤal-a: ,	ya:mo . . .	yaʕni:
	yes	yes	he.gave.up-it ,	mother . . .	this.mean

bas   tarak   ʒo:z   la-l-tisla:ye .
only   he.kept   a.pair   for-the-entertainment .
baʕd   l-ɣada: ,   byitˤlaʕ   ʕa-l-ʔustˤu:h ,   byiʃrab
after   the-lunch , he.go.up   to-the-roof ,   drink
si:ka:ra   w-ka:set   ʃa:y ,   w-byitsalla:-lo   ʃwayy .
cigarette   and-cup   tea ,   and-have.fun-**him.D**   a.little .

'Yes, yes, he gave it up, Mother. I mean, he has kept a couple of them just for fun. After lunch, he goes up to the roof, smokes a cigarette, drinks a cup of tea, and relaxes **[him]** for a bit (flying his pigeons).'

From *ba:b l-ha:ra* 'the neighborhood gate' – Season 1 – Episode 25 – 00:38:50 – SYR   5.9

Example (10) is from a Lebanese show about marital disloyalty. The speaker describes how he goes about his extramarital affairs. The speaker, we find out a few minutes after the utterance, is in a unilateral open relationship with his wife: that is, he is allowed to have relations with other women, but his wife is not allowed to have relations with other men. Both he and his wife have agreed to this arrangement. In (10), he tells the interviewer that he travels to Ukraine for fifteen days every year for sexual tourism. Importantly, he uses a SUBJ-AD twice in order to trivialize the gravity of his behavior. He later tells the interviewer that the fifteen-day trips are presents he gives to himself, just like a man might give his girlfriend a watch or a cellphone as a present. The speaker's evaluation of the event as trivial is anchored to his identity as a man. Later in the program, when the speaker is asked how he would react if his wife behaved in the same way, his response is that he would divorce her.

10   Context: In an interview, a man explains his extramarital affairs.
ʔana: bse:fir . . .   bru:h   ʕa-ʔukra:nya: . . .   biʔʕid-**li:**
I   travel . . .   I.go   to-Ukraine . . .   I.stay-**me.D**
xamstaʕʃar   yo:m . . .   brih-**li:** ,   xamstaʕʃar
fifteen   day . . .   I.go-**me.D**   fifteen
yo:m   binbisitˤ-un .
day   I.enjoy-them .

'I travel, I go to Ukraine; I stay **[me]** fifteen days; I go **[me]** fifteen days and I enjoy them.'

From *tahqi:q* 'investigations' – *Extramarital Affairs in Lebanon* – 00:20:40 – LEB   5.10

In the three examples above, in order for the hearers to align positively with the speakers, they have to accept the identity of 'a man' that the speakers attribute to the referent of the SUBJ-AD. In (8) and (9), the hearers do not believe that men are entitled to the behavior that the speakers anchor to the SUBJ-ADs. This results in negative alignment. In (10), the wife accepts the identity attributes that the speaker attaches to the SUBJ-AD and, by association, to all men. However, not all viewers of the show – and I certainly hope not many – evaluate men and extramarital affairs in the same way.

Speakers may also use a SUBJ-AD to diminish the importance of an accomplishment. In doing so, they instruct the hearer not to think too highly of the accomplishment, and to conclude that the referent of the SUBJ-AD could do better. When the referent is the speaker herself or someone dear to the speaker (daughter, brother, and so on), the speaker is normally using a SUBJ-ADC as an attempt to be modest. In this respect, a SUBJ-ADC is the mirror image of a HR-ADC used for bragging; see Chapter 4. Using a SUBJ-AD allows the speaker to talk about a certain accomplishment without giving the impression that she is bragging about it. By doing so, she often gives the hearer the chance to counter her modesty and praise her for her work. For example, the speaker in (11) uses two SUBJ-ADs in reference to a plan that he and his partner will carry out. Their plan is to collect donations to support the Palestinian rebels against foreign occupation, something that most of the people in their community consider an important act of patriotism. By using these datives, the speaker implies that his utterance is meant only to inform and that it is not meant to brag. It also implies that the accomplishment will be minor, compared to what he and his partner could do or have done in the past.[1]

11 Context: Abu Esam tells the mayor of the neighborhood, Abu Saleh, that he and Abu Shihab plan to make a tour to a number of neighborhoods and collect money to support the Palestinian rebels against the British occupation.
ʔana: w-ʔabu: ʃha:b ,   zaʕi:m ,   raħ   naʕmil-**lna**:
I   and-Abu Shihab , chief ,   will   make-**us.D**
makku:k w-fatle   bi-ha-l-ħa:ra:t ,   niʒmaʕ-**ilna**:
a.go.around   in-these-the-neighborhoods , collect-**us.D**
ʃwayyet   masʕa:ri: .
some   money .
'Abu Shihab and I will make [us] a tour to the surrounding neighborhood and collect [us] some money.'

5.11 From *ba:b l-ħa:ra* 'the neighborhood gate' – Season 1 – Episode 24 – 00:25:20 – SYR

In addition to the above uses, speakers may occasionally use a SUBJ-AD in association with an epistemic possibility, an event that they believe has happened or will happen but are not certain if it actually has or will. In this case, the SUBJ-AD may evaluate the event in terms of the likelihood of its occurrence as 'not unexpected.' Again, the evaluation is based on the speaker's expectations of the subject.

Consider (12), for example. In a conversation about a recent burglary in the community, the chief of the police district, Abu Jawdat, and his subordinate, Nuri, talk about the neighborhood guard, Abu Samo, as a potential suspect. Abu Samo disappeared the night of the burglary. The audience of the show know that he was murdered, but the residents and police believe he stole fifty gold coins and ran away. After several days of search and inquiry, Abu Jawdat arrives at the conclusion that the disappearance of Abu Samo is not necessarily enough reason to suspect that he is the burglar. He goes on to say that the guard probably disappeared because he got married to a second wife, a practice that is allowed in Islam. The speaker uses a SUBJ-AD to indicate that this hypothetical scenario would not be totally unexpected and thus would be unsurprising if true. The evaluation is based on the speaker's familiarity with Abu Samo's group identity as a Muslim man who is allowed by religion and law to have up to four wives and who lives in a community that considers the behavior as not only religiously legal or *hala:l* but also culturally normal. The sheikh in the neighborhood, for example, has two wives. The same behavior would not be considered unsurprising in a different sociocultural context, such as in present-day Tunisia, a Muslim country where polygamy is outlawed. It would not be considered unsurprising either if the subject were a woman or a Christian man.

12 Context: A burglary occurred in the neighborhood, and the neighborhood guard, Abu Samo, is a suspect. Abu Samo disappeared (in fact, he was murdered), and the police assumed at first that it was he who committed the burglary. After a while, however, the chief of the police district, Abu Jawdat, starts doubting the idea that Abu Samo is involved at all. In a conversation with his subordinate, Nuri, he says:
ʔamma: bxsˤu:sˤ   ha:da: ʔabu: samˤo   ha:res
as.to   this   Abu Samo   guard
ħa:ret   l-dˤabeʕ,   w-sabab   ɣya:b-o,   yaˤni:
neighborhood   the-hyena,   and-reason   absence-his,   I.mean
ʃu: biˤarrif-na:.   yimken   l-riʒʒa:l   haʒʒ
what   inform-us.   perhaps   the-man   got.fed.up.and.left
min   l-ħa:ra,   walla: harba:n   min   mart-o
from   the-neighborhood,   or   escaping   from   wife-his
w-wla:d-o,   ya: si:d-i: .   ʔaw   tˤaʔʔ-**allo**
and-children-his,   VOC   sir-my.   or   snapped-**him.D**
ʒwa:ze   ta:nye   .   ˤa:di: !
marriage   second   .   normal !
'As for Abu Samo, the guard of the neighborhood of the hyena, and the reason behind his absence, how are we supposed to know (that he disappeared because he committed the burglary)? Perhaps the man got fed up with the neighborhood and fled, or he ran away from his wife and kids, my good sir, or perhaps he went [him] for another marriage. These things happen!'
From *ba:b l-ha:ra* 'the neighborhood gate' – Season 1 – Episode 4 – 00:10:50 – SYR   5.12

Unlike in (12), in which the evaluation is based on the subject's group identity, the evaluation in (13) is based on the individual identity of the subject, who in this case is also the hearer. The speaker in (13) has seized the poniard of a teenage boy. When the latter goes to the speaker's house to get it back, the speaker refuses to return it because he believes that the boy may use it to stab someone. The use of a SUBJ-AD signifies that this hypothetical situation is not completely unexpected. As the speaker explicitly states, it has happened before and thus it may happen again. If the teenage boy did not have a history of stabbing, the use of the SUBJ-AD would be infelicitous.

Note that in this case the evaluation expressed via the SUBJ-AD does not target the event itself but the likelihood of its occurrence.

13 Context: Samo, the teenage son of Abu Samo, gets into a fight with a boy who taunts him about his father being a thief. Samo ends up stabbing the boy in the arm. Idaashari sees him and grabs his poniard. Samo later goes to ask Idaashari to return his father's poniard. Idaashari refuses to give it back and explains:

l-ʃibriyye   ma: ha-ʔaʕtˤi:-k   yya:ha: ,   miʃa:n
the-poniard   NEG   will-I.give-you   it ,   so.that
ma: tibtili:-**lak**   bi-walad   ta:ni:
NEG   you.get.in.trouble-**you.D**   with-boy   another
mitil   ma: btale:t   bi-walad   ʔabu: ka:mel .
like   that   you.got.in.trouble   with-boy   Abu Kamel .

'I'm not going to give you the poniard back so that you don't get [you] in trouble with another boy as you did when you stabbed Abu Kamel's boy.'

5.13 From *ba:b l-ha:ra* 'the neighborhood gate' – Season 1 – Episode 22 – 00:03:20 – SYR

The utterance in (13) is performed in relation to the subject's individual identity and individual history. Alternatively, it is possible to perform an utterance like (13) in relation to the subject's group identity. Consider the constructed example in (14). In this case, the speaker spots a gun in the hands of a toddler and indicates that the gun should be taken away from him before he shoots someone. The SUBJ-AD expresses the sentiment that if the toddler in fact shoots someone, that will not be completely unexpected. The evaluation is based not on the toddler's history of shooting people but rather on the history of gun accidents that involve toddlers as shooters. In other words, the evaluation expressed via the SUBJ-AD is based on the toddler's group rather than individual identity.

14 Context: A toddler finds his father's gun, so he starts playing with it. A guest sees him, so she says to the father:

xo:d   l-fared   minn-o ,   yʔu:m   yʔawwisˤ-**lo**
take   the-gun   from-him ,   he.may   shoot-**him.D**
hada: bi-l-ɣalatˤ
someone   by-the-mistake

'Take the gun away from him; he may shoot [him] someone by accident.'

2.2 SUBJ-ADCs about surprising events

As I pointed out in the introduction to this chapter, speakers of Levantine Arabic use a SUBJ-ADC to evaluate an event as either insignificant (falling short of expectations) or as surprising (exceeding expectations). SUBJ-ADCs of the former type are more common, but those of the latter type are also attested. We already saw an example from Jordanian Arabic in (3) above. In this section, I provide and discuss additional examples.

Consider the Syrian example in (15). The dialog is part of a more elaborate gossip event presented in Chapter 4, example (21). The speaker, a street vendor called Abu Ghaleb, tells an acquaintance, a garbage collector called Abu Ahmad, about a recent robbery in the neighborhood. The suspect is the poor guard Abu Samo, who features in (12) above. Some residents believe that Abu Samo broke into one of the houses in the neighborhood and stole fifty Ottoman gold coins. The number of coins is exaggerated in (15). Abu Ghaleb uses a SUBJ-AD to evaluate the event as surprising – even shocking – rather than insignificant. This interpretation is confirmed by the idiomatic expression *le:ra tʕintʕah le:ra* 'one pound pokes another,' which is used when speakers make reference to (subjectively) large amounts of money. The speaker may evaluate the robbery event as shocking, based on his familiarity with and expectations of Abu Samo as a guard who should protect the neighborhood rather than violate it, or as a poor man to whom two hundred gold coins mean a lot of money.

15 Context: Abu Ghaleb is a street vendor who is interested in gossip, often maliciously so in order to cause trouble. He tries to involve Abu Ahmad, a garbage collector, in a gossip situation about recent events in a rich neighborhood where they work.

Abu Ghaleb: mazbu:tʕ   mitil   ma: smiʕit ,   ʔabu: ʔaḥmad ?
              true   like   that   I.heard ,   Abu   Ahmad ?
              'Is it true what I heard, Abu Ahmad?'

Abu Ahmad: ʃu: smiʕit ,   ta:ʒ   ra:s-i: ?
              what   you.hear ,   crown   head-my?
              'What did you hear, my man?'

Abu Ghaleb: smiʕt-**illak**   ʔinno   l-ḥa:ra   ʔa:yme   ʔa:ʕde . . .
              I.heard-**you.D**   that   the-neighborhood   upside   down . . .
              w-ʕam-biʔu:lu: kama:n   ʔinno   ʔabu: samʕo
              and-PROG-they.say   also   that   Abu Samo
              sʕar-lo   mixtifi   yawme:n   tla:te   mu:
              happen-him.D   unfound   two.days   three   NEG
              mbayyen   w-ʕam-biʔu:lu: kama:n   ʔinno
              showing   and-PROG-they.say   also   that
              ḥa:fif-**lo**   mi:te:n   le:ra   dahab ,   le:ra
              he.stole-**him.D**   two.hundred   liras   gold ,   lira
              tʕintʕah   le:ra !
              poking   lira !
              'I heard [you] that the neighborhood is in turmoil . . . and they're saying that Abu Samo has been gone for two or three days and no one knows where he is, and they are saying that he stole [him] two hundred gold coins, a king's ransom.'

From *ba:b l-ḥa:ra* 'the neighborhood gate' – Season 1 – Episode 2 – 00:37:00 – SYR   5.15

The utterances in (16) and (17) are additional examples from Jordanian and Lebanese Arabic respectively. In (16) the speaker, Abu Karim, tries to convince his friend, Abu Raad, not to buy a new satellite dish. Rather, he suggests that Abu

Raad should give him the satellite dish to fix it. Abu Karim uses a SUBJ-AD to evaluate new satellite dishes as shockingly expensive. This evaluation may be based on the speaker's familiarity with Abu Raad as a middle-class person who should be careful with his budget. It may also be based on a broader group identity of Abu Raad as a consumer. In the latter case, we can say that Abu Karim evaluates satellite dishes as expensive for any person who fits in the category of consumers, with Abu Raad as one such person.

> 16 Context: Abu Raad wants to sell his satellite dish and buy a new one. Abu Karim objects to this. He says:
> maʕʔu:l,   maʕʔu:l,   ya: ʔabu: raʕed !   biddak
> possible   possible   VOC   Abu Raad !   you.want
> tbi:ʕ-u   w-thitʕtʕ-**illak**   mablaɣ   w-qadr-u
> sell-it   and-pay-**you.D**   amount.of.money and-value-it
> ʕala: satellite   ʒdi:d ?   ʔay   ʔana: basʕalliḥ-lak
> on   satellite   new ?   INTER   I   fix-you.D
> yya: ,   w-baraʒʒiʕ-lak   yya: ʒdi:d .
> it ,   and-make.again-you.D   it   new .
>
> 'You can't be serious, Abu Raad! You want to sell it and pay [you] a large amount of money for a new one?! I can fix it for you and make it new again.'

5.16 From *naḥafa:t ʕaylitna*: 'our family anecdotes'– *l-ʔiqtisʕa:d wa:ʒib* 'economy is a duty' – 00:02:45 – JOR

Similarly, in (17), the speaker attaches a SUBJ-AD to the at-issue content of his utterance and the twelve lawsuits he won against former employers. To him, the fact that he won so many lawsuits is shocking, and he wants his hearer to have the same perspective. The evaluation may be based on his identity as a poor employee who is unlikely to win so many lawsuits. Alternatively, he may consider twelve wins to be rather surprising, no matter who is suing whom. In this case, the group identity becomes broader, including all humans eligible to file lawsuits.

> 17. Context: A new employee is upset because his boss would not sign him up for health care and social security benefits. He complains to his colleagues and tells them that he plans to sue his boss. He adds that he is certain that he will win the case. An older colleague replies that he will probably win the case but not much more, suggesting that he will likely lose his job.
> btirbaḥ   l-daʕwe   bas ,   w-byitʕlaʕ   ʔinno
> you.win   the-lawsuit   only ,   and-it.be.decided   that
> le:zim   tku:n   madʕmu:n . bas   min   baʕd   l-daʕwe
> you.must   be   insured .   but   from   after the-lawsuit
> w-bi-l-ra:yeh ,   ma: biʕu:d   fi: ʃi: madʕmu:n .
> and-from-the-thereof ,   NEG   return   there anything secured .
> sʔal-ni   ʔana: ,   bas   kint   b-ʕimr-ak ,   ya   rayyis ,
> you.ask-me   I ,   when   I.was   in-age-your , VOC   chief ,

ribhan-**li:**	ʃi	tnaʕʃar	daʕwe !
I.won-**me.D**	some	twelve	lawsuit !

'You will win the lawsuit and nothing else. It will be decided that you must receive social security benefits, but after that, there will be no (job) security. Trust me, chief, when I was your age, I won [**me**] some twelve lawsuits.'

From *bi-l-nisbe la-bukra ʃu:* 'what are the plans for tomorrow' – 00:37:30 – LEB   5.17

The above examples go against Al-Zahre and Boneh's (2016) generalization that Syrian Arabic SUBJ-ADCs (which they label as coreferential dative constructions) may be used only to express a dismissive stance toward an event as insignificant. The examples clearly show that SUBJ-ADs may be used in relation to events that, according to the speaker, exceed expectations.

In their article, Al-Zahre and Boneh also dismiss the idea that the speaker's evaluation of events in SUBJ-ADCs may be anchored to her expectations of the subject. To the authors, the event in a SUBJ-AD is evaluated as insignificant, regardless of who the subject is. I believe this dismissal to be too hasty, as the examples we have seen so far show. In Haddad (to appear), I conceded Al-Zahre and Boneh's claim is one possibility, and maintained that in addition to the possibility of using a SUBJ-ADC to evaluate an event as insignificant or unexpected based on the speaker's familiarity with and expectations of the subject, a speaker may use a SUBJ-AD to evaluate a profiled event based on her expectations of and experience with events of the same type in general terms.

Here, I will reassert my original statement that SUBJ-ADCs always involve an evaluation that is based on the speaker's knowledge and expectations of the subject. As I mentioned earlier, the speaker's familiarity with the subject may target one or more aspects of the subject's individual, group, or relational identities. There are behaviors that may be evaluated as shocking or insignificant, for example, only when they are carried out by a shy man (individual identity), an Arab woman (group identity), or a son (relational identity). At the same time, there are behaviors that may be evaluated as surprising or unimportant if they are carried out by any human but not, say, by an elephant. Thus, [+human] becomes a group identity – or, in more accurate terms, a collective identity (see Brewer and Gardner 1996: 83 and Chapter 2) – involving all humans. For example, if I write *Aslan ate five pounds of meat yesterday*, the reader's reaction as to whether the eating event falls short of or exceeds expectations will depend on whether Aslan is my human friend or whether he is a lion in a zoo named after the main character in C. S. Lewis's *The Chronicles of Narnia* series. Lions typically eat about fifteen pounds of meat per day.

Similarly, as we saw above, evaluations of events such as buying a satellite dish or winning twelve lawsuits may be considered significant or shocking, based on the subject in terms of her or his individual identity. Alternatively, they may be evaluated as exceeding expectations, based on the subject's group identity as a customer, employee, or simply a human being within a certain sociocultural context.

Al-Zahre and Boneh use statements about the weather such as (18) to make their point. To them, when speaking about the weather, the word *it* is vacuous, and thus the evaluation of a rain event cannot be based on *it* as a subject. In fact, 'weather *it*' is not as vacuous as Al-Zahre and Boneh claim it is. This is especially true of Levantine Arabic, in which words like *l-sama:* 'the sky' or *l-dini:* 'the world' may be used as subject with weather predicates.[2] Importantly, the evaluation of the rain event in (18) depends on the identity of weather *it*, and whether the speaker refers to *l-sama:* 'the sky' or *l-dini:* 'the world' in Dubai (United Arab Emirates) in the summer, where it hardly ever rains, or in Tallahassee (Florida, United States) in the summer, where it rains almost every afternoon. If the speaker is in Dubai, then the statement will be uttered with a rising, surprise tone, and the SUBJ-ADC evaluates the rain event as unexpected or shocking. The opposite would be true if this speaker is in Tallahassee. In both of these cases, the focus is on the individual local identity of weather *it*.

18. ʃattit-**la:**   ʃi   se:ʕa   lyo:m
    it.rained-**it.D** some   hour   today
    'It rained [it] for about an hour today.'

SUBJ-ADCs may be realized as other types of speech act as well, as we will see in the next section.

3 SUBJ-ADCs as directives

SUBJ-ADCs are frequently used as directives. Two types stand out in particular: requests and suggestions. SUBJ-ADCs are also not uncommon as dares or challenges, which, according to Searle (1976: 11), also qualify as directives. In all these cases, the speaker uses a SUBJ-AD to evaluate the action she instructs the hearer to do, along with any potential effort involved, as insignificant compared to what the hearer is fully capable of doing. If the directive is a suggestion or a piece of advice that would benefit the hearer, the speaker uses a SUBJ-AD to evaluate the potential cost of the suggested action as minimal compared to any potential gain. Importantly, the speaker invites the hearer to view the directive from this perspective, as Figure 5.2 schematically illustrates.

3.1 SUBJ-AD directives as requests

Speakers may employ a SUBJ-AD in requests in order to make them sound minimally imposing. In Brown and Levinson's (1987) terms, the SUBJ-AD has a redressive effect, making the request less face-threatening. Roughly, the SUBJ-AD has the effect of such English expressions as *I hope I am not asking for too much* or *I hope I am not asking too much from you*, as illustrated in (19) and (20).

19. **I hope I am not asking for too much** but could you look up my friend's perfume purchase to make absolutely sure I have the same perfume.
From *The Killfile* by Dan Danov (2009: 33)

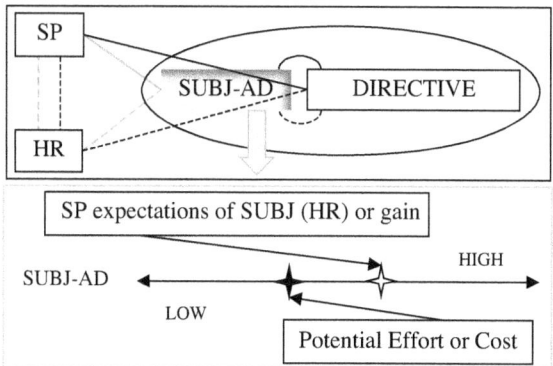

Figure 5.2 Stancetaking stage model of SUBJ-AD directives

20. **I hope I am not asking too much from you**, but will you put in another bill for my wife in January.

From a letter by J. D. Lewis to Senator Walter George on October 21, 1955, in *House Reports, United States Congressional Serial Set, Volume 11904* (1956: 15).

The directive in (21) is an example from Syrian Arabic. The speaker, Idaashari, attaches two SUBJ-ADs to two requests he performs in the neighborhood's coffee shop. He requests a cup of tea for himself and a bucket of water for his donkey. The hearer is Msallam, the waiter at the shop. The speaker chooses to sound polite and minimally imposing with his requests, which is why he uses SUBJ-ADs. He also invites the hearer to view the requests from the same perspective. For Msallam, the first request is business as usual; thus, it is insignificant in terms of the effort it requires and its implied expectations of him as a waiter. The second request, however, does not match Msallam's job description. It clashes with his identity as a waiter who serves people and not donkeys, which is why he does not view the request as insignificant or minimally imposing in relation to what a customer should expect of him. The eventual outcome is positive alignment regarding the first request but confrontation and negative alignment regarding the second.

21. Context: Idaashari, a peddler of lower socio-economic status, comes to the neighborhood coffee shop and asks the waiter, Msallam, for two things:
    Idaashari: msallam (.)   hat-**lak**   ka:set   ʃa:y . . .
              Msallam (.)   bring-**you.D**   cup   tea . . .
              ʒib-**lak**   satˤel   mayy   la-ha-l-hma:r
              bring-**you.D**   bucket   water   for-this-the-donkey
              xalli-i   yiʃrab .
              let-it   drink .
              'Msallam, bring [you] me a cup of tea . . . and bring [you] a bucket of water for the donkey to drink.'

	Msallam:	leːʃ	min	ʔeːmta:	sˤaːret	l-ʔahwe
		why	since	when	became	the-coffee.shop
		baːyke,	nʃarreb		w-ntˤaˤmi:	fiː-ha:	l-hamiːr?
		barn,	we.give.water		and-we.feed	in-it	the-donkeys?
		'Since when is the coffee house a barn for giving food and water to donkeys?'

5.21 From *baːb l-haːra* 'the neighborhood gate' – Season 1 – Episode 2 – 00:05:30 – SYR

SUBJ-AD requests are common when the speaker and hearer view each other as equals. This is the case between Idaashari and Msallam in (21) above. Additional examples are provided in (22) and (23). In both cases, the speaker – a husband in (22) and a friend in (23) – perceives the hearer as an equal and thus uses a SUBJ-ADC to sound less imposing.

22. Context: Abu Nizar and Um Nizar, husband and wife, are having visitors over. They plan to sit outside on the patio. Abu Nizar asks his wife:
    haːtiː-**lik** kam kirsiː min ʒuwwaː, ya ʔim Nizaːr.
    bring-**you.D** some chair from inside, VOC Um Nizar.
    'Bring [you] some chairs from inside, Um Nizar.'

5.22 From *lammaː hikyit Maryam* 'when Mariam spoke out' – 00:42:45 – LEB

23. Context: There is a demonstration outside a hotel, and the police are trying to contain it by hosing the demonstrators down. A man asks his friend:
    ftah-**lak** ha-l-beːb ʃway ʔallah, barki
    you.open-**you.D** this-the-door a.little by.God, perhaps
    byiʒi raʃʃe ʕlay-naː, ʕabbaʔnaː rah niftˤus.
    come splash on-us, we.are.burdened.by.heat will we.suffocate.
    'Open [you] the door a little please; perhaps we will be splashed with some water. The heat in here is about to kill us.'

5.23 From *nazl l-suruːr* 'the Surour Inn' – 00:11:15 – LEB

Of course, the request must be reasonable and must not clash with the hearer's identity. For example, if the wife in (22) happens to have a bad backache that day and her husband is aware of it, his SUBJ-AD may backfire. She may answer something like (24) with stress on the verb with the dative. By doing so, she means to isolate the dative in an attempt to ask the question: *X? What do you mean X?* à la Potts (2011).

24. haːtiː-**lik** kam kirsiː? ʔanaː riːʃe bi-l-keːd
    bring-**you.D** a.few chair? I feather in-the-difficulty
    fiyy-i ʔihmul!
    in-me carry!
    'Bring [you] a few chairs? I can hardly carry a feather!'

Let us look at (21) one more time. The exchange is interesting for another reason. The speaker, Idaashari, has no choice but to be polite – or to fake politeness – with Msallam if he does not want to be confrontational. This is so because, at this point in the Syrian show, his public identity is that of a poor peddler who has authority only over his wife and children. In (21), he is of equal status compared to his hearer and as such his linguistic choices are limited. He has not established himself as a 'tough guy' yet, and thus has not qualified for the use of tougher language, such as the use of SP-AD directives, something that we witnessed in Chapter 3, example (22).

Unlike the speaker in (21), speakers of a higher status compared to their hearers have more linguistic choices. Consider (25), for example. The speaker, Abu l-Nar, normally uses SP-AD directives with his employee, Abu Draa, even when he asks him to do things that are not strictly part of his job description as a farrier. Abu Draa does not mind and he is normally happy to please his boss. The exchange in (25) takes place right after Abu l-Nar has unfairly reprimanded Abu Draa. To make it up to him, Abu l-Nar chooses to soften his tone and use a SUBJ-AD directive. He could have chosen to keep the same tone and used a SP-AD directive without being penalized. The unequal status between him and his hearer allows him to go either way.

25. Context: Abu l-Nar, a farrier, reprimands his employee, Abu Draa, for being late. When Abu Draa gives a legitimate excuse, Abu l-Nar says that all is fine and then the two have the following exchange:
    Abu l-Nar: saːwiː-**lak**   kaːset   ʃaːy .
                 make-**you.D**   cup   tea .
                 'Make [you] a cup of tea.'
    Abu Draa: btiʔmur ,   ʕadiːd .
                 at.your.service ,   boss .
                 'Right away, Boss.'
From *baːb l-ḥaːra* 'the neighborhood gate' – Season 1 – Episode 13 – 00:03:20 – SYR   5.25

The observation that social actors who enjoy a certain level of authority over their hearers have more choices is also evident in (26) and (27). The former is a repetition of example (23) in Chapter 3. The example features a belligerent man in a pub bossing the pub manager around and ordering him to inform the pub employees that they must not mess with him. About twelve minutes earlier in the play, this same man had walked into the pub, except at that time he was in a good mood. He does not use a SP-AD order. Instead, he performs the SUBJ-AD request in (27). The dative in (27) is anchored to the speaker's evaluation of his request for a fan as a minor ordeal. In effect he is saying: at least install a fan, something a pub like this should be able to afford. He could have equally chosen to play the belligerent man and used a SP-AD in (27) as well.

26. Context: During the war in Lebanon, it was common for men with weapons and connections to act tough in public. In this scene, a tough guy in a pub has become

upset with one of the waiters. He is about to start a fight when the pub manager tries to calm him down. The customer says with indignation and a patronizing tone:

fahhim-**li:** ʃayyi:l-tak , ʔana ma: hada: byitʕa:tˤa:
explain-**me.D** workers-your , I no one interfere
maʕ-i: ʔabdan .
with-me ever .

'Explain [me] to your employees that they should never mess with me.'

5.26 From *bi-l-nisbe la-bukra ʃu:* 'what are the plans for tomorrow' – 00:52:20 – LEB

    27. Context: A man walks into a pub. He complains about how stuffy and full of smoke the place is. He says:

wlo: ! wlo: ʃu: ha-l-ʕabʔa ha:y !
INTER ! INTER what this-the-stuffiness this !
rakbu:-**lkun** ʃi: asberate:r .
you.install-**you.D** some aspirator .

'Come on! It's so stuffy in here! Install [you] a fan.'

5.27 From *bi-l-nisbe la-bukra ʃu:* 'what are the plans for tomorrow' – 00:40:00 – LEB

3.2 SUBJ-ADCs as suggestions

SUBJ-ADCs may also be used as suggestions, taking the form of advice or offers that would benefit the hearer/subject: that is, the speaker performs these suggestions with the hearer/subject's best interest in mind. By attaching a SUBJ-AD to the suggestion, the speaker expresses the belief that the suggested action is insignificant in terms of effort or cost compared to what the hearer/subject could do or to the potential gain he or she would receive.

Consider (28) as an example. The speaker is the neighborhood doctor, Abu Esam. He is checking on a patient, Idaashari, who has recently had his arm amputated because of gangrene. Abu Esam finds out that Idaashari is weak and depressed. He suggests that Idaashari will have to endure the pain for a few days. To cheer him up, he attaches a SUBJ-AD to the suggestion, implying that enduring a few days of pain should be really easy for a tough guy, or a 'horse,' like Idaashari. Idaashari agrees that a few days of pain should be easy for a tough guy, but he updates the ground by saying that he no longer is the tough guy he used to be and that he is now a 'broken horse.' He thus implies that Abu Esam's evaluation of enduring the pain as easy or reasonable, based on the expectations that he has of Idaashari, no longer holds. The outcome is negative alignment, at least on the surface. Abu Esam uses the SUBJ-ADC and the horse metaphor only for encouragement, but in reality he knows that Idaashari is not doing well, as he later reveals to Idaashari's son.

    28. Context: Idaashari feels really sick after he had his arm amputated because of gangrene. Abu Esam, the neighborhood physician, is checking on him to make sure he is doing OK. They have this conversation:

Idaashari: ʔana: taʕba:n , ya: haki:m ...
 I tired , VOC doctor ...
 'I'm tired, doctor.'
Abu Esam: ... baddak tithammal-**lak** kam yo:m .
 ... you.need endure-**you.D** a.few day .
 wlek ʕala: ʔasa:s ʔinte mitil l-hsˤa:n ,
 INTER on principle you like the-horse ,
 ʃu: ba-na: ?
 what with-us ?
 'You need to endure [**you**] the pain for a few days. I thought you were tough like a horse. What's going on?'
Idaashari: ... l-hsˤa:n bas nkasar (.) bisˤi:r
 the-horse when break (.) become
 mo:t-u ʔarḥam .
 death-its more.merciful .
 'When a horse is broken, death becomes more merciful.'
From *ba:b l-ḥa:ra* 'the neighborhood gate' – Season 1 – Episode 30 – 00:17:00 – SYR 5.28

Similarly, in (29) one woman, Im Ziki, tries to convince her friend, Firyal, to hire a tailor or two to help her out with sewing dresses for Firyal's daughter Jamileh's wedding. By using a SUBJ-ADC, the speaker expresses her evaluation of the suggestion as easy and doable for two reasons: first, there are plenty of tailors in Damascus, and thus it is not hard for Firyal or any resident of Damascus to find one; and second, Firyal is well off and can afford to hire tailors. In addition, the gain is substantially larger than the cost: by hiring tailors, Firyal will be able to finish faster and the wedding will not be delayed.[3]

29. Context: Firyal has an only daughter, Jamileh, who is soon to be married. Firyal wants to sew all her daughter's dresses herself in preparation for the wedding, but Im Ziki is trying to convince her to hire a couple of tailors to help her out. She argues that Firyal will not be able to finish on time for the wedding if she works on the dresses all by herself.
 sˤaʕb ʕle:-ki tiʃtiɣli: kil ha-l-ʃiɣil .
 difficult for-you work all this-the-work .
 ʔillet xayya:tˤat bi-l-ʃa:m ? la:ʔi:-**lek**
 shortage tailors in-the-Damascus ? find-**you.D**
 ʃi: xayya:tˤa tinte:n ysaʕdu:-ki , minnu
 some tailor two help-you , on.the.one.hand
 bitʃaheʃlu: , w-minnu l-binit
 you.finish.fast , and-on.the.other.hand the-girl
 bitru:ḥ ʕala: be:t ʒo:z-a: bisirʕa .
 go to house husband-her quickly .
 'It will be difficult for you to do all this work. And for what? Is there a shortage of tailors in Damascus? Find [**you**] a tailor or two who can help you. For one, you'll

finish faster, and for two, your daughter will be able to move into her husband's house sooner.'

5.29 From *ba:b l-ha:ra* 'the neighborhood gate' – Season 1 – Episode 19 – 00:07:40 – SYR

SUBJ-AD suggestions are often used in offers of food or drink. The speaker employs a dative to evaluate the food or drink offer as minor (inexpensive, insignificant) when compared to potential gains. Sometimes, the gains are explicitly stated, as (30) and (31) illustrate. In situations like (30), in which the speaker invites the hearer to have a drink or meal, the SUBJ-ADC implies that the offer is insignificant compared to the treatment that the hearer deserves as a guest: that is, the speaker effectively tells the hearer that he deserves better. The expression in Levantine Arabic is usually *ma: fi: ʃi: min ʔi:mt-ak* 'none is a match to your status.' As to (31), the speaker soliloquizes about his plan for breakfast. He refers to himself in the first person plural, as if he is having a conversation with himself. To him, a plate of chickpeas is affordable in terms of cost, and the satisfaction he may get from it is substantial, as he explicitly states.

30. Context: The neighborhood doctor, Abu Esam, invites his brother-in-law, Abu Shihab, to share a cup of tea.

fu:t	ʕo:d,	ʔax-i: .	ʃrab-**lak**
enter	sit,	brother-my .	drink-**you.D**
ka:set	ʃa:y	he:k	w-rayyeh .
cup	tea	like.this	and-relax .

    'Come in, brother, and sit down. Have **[you]** a good cup of tea and relax.'

5.30 From *ba:b l-ha:ra* 'the neighborhood gate' – Season 1 – Episode 17 – 00:08:00 – SYR

31. Context: Abdo, an employee at the public bath in the neighborhood, is subbing as a night guard after the neighborhood guard, Abu Samo, disappeared. Early in the morning, right after his shift is over, he says to himself:

walla:	ʔahsan	ʃi:	halla?	
by.God	best	thing	now	
nru:h,	naʕmil-**lna**:	sˤahn	msabbaha	
we.go,	we.do-**us.D**	plate	chickpeas	
ʕind	ʔabu: sami:r,	maʕ	ʃwayyit	basˤal w-fiʒil ,
at	Abu Samir,	with	a.little	onion and-radish ,
ʔe	btiswa:	l-dinye:	w-ma:	fi:-ha: !
INTER	worth	the-world	and-what	in-it !

    'The best thing to do now is go **[us]** to Abu Samir's and have a plate of chickpeas with some onions and radishes on the side. That will be better than anything in the world!'

5.31 From *ba:b l-ha:ra* 'the neighborhood gate' – Season 1 – Episode 3 – 00:14:50 – SYR

Examples (32) and (33) are from Lebanese Arabic. In both cases, the speakers use a SUBJ-ADC to evaluate the cost of the profiled suggestion as negligible compared to the potential gain. Importantly, the evaluation is based on the speakers' knowledge and expectations of the hearers/subjects. The suggestion in (32) that the hearer should travel abroad and work for two or three years may be considered reasonable and affordable only if the hearer is a young person. The older the hearer is, the less reasonable the suggestion becomes. If the same suggestion is addressed to a sixty-year old, the attachment of the SUBJ-AD to the suggestion is judged as infelicitous or sarcastic. Similarly, the speaker in (33) implies that women in general should have *nʕu:me* 'gentleness/softness'; he further implies that the hearer, as a woman, should have at least a little *nuʕu:me*, an insignificant amount that may be considered barely enough for her to find a husband. The second part of example (33) is a clear indication that the speaker's stance toward his co-worker's blunt response is anchored to his expectations of her as a woman, more specifically as a single woman who would like to get married one day.

32. Context: In this scene from a political/social comedy show, a woman tells a man that his only solution to his financial problems is to migrate to Germany (alluding to the migration of Syrians to Germany during the Syrian civil war). She says:
    bitrih-**lak**   sinte:n   tle:te   ʔarbʕa ,
    you.go-**you.D**   two.years   three   four ,
    bte:xud   ʒinsiyye   honi:k ,   w-btiʒi:
    you.obtain   citizenship   there ,   and-you.come
    la-ho:n ,   maʔarriʃ   bi-l-masʕa:re !
    to-here ,   rich   with-the-money !
    'You could spend [you] two to four years there, get citizenship, and come back filthy rich!'
    From *Ktir Salbeh Show* – Season of 2015 – Episode 7 – 00:01:20 – LEB   5.32

33. Context: The conversation is between two workers, a woman and a man, in a factory during lunch time. The man asks the woman to prepare a cup of tea. She refuses, expressing rather forcefully that she is not his maid. The man answers:
    daxlik ʃu: ʒifsʕa !   tʕallami:-**lik**   ʃwayyit   nʕu:me .
    how blunt !   learn-**you.D**   some   gentleness .
    bukra   ki:f   baddik   titʒawwazi: ?
    tomorrow   how   you.want   marry ?
    'How rude! Learn [you] how to be a bit gentle. Otherwise, how do you expect to get married?'
    From *lamma: hikyit Maryam* 'when Mariam spoke out' – 00:06:25 – LEB   5.33

In (34), a Facebook user posts a conversation between himself and his mother to illustrate how biased mothers can be in their judgments of their children's potential. This example is interesting because it contains two SUBJ-ADs that perform complementary functions. The first SUBJ-AD is attached to the cost of the suggestion and the second is attached to the gain. The mother suggests that her son should have studied medicine or engineering instead of pursuing an acting major. In her eyes, her son could have pursued any major and succeeded. She uses the first SUBJ-AD to emphasize her view that the costs involved (that is, effort, time) are minimal in comparison to the gains he could receive with a job in one of these fields. As to the second SUBJ-AD, it emphasizes the mother's belief that her son is so perfect he could become a president or a minister and this would not be unexpected at all. Both SUBJ-ADs are attached to the mother's positive appreciation of her son. The son does not evaluate himself in the same way, however. He does not seem to believe that he could have successfully pursued any major or become a minister or president as his mother says. The outcome is negative alignment.

34. Context: A Syrian man who claims he is an actor posts a typical conversation between him and his mother on Facebook:

    l-ʔirid   bi-ʕe:n   ʔimm-o   ɣaza:l
    the-monkey   in-eye   mother-his   gazelle

    'A monkey in his mother's eyes is a gazelle. (That is, a mother believes her child to be much better or prettier that she or he actually is.)'

    Mother: law   darast-**illak**   ʃi: ʃaɣle   mitil
             had.you   studies-**you.D**   some   thing   like
             l-tˁibb   ʔaw   l-handase   w-sˁirt-**illak**
             the-medicine   or   the-engineering and-became-**you.D**
             ʃi: raʔi:s   ʔaw   wazi:r   mu: ʔahsan-lak?
             some   president   or   minister   NEG   better-you.D?

    'Had you studied [you] something else like medicine or engineering and become [you] a president or minister or something like that, wouldn't that have been better for you?'

    Actor: mbala:
             of.course
             'Of course!'

القرد بعين أمو غزال ..
قالتي أمي : لو درستلك شي شغلة متل الطب أو الهندسة وصرتلك شي رئيس أو وزير مو أحسنلك ؟
أنا : مبلا ...

Speakers may also use a SUBJ-ADC to make their suggestion sound more convincing. Sometimes they do so in an attempt to con the hearer, as the Jordanian example in (35) illustrates. The speaker tries to trick the hearer into running for public office in order to take his money. In this example, the speaker asks for two hundred pounds. He uses a SUBJ-ADC, implying that two hundred pounds is not a large amount of money compared to the gains the hearer will reap from it. The speaker makes similar comments, using the same dative, at least two more times in the episode (at 00:29:40 and again at 00:33:20), and the hearer ends up paying the money each time. The speaker would not use a SUBJ-ADC, however, to ask this particular hearer for six hundred pounds in a single event. The speaker is aware of the hearer's socio-economic status, and thus he knows the threshold beyond which a SUBJ-ADC becomes infelicitous for this speaker.

35. Context: A man tries to con Abu Awwad, a lower-middle-class man, by convincing him that he should run for a position as a city official. In this scene, he asks Abu Awwad for money:

hat-**lak** mite:n le:ra
give-**you.D** two.hundred pounds
. . .
fi: ʃwayyet manʃu:ra:t w-matˤbu:ˤa:t ,
there a.few flyers and-printed.material ,
ˤaʃa:n nlazzig ʔism-ak ˤala: kul l-hitˤa:n ,
in.order.to we.post name-your on all the-walls ,
bi-l-ʒara:yed , w-l-ʔi:za:ˤa , w-l-televizyo:n .
in-the-newspapers , and-the-radio , and-the-television .
'Give [you] me two hundred pounds. There are some flyers and other printed material we need to advertise your name by posting it on walls and including it in newspapers, on the radio, and on TV.'
From *ʔabu: ˤawwa:d* 'Abu Awwad' – Season 1 – Episode 3 – 00:10:20 – JOR 5.35

3.3 SUBJ-ADCs as challenges

Speakers may use SUBJ-AD directives to challenge the hearer to an action that he is likely to fail at despite its insignificance. Effectively, the speaker says to the hearer, 'I challenge you to do X, and if you do, you win.' The use of a SUBJ-AD may imply one of two things: first, the challenge is so hard for the hearer to perform that even performing one instance of it (an insignificant number) is impossible; or second, the challenge is so easy, but the speaker's expectations of the hearer are so low that she does not think he will succeed.

The Facebook posts in (36) and (37) are examples. First, observe (36). The writer finds it bizarre that a Lebanese citizen should carry a foreign flag in Lebanon. He challenges his fellow Lebanese citizens to find at least one person from another country carrying the Lebanese flag. The SUBJ-AD expresses the speaker's judgment that the challenge is impossible to the point that finding even one instance of it (an insignificant number) is unlikely to happen. Effectively, the Facebook user says the following: if Lebanese citizens think it is acceptable to carry an Iranian or French flag, it should not be difficult to find at least one Iranian or French citizen carrying a Lebanese flag. In reality it is, however, and therefore there is no reason for a Lebanese to carry the flag of another country.

36. Context: A Lebanese man posts the following challenge on Facebook. He intends to urge other Lebanese citizens who show loyalty to other countries to be loyal to their own country instead.

ʃift-**illak** ʃi: ʔira:ni: he:mil ˤalam libne:n ?
see-**you.D** any Iranian carrying flag Lebanon ?
ʃift-**illak** ʃi: suˤu:di: he:mil ˤalam libne:n ?
see-**you.D** any Saudi carrying flag Lebanon ?

ʃift-illak   ʃi: frinse:we: he:mil   ʕalam   libne:n ?
see-you.D   any   French   carrying   flag   Lebanon ?
hiz   tˤu:l-ak   w-ku:n   libne:ne: ...   min ɣe:r
shake   posture-your   and-be   Lebanese ...   without
ma: tku:n   te:biʕ   la-fle:n   w-ʕlte:n
that   you.be   follower   for-this   and-that

'Have you ever seen [you] an Iranian holding a Lebanese flag? Have you ever seen [you] a Saudi holding a Lebanese flag? Have you ever seen [you] a French person holding a Lebanese flag? Wake up already and be Lebanese without being a follower of this side or that.'

شفتلك شي ايراني حامل علم لبنان ؟؟
شفتلك شي سعودي حامل علم لبنان ؟؟
شفتلك شي فرنساوي حامل علم لبنان ؟؟
هز طولك و كون لبناني مرة و طالب بحقك كمواطن من غير ما تكون تابع لفلان و علان

Now observe the Facebook post in (37) by a Syrian woman. The writer tells men that they have the right to complain about women driving only if they are able to cook a meal. The writer uses a SUBJ-AD, implying that she has such low expectations of men's ability to cook that she believes they will not be able to pull the challenge off. The Facebook user seems to agree that women do not drive well, but she uses this challenge to make men aware that they also have problems. As the last part shows, she had other women in mind when she wrote the post. She invokes her group identity as a woman against her addressees' group identity as men. In the process, she seems to confirm the sociocultural belief that driving is a male activity and cooking is a female activity. Needless to say, not all residents of the Levant embrace this way of thinking. For example, while my mother thought the challenge was fair, my sisters rejected the whole premise, as do I.

37. Context: A Syrian woman posts the following challenge on Facebook, targeting men who complain about women driving.

ʕazi:z-i: lli: bitdˤa:l-lak   titxawwat
dear-my   who   you.keep-you.D   complain
ʕala: swa:ʔet   l-niswa:n ,   ru:h   ʒarreb
about   driving   the-women ,   go   try
tˤbix-lak   tˤabxa   w-xabber-ni: ʃu:
cook-you.D   meal   and-tell-me   what
bitˤlaʕ   maʕ-ak .   kaf-kun ,   sˤaba:ya: !
come.up   with-you .   palm-your ,   ladies !

'Dear men who keep complaining about women's driving, try and cook [you] a meal and let me know what the outcome is. High five, ladies!'

عزيزي الي بتضلك تتخوث على سواقة النسوان !
روح جرب اطبخلك طبخه !
وخبرني شو بطلع معك !
كفكم صبايا ^_* !

4 Conclusion

This chapter has discussed the pragmatic contributions and social functions of SUBJ-ADs. It has shown that these datives are anchored to events that the speaker evaluates in one of two ways: first, as insignificant/not worth mentioning; or second, as surprising/shocking. If the SUBJ-AD is attached to an epistemic possibility, the evaluation may focus on the likelihood of the occurrence of the event rather than on the event itself; in this case, the speaker evaluates the occurrence of the event as probable and 'not unexpected.' The evaluation is always based on the speaker's familiarity with and expectations of the subject in relation to any individual, group, and/or relational identities that are instantiated by the context, and often in relation to the rights and obligations that are associated with these identities.

Notes

1. The utterance in (11) may be considered a commissive rather than a representative. However, when we observe it in context, we can see that it is stated only to inform.
2. Even in English, weather *it* behaves differently than other expletives. For example, it may participate in control structures – *It never snows without raining.* Other expletives may not behave in the same way.
3. Im Ziki refers to Firyal's daughter as *binit* 'girl.' In the Levant, as well as in most (if not all) Arab countries, the word *mara:* 'woman' is reserved for married women or women who have been married. If a woman has never been married, no matter how old she is, she is referred to as *binit* 'girl.'

6

Final Remarks

This study started with the premise that language use necessarily interacts with contextual factors. It focused on attitude datives (ADs) in Levantine Arabic as interpersonal pragmatic markers and analyzed them from this perspective. Pragmatists, especially those who work within the Continental school of pragmatics and who emphasize 'the functional perspective on language behavior' (LoCastro 2012: 7), consider this premise a universal in that it applies to any language used in human communication. However, as Attardo (1998: 634) maintains, 'it should be observed that the existence of universals of language, be it at the phonetic or at the pragmatic level, is an empirical issue, not one that can be solved by one's philosophy.' The question of what contextual factors (for example, identities of social actors, activity type) are most relevant for the sociopragmatic analysis of ADs, as well as the question of how they are relevant, 'is not given a priori,' as Verhagen (2010: 48) puts it, 'and thus requires empirical investigation.' This study has intended to do just that, approaching ADs from an empirical perspective and analyzing them in their local contexts. This approach aligns with Aijmer and Anderson (2012: 1), who hold that the main purpose of sociopragmatics is to account for the instantiation of pragmatic markers like the ADs examined here, as well as other pragmatic phenomena, 'in empirical socio-cultural contexts and to present cultural, social and situational differences in their manifestation.'

The previous chapters have examined four types of AD: topic/affectee-oriented or TOP/AFF-ADs, speaker-oriented or SP-ADs, hearer-oriented or HR-ADs, and subject-oriented or SUBJ-ADs. These ADs may be added to utterances by cliticizing to verbal elements. They do not alter the truth conditions of these utterances. Rather, they function as attitudinal and/or relational interpersonal pragmatic markers that instruct the hearer to view the at-issue content of an utterance from the perspective identified by the speaker. As such, they serve as perspectivizers, allowing the speaker to transform the at-issue content of an utterance into a perspectivized thought. Each type of AD offers a different perspective.

FINAL REMARKS

The use of these ADs, this study has shown, interacts with elements of an utterance's context. Context may be divided into three types:

- the co-textual context, which includes the type of speech act an AD is embedded in, along with other linguistic and non-linguistic contextualization cues
- the situational context, which includes the speaker's and hearer's identities and the type of activity they are involved in
- the sociocultural context, along with the shared values, beliefs, and norms that the speaker and hearer and other members of their community live by and take for granted.

Social actors may use ADs in accordance with the elements of the context, affirming and enhancing them. Alternatively, they may use ADs to challenge these elements, negotiate them, or redefine them.

A sociopragmatic analysis of this type is important from a learnability perspective, including foreign language education. Ochs (1996: 428) writes:

> For a newcomer to a culture, be that a newborn or second/foreign language learner, one of the challenges is to learn the grammar of the language spoken/used in that culture. Another challenge is to learn how language is used to structure and define the local cultural environment.

In recent years, universities in the United States and other countries around the world have been incorporating Arabic dialects into their foreign language curricula. This study hopes to have illustrated the bidirectional interaction between language and culture in a way that will be useful to teachers of Arabic as a foreign language.

Finally, this study focuses on Levantine Arabic to the exclusion of other varieties. This is so because ADs in other Arabic varieties may be slightly or radically different from ADs in Levantine Arabic at the level of structure, meaning contribution, and/or social function. These differences are worth examining closely and systematically. My intention is to take on this project next . . . unless another linguist gets to it first!

Bibliography

Aijmer, Karin. 2013. *Understanding Pragmatic Markers: A Variational Pragmatic Approach*. Edinburgh: Edinburgh University Press.

Aijmer, Karin and Gisle Anderson. 2012. Introducing the pragmatics of society. In Gisle Anderson and Karin Aijmer (eds), *Pragmatics of Society*, 1–27. Berlin: Mouton de Gruyter.

Alba-Juez, Laura and Geoff Thompson. 2014. The many faces and phases of evaluation. In Geoff Thompson and Laura Alba-Juez (eds), *Evaluation in Context*, 3–24. Amsterdam: Benjamins.

Al-Wer, Enam. 2007. The formation of the dialect of Amman: From chaos to order. In Catherine Miller, Enam Al-Wer, Dominique Caubet, and Janet C. E. Watson (eds), *Arabic in the City: Issues in Dialect Contact and Language Variation*, 55–76. New York: Routledge.

Al-Zahre, Nisrine and Nora Boneh. 2010. Coreferential dative constructions in Syrian Arabic and Modern Hebrew. *Brill's Annual of Afroasiatic Languages and Linguistics* 2: 248–82.

Al-Zahre, Nisrine and Nora Boneh. 2016. Pronominal non-core datives in Syrian Arabic. *Brill's Journal of Afroasiatic Languages and Linguistics* 8: 3–36.

Anscombre, Jean-Claude and Oswald Ducrot. 1989. *L'Argumentation dans la langue*. Liège, Brussels: Mardaga.

Attardo, Salvatore. 1998. Are socio-pragmatics and (Neo)-Gricean pragmatics incompatible? *Journal of Pragmatics* 30: 627–36.

Austin, J. L. 1962. *How to Do Things with Words*. Cambridge, MA: Harvard University Press.

Bakhtin, M. M. 1981. *The Dialogic Imagination* (translated by Caryl Emerson and Michael Holquist). Austin: University of Texas Press.

Baumeister, Rot F., Liqing Zhang, and Kathleen D. Vohs. 2004. Gossip as cultural learning. *Review of General Psychology* 8: 111–21.

BIBLIOGRAPHY

Bayertz, Kurt. 1999. Four uses of 'solidarity.' In Kurt Bayertz (ed.), *Solidarity*, 3–28. The Netherlands: Kluwer Academic Publishers.

Beeching, Kate. 2016. *Pragmatic Markers in British English: Meaning in Social Interaction*. Cambridge: Cambridge University Press.

Bolinger, Dwight. 1979. To catch a metaphor: You as norm. *American Speech* 54: 194–209.

Bosse, Solveig, Benjamin Bruening, and Masahiro Yamada. 2012. Affected experiencers. *Natural Language and Linguistics Theory* 30: 1185–230.

Brewer, Marilynn B. and Wendi Gardner. 1996. Who is this 'we'? Levels of collective identity and self representations. *Journal of Personality and Social Psychology* 71: 83–93.

Brinton, Laurel J. 1996. *Pragmatic Markers in English: Grammaticalization and Discourse Functions*. Berlin: Mouton de Gruyter.

Brown, Penelope and Stephen C. Levinson. [1978] 1987. *Politeness: Some Universals in Language Usage*. Cambridge: Cambridge University Press.

Brown, Roger and Albert Gilman. [1987] 2003. The pronouns of power and solidarity. In Christine Bratt Paulston and G. Richard Tucker (eds), *Sociolinguistics: The Essential Readings*, 156–76. Oxford: Blackwell.

Brummel, Bradley J. and Kelsey N. Parker. 2015. Obligation and entitlement in society and workplace. *Applied Psychology* 64: 127–60.

Brustad, Kristen. 2000. *The Syntax of spoken Arabic: A Comparative Study of Moroccan, Egyptian, Syrian, and Kuwaiti Dialects*. Washington, DC: Georgetown University Press.

Culpeper, Jonathan. 2009. Historical sociopragmatics: An introduction. *Journal of Historical Pragmatics* 10: 176–86.

Culpeper, Jonathan. 2011. *Impoliteness: Using Language to Cause Offence*. Cambridge: Cambridge University Press.

Culpeper, Jonathan and Michael Haugh. 2014. *Pragmatics and the English Language*. China: Palgrave–Macmillan.

Deal, Amy Rose. 2013. Possessor raising. *Linguistic Inquiry* 44: 391–432.

Dickerson, Mark O., Thomas Flanagan, and Brenda O'Neill. 2009. *An Introduction to Government and Politics: A Conceptual Approach*. 9th edn. Ontario: Nelson College Indigenous.

Du Bois, John W. 2007. The stance triangle. In Robert Englebretson (ed.), *Stancetaking in Discourse: Subjectivity, Evaluation, Interaction*. Amsterdam: Benjamins.

Dunbar, R. I. M. 2004. Gossip in evolutionary perspective. *Review of General Psychology* 8: 100–10.

Edwards, Derek. 1999. Emotion discourse. *Culture and Psychology* 5: 271–91.

Foster, Eric K. 2004. Research on gossip: Taxonomy, methods, and future directions. *Review of General Psychology* 8: 78–99.

Fraser, Bruce. 1990. Perspectives on politeness. *Journal of Pragmatics* 14: 219–36.

Fraser, Bruce. 1996. Pragmatic markers. *Pragmatics* 6: 167–90.

Freadman, Anne. 1999. The green tarpaulin: Another story of the Ryan hanging. *The UTS Review* 5: 1–67.

Goffman, Erving. [1964] 1972. The neglected situation. In Pier P. Giglioli (ed.), *Language and Social Context*, 61–6. Harmondsworth: Penguin.

Goffman, Erving. 1967. *Interaction ritual: Essays on Face-to-Face Behavior*. New York: Pantheon Books.

Goffman, Erving. 1981. *Forms of Talk*. Philadelphia: University of Pennsylvania Press.

Goldsmith, Joh and Erich Woisetschlaeger. 1982. The logic of the English progressive. *Linguistic Inquiry* 13: 79–89.

Gumperz, John J. 1982. *Discourse Strategies*. Cambridge: Cambridge University Press.

Gumperz, John J. 2001. Interactional sociolinguistics: A personal perspective. In Deborah Schiffrin, Deborah Tannen, and Heidi E. Hamilton (eds), *The Handbook of Discourse Analysis*, 215–28. Oxford: Blackwell.

Haddad, Youssef A. 2013. Pronouns and intersubjectivity in Lebanese Arabic gossip. *Journal of Pragmatics* 49: 57–77.

Haddad, Youssef A. 2014. Attitude datives in Lebanese Arabic and the interplay of syntax and pragmatics. *Lingua* 145: 65–103.

Haddad, Youssef A. 2016. Possessively construed attitude dative constructions in Lebanese Arabic. *Brill's Journal of Afroasiatic Languages and Linguistics* 8: 37–75.

Haddad, Youssef A. To appear. The pragmatics–syntax division of labor: The case of personal datives in Lebanese Arabic. In Elabbas Benmamoun and Reem Bassiouney (eds), *The Routledge Handbook on Arabic Linguistics*. New York: Routledge.

Haddington, Pentti. 2004. Stance taking in news interviews. *SKY Journal of Linguistics* 17: 101–42.

Halliday, Michael A. K. 1970. Language structure and language function. In John Lyons (ed.), *New Horizons in Linguistics*, 140–65. Harmondsworth: Penguin Books.

Halliday, Michael A. K. 1973. *Explorations in the Functions of Language*. London: Edward Arnold.

Hanks, William F., Sachiko Ide, and Yasuhiro Katagiri. 2009. Towards an emancipatory pragmatics. *Journal of Pragmatics* 41: 1–9.

Hole, Daniel. 2004. Extra argumentality – a binding account of 'possessor raising' in German, English, and Mandarin. In Ji-Yung Kim, Yuri A. Lander, and Barbara H. Partee (eds), *Possessives and Beyond: Semantics and Syntax*, 365–83. Amherst, MA: GLSA Publications.

Hole, Daniel. 2005. Reconciling 'possessor' datives and 'beneficiary' datives: Towards a unified voice account of dative binding in German. In Claudia Maienborn and Angelika Wöllstein (eds), *Event Arguments: Foundations and Applications*, 213–42. Berlin: Mouton de Gruyter.

Holes, Clive. 2016. *Dialects, Culture, and Society in Eastern Arabia 3: Phonology, Morphology, Syntax, Style*. Leiden: Brill.

Holtgraves, Thomas. 1994. Communication in context: Effects of speaker status on the comprehension of indirect requests. *Journal of Experimental Psychology: Learning, Memory and Cognition* 20: 1205–18.

Horn, Laurence R. 2008. '*I love me some him*': The landscape of non-argument datives. In Olivier Bonami and Patricia Cabredo-Hofherr (eds), *Empirical Issues in Syntax and Semantics 7*, 169–92. Online publication: http://www.cssp.cnrs.fr/eiss7/horn-eiss7.pdf (accessed November 16, 2010).
Horn, Laurence R. 2013. I love me some datives: Expressive meaning, free datives, and F-implicature. In Daniel Gutzmann and Hans-Martin Gärtner (eds), *Beyond Expressives: Explorations in Use-Conditional Meaning*, 151–99. Leiden: Brill.
Huang, Yan. 2014. *Pragmatics*. Oxford: Oxford University Press.
Iwasaki, Shoichi and Foong Ha Yap. 2015. Stance-marking and stance-taking in Asian languages. *Journal of Pragmatics* 83: 1–9.
Johnstone, Barbara. 2009. Stance, style, and the linguistic individual. In Alexandra Jaffe (ed.), *Sociolinguistic Perspectives on Stance*, 29–52. Oxford: Oxford University Press.
Jouitteau, Melanie and Milan Rezac. 2007. The French ethical dative, 13 syntactic tests. *Bucharest Working Articles in Linguistics* IX: 97–108.
Kärkkäinen, Elise. 2006. Stance taking in conversation: From subjectivity to intersubjectivity. *Text and Talk* 26: 699–731.
Kitagawa, Chisato and Adrienne Lehrer. 1990. Impersonal uses of personal pronouns. *Journal of Pragmatics* 14: 739–45.
Laberge, Suzanne and Gillian Sankoff. 1979. Anything you can do. In Givon Talmy (ed.), *Discourse and Syntax*, 419–40. New York: Academic Press.
Labov, William. 1972. The transformation of experience in narrative syntax. In William Labov (ed.), *Language in the Inner City: Studies in the Black English Vernacular*, 354–96. Philadelphia: University of Pennsylvania Press.
Labov, William and Joshua Waletzky. 1967. Narrative analysis: Oral versions of personal experience. *Journal of Narrative and Life History* 7: 3–38.
Langacker, Ronald W. 2000. A dynamic usage-based model. In Michael Barlow and Suzanne Kemmer (eds), *Usage-Based Models of Language*, 1–63. Stanford, CA: CSLI Publications.
Langacker, Ronald W. 2008. *Cognitive Grammar: A Basic Introduction*. Oxford: Oxford University Press.
Langacker, Ronald W. 2009. *Investigations in Cognitive Grammar*. Berlin: Mouton de Gruyter.
Langacker, Ronald W. 2010. Cognitive grammar. In Dirk Geeraerts and Hubert Cuyckens (eds), *The Oxford Handbook of Cognitive Linguistics*, 421–62. Oxford: Oxford University Press.
Leech, Geoffrey N. 1983. *Principles of Pragmatics*. London: Longman.
Lee-Schoenfeld, Vera. 2006. German possessor datives: Raised and affected. *Journal of Comparative Germanic Linguistics* 9: 101–42.
Levinson, Stephen C. 1988. Putting linguistics on a proper footing: Explorations in Goffman's participation framework. In Paul Drew and Anthony J. Wootton (eds), *Goffman: Exploring the Interaction Order*, 161–227. Oxford: Polity Press.
Levinson, Stephen C. 1979. Activity types and language. *Linguistics* 17: 365–99.

LoCastro, Virginia. 2003. *An Introduction to Pragmatics: Social Action for Language Teachers*. Ann Arbor: University of Michigan Press.

LoCastro, Virginia. 2012. *Pragmatics for Language Educators: A Sociolinguistic Perspective*. New York: Routledge.

Lyons, John. 1982. Deixis and subjectivity: *Loquor, ergo sum*? In Robert J. Jarvella and Wolfgang Klein (eds), *Speech, Place, and Action: Studies in Deixis and Related Topics*, 101–24. New York: Wiley.

McCawley, James D. 1999. Participant roles, frames, and speech acts. *Linguistics and Philosophy* 22: 595–619.

Maldonado, Ricardo. 2002. Objective and subjective datives. *Cognitive Linguistics* 13: 1–65.

Martin, J. R. 2003. Introduction. *Text* 23: 171–81.

Martin, J. R. and P. R. R. White. 2005. *The Language of Evaluation: Appraisal in English*. New York: Palgrave–MacMillan.

Mey, Jacob L. 2001. *Pragmatics. An Introduction*. Oxford: Blackwell.

Mey, Jacob L. 2016. Pragmatics seen through the prism of society. In Alessandro Capone and Jacob L. Mey (eds), *Interdisciplinary Studies in Pragmatics, Culture and Society. Perspectives in Pragmatics, Philosophy and Psychology* 4, 15–24. Dordrecht and London: Springer.

Myers, Greg and Sofia Lampropoulou. 2012. Impersonal you and stance-taking in social research interviews. *Journal of Pragmatics* 44: 1206–18.

Nazzal, Rima. 2007. sˤuratu l–marʔati fi: musalsali ba:b l–ha:ra 'The image of women in the soap opera "the neighborhood gate."' *l–ḥiwa:r l–mutamaddin 'Civilized Debate'* 2081. http://www.ahewar.org/debat/show.art.asp?aid=113483 (last accessed September 2016).

Norén, Kerstin and Per Linell. 2007. Meaning potentials and the interaction between lexis and contexts: An empirical substantiation. *Pragmatics* 17: 387–416.

Ochs, Elinor. 1996. Linguistic resources for socializing humanity. In John J. Gumperz and Stephen C. Levinson (eds), *Rethinking Linguistic Relativity*, 407–37. Cambridge: Cambridge University Press.

O'Connor, Patricia E. 1994. 'You could feel it through the skin': Agency and positioning in prisoners' stabbing stories. *Text* 14: 45–75.

Östman, Jan-Ola. 1982. The symbiotic relationship between pragmatic particles and impromptu speech. In Nils Erik Enkvist (ed.), *Impromptu Speech: A Symposium*, 147–77. Åbo: Åbo Akademi.

Owings, Donald H. and Eugene S. Morton. 1998. *Animal Vocal Communication: A New Approach*. Cambridge: Cambridge University Press.

Potter, Jonathan. 1996. *Representing Reality: Discourse, Rhetoric, and Social Construction*. London: Sage.

Potts, C. 2011. Conventional implicature and expressive content. In Claudia Maienborn, Klaus Von Heusinger, and Paul Portner (eds), *Semantics: An International Handbook of Natural Language Meaning*, vol. 3, 2516–36. Berlin: Mouton de Gruyter.

Rákosi, György. 2008. Some remarks on Hungarian ethical datives. In József Andor, Béla Hollósy, Tibor Laczkó, and Péter Pelyvás (eds), *When Grammar Minds Language and Literature: Festschrift for Prof. Béla Korponay on the Occasion of His 80th Birthday*, 413–22. Debrecen: Institute of English and American Studies.

Rieschild, Verna Robertson. 1998. Lebanese Arabic reverse role vocatives. *Anthropological Linguistics* 40: 617–41.

Riordan, Jan. 2005. *Breastfeeding and Human Location*. Canada: Jones and Bartlett Publishers.

Sabini, John and Maury Silver. 1982. *Moralities of Everyday Life*. Oxford: Oxford University Press.

Sadiqi, Fatima. 2003. *Women, Gender, and Language in Morocco*. Leiden: Brill.

Schieffelin, Bambi and Elinor Ochs. 1986a. Language socialization. *Annual Review of Anthropology* 15: 163–246.

Schieffelin, Bambi and Elinor Ochs. 1986b. *Language Socialization across Cultures*. Cambridge: Cambridge University Press.

Schiffrin, Deborah. 1987. *Discourse Markers*. Cambridge: Cambridge University Press.

Scollon, Ron, Suzanne Wong Scollon, and Rodney H. Jones. 2012. *Intercultural Communication: A Discourse Approach*. Oxford: Blackwell.

Searle, John R. 1976. A classification of illocutionary acts. *Language in Society* 5: 1–23.

Sinha, Chris and Cintia Rodriguez. 2008. Language and the signifying object: From convention to imagination. In Jordan Zlatev, Timothy Racine, Chris Sinha and Essa Itkonen (eds), *The Shared Mind: Perspectives on Intersubjectivity*, 358–78. Amsterdam: Benjamins.

Spencer-Oatey, Helen. 2000. Rapport management: A framework for analysis. In Helen Spencer-Oatey (ed.), *Culturally Speaking: Managing Rapport through Talk across Cultures*, 11–46. New York: Continuum.

Spencer-Oatey, Helen. 2002. Managing rapport in talk: Using rapport sensitive incidents to explore the motivational concerns underlying the management of relations. *Journal of Pragmatics* 34: 529–45.

Spencer-Oatey, Helen. 2005. (Im)Politeness, face and perceptions of rapport: Unpackaging their bases and interrelationships. *Journal of Politeness Research: Language, Behavior, Culture* 1: 95–119.

Spencer-Oatey, Helen. 2008. *Culturally Speaking: Managing Rapport through Talk across Cultures*, 2nd edn. New York: Continuum.

Stirling, Leslie and Lenore Manderson. 2011. About you: Empathy, objectivity, and authority. *Journal of Pragmatics* 43: 1581–602.

Taylor, John R. 2010. *Cognitive Grammar*. Oxford: Oxford University Press.

Thomas, Jenny A. 1983. Cross-cultural pragmatic failure. *Applied Linguistics* 4: 91–112.

Thompson, Geoff and Susan Hunston. 2000. Evaluation: An introduction. In Susan Hunston and Geoff Thompson (eds), *Evaluation in Text*, 1–27. Oxford: Oxford University Press.

Tomasello, Michael. 1999. *The Cultural Origins of Human Cognition*. Cambridge, MA: Harvard University Press.
Traugott, Elizabeth Closs. 2003. From subjectification to intersubjectification. In Raymond Hickey (ed.), *Motives for Language Change*, 124–39. Cambridge: Cambridge University Press.
Traugott, Elizabeth Closs. 2010. (Inter)subjectivity and (inter)subjectification: A reassessment. In Hubert Cuyckens, Kristin Davidse, and Lieven Vandelotte (eds), *Subjectification, Intersubjectification and Grammaticalization*, 29–71. Berlin: Mouton de Gruyter.
Traugott, Elizabeth Closs and Richard Dasher. 2002. *Regularity in Semantic Change*. Cambridge: Cambridge University Press.
Verhagen, Arie. 2005. *Constructions of Intersubjectivity. Discourse, Syntax and Cognition*. Oxford: Oxford University Press.
Verhagen, Arie. 2010. Construal and perspectivization. In Dirk Geeraerts and Hubert Cuyckens (eds), *The Oxford Handbook of Cognitive Linguistics*, 48–81. Oxford: Oxford University Press.
Voloshinov, V. N. 1995. *Marxism and the Philosophy of Language, Bakhtinian Thought – an Introductory Reader* (translated by S. Dentith, Ladislav Matejka, and I. R. Titunik). New York: Routledge.
Watts, Richard J. 2003. *Politeness*. Cambridge: Cambridge University Press.
Wichmann, Anne. 2012. Prosody and pragmatic effects. In Gisle Anderson and Karin Aijmer (eds), *Pragmatics of Society*, 181–213. Berlin: Mouton de Gruyter.
Wilson, John and Karyn Stapleton. 2010. Authority. In Jürgen Jaspers, Jan-Ola Östman, and Jef Verschueren (eds), *Society and Language Use*, 49–70. Amsterdam: Benjamins.
Zlatev, Jordan, Timothy P. Racine, Chris Sinha, and Esa Itkonen. 2008. Intersubjectivity: What makes us human? In Jordan Zlatev, Timothy Racine, Chris Sinha, and Essa Itkonen (eds), *The Shared Mind: Perspectives on Intersubjectivity*, 1–14. Amsterdam: Benjamins.

Literary works

Chesbro, George C. 2004. *Strange Prey and Other Tales of the Hunt*. New Baltimore, NY: Apache Beach Publications.
Danov, Dan. 2009. *The Killfile*. Bloomington, IN: iUniverse.
Khalifeh, Sahar. 1997. *l-mira:θ* 'the inheritance.' Beirut: Da:r l-ʔadab.
Lewis, J. D. 1956. A letter to Senator Walter George on October 21, 1955. In *House Reports, United States Congressional Serial Set, Volume 11904*. Washington: United States Government Printing Office.
Ora, Nulli Para. 2012. *Dragon Moon, Book One*. Indiana: Liquid Silver Books.

Bibliography

Feature films, plays, series, and talk shows

Jordanian

ha:l l-dunya: 'this is life,' TV series, directed by Nader Ammar. Jordan Radio and Television Corporation, 2013. Three episodes:

- *baʕdˤ l-ðanni ʔiθm* 'suspicion is sometimes a sin'
- *fa:res ʔahla:mi:* 'my prince charming'
- *farsˤa w-xarsa:* 'Farsa and Kharsa'.

nahafa:t ʕaylitna: 'our family anecdotes,' animated TV show, directed by Muead Zaydan. Roya TV, 2016. Five episodes:

- *Entrepreneur*
- *Facebook*
- *l-ʔiqtisˤa:d wa:ʒib* 'economy is a duty'
- *mawʕed yara:mi:* 'a love date'
- *tanfi:x* 'inflating'.

ʔabu: ʕawwa:d 'Abu Awwad,' soap opera, Season 1, Episodes 1, 3–6, 8–9, directed by Rufael Bukayli. Jordan Radio and Television Corporation, 1981.

Lebanese

bi-l-nisbe la-bukra ʃu: 'what are the plans for tomorrow,' play, directed by Ziad al-Rahbani, 1978.
El Professeur 'the professor,' play, directed by George Khabbaz, 2010.
fi:lm ʔameriki: tˤawi:l 'a long American movie,' play, directed by Ziad al-Rahbani, 1980.
hallaʔ la-we:n 'where do we go now,' film, directed by Nadine Labaki, produced by Anne-Dominique Toussaint, 2011.
kizze:b kbi:r 'a big liar,' play, directed by George Khabbaz, 2006.
Ktir Salbeh Show, comedy show, Season of 2015, Episode 7, directed by Nabil Assaf. Lebanese Broadcasting Corporation International, 2015.
lamma: hikyit Maryam 'when Mariam spoke out,' film, directed by Assad Fouladkar, produced by Assad Fouladkar and the Lebanese American University, 2001.
l-sayyida l-θa:niya 'the second lady,' film, directed by Philip Asmar. Eagle Films, 2015.
matˤlu:b 'wanted,' play, directed by George Khabbaz, 2011.
Meryana, soap opera, Episodes 1, 7 and 10, directed by Jinan Mandour. MGN Production, 1998.
Nazl l-suru:r 'the Surour Inn,' play, directed by Ziad al-Rahbani, 1974.
tahqi:q 'investigations,' *28% of the Lebanese Live Below Poverty Line*, talk show, directed by Fadi Haddad, Murr Television, Lebanon, 2016.

tahqi:q 'investigations,' *Extramarital Affairs in Lebanon*, talk show, directed by Fadi Haddad. Murr Television, Lebanon, 2011.

te:ta: ʔalef marra 'grandma, a thousand times', documentary, directed by Mahmoud Kaabour. Veritas Films, 2010.

ʔahmar bi-l-xatˤ l-ˤari:dˤ 'a red line with a thick stroke,' talk show, Season 5, *Daughter-in-Law and Mother-in-Law*, directed by Elie Abi Aad. Lebanese Broadcasting Corporation International, 2011.

Palestinian

maʃruː:ˤ tawfi:r 'a saving project,' Youtube series, Episode 1, directed by Lama Rabah, produced by Rabih l-Haj Abd, 2013.

watˤan ˤa-watar 'a nation on a string,' Youtube series, produced by One Shot Productions and the Palestinian, 2013. Three episodes:

- *dawa:wi:n ʃaba:b* 'young people's anthologies'
- *l-ˤa:ʔila* 'the family'
- *ʔiftita:h l-xa:zu:q* 'the opening ceremony of the screw'.

Syrian

ba:b l-ha:ra 'the neighborhood gate,' soap opera, Season 1, Episodes 1–13, 15–22, 24–25, 28–29, 30, 33, directed by Bassam al-Mulla. Aj Co. for Art Production and Distribution, 2006.

l-fusˤu:l l-ʔarbaˤa 'the four seasons,' TV series, Season 1, Episodes 1, 5–6, directed by Hatem Ali. Ugarit Co. for Art Production, 1999.

Index

acquisition, 15; *see also* learnability
activity, type of, 2, 15, 21, 27, 29, 30–1, 40, 56, 65, 68, 76, 156, 157; *see also* context
Aijmer, Karin, 14, 15, 22n, 29, 156
Alba-Juez, Laura, 32, 34,
Al-Wer, Enam, 19
Al-Zahre, Nisrine, 4, 14, 22n, 132–3, 143 4
Anderson, Gisle, 14, 29, 156
Attardo, Salvatore, 156
attitude datives, 3–4, 156–7
    hearer-oriented, 10–12, 13, 21, 70, 98–130, 132, 138, 156
    possessively construed, 6–7, 24
    speaker-oriented, 8–10, 21, 53–96, 101–7, 119, 124–5, 147, 156
    subject-oriented, 12–14, 16, 21, 73, 89, 115, 131–55, 156
    topic/affectee-oriented, 4–8, 21, 22n, 23–51, 63, 156
Austin, J. L., 104
authority, 8, 9, 19, 53–7; *see also* power
    hierarchical, 58–78, 87, 88
    knowledge, 83–7, 89
    moral, 87–96
    reciprocal, 78–83, 87, 88

Bakhtin, M. M., 130n
Baumeister, Rot F., 91

Bayertz, Kurt, 79
Beeching, Kate, 2, 14, 15, 22n, 26
Boneh, Nora, 4, 14, 22n, 132–3, 143–4
Brewer, Marilynn B., 30, 143
Brinton, Laurel J., 2, 34, 36
Brown, Penelope, 76, 144
Brown, Roger, 56, 79
Brummel, Bradley J., 31, 57

Cognitive Grammar, 39
context 2, 7, 14, 15, 17, 18, 19, 20, 21, 23, 24, 27, 28–33, 36, 37, 38, 40, 45, 46, 51, 54, 55, 56, 57, 59, 64, 65, 68, 71, 73, 75, 76, 81, 87, 88, 90, 100, 103, 108, 125, 133, 136, 155, 156–7
    co-textual, 27, 31–2, 38, 51, 56, 57, 157
    situational, 27, 29–31, 33, 38, 51, 56, 57, 156–7; *see also* activity type; identity
    sociocultural, 15, 27, 29, 38, 51, 56, 57, 68, 87, 139, 156–7
contextualization cues, 67, 70, 107, 121, 128, 143
Culpeper, Jonathan, 2, 14, 23, 28, 29, 35, 76, 109

Dasher, Richard, 35
Du bois, John W., 28, 34, 35, 37–9, 41, 42, 43
Dunbar, R. I. M., 114

Egyptian Arabic, 16
engagement, hearer, 10, 11, 12, 41, 100–2, 109–11, 118, 119, 121, 129
entitlement, 31, 57, 78, 91, 91–2, 124, 128; *see also* rights and obligations
evaluation, 21, 23, 27, 28, 29, 33–8, 41, 42, 45, 46, 49, 51, 54, 86, 87, 101, 102, 109, 110, 122, 124, 125, 128, 133, 134, 136, 137, 138, 139, 140, 142, 143, 144, 147, 148, 149, 150, 155; *see also* stancetaking
   affect, 35–6, 41, 53, 87, 109, 122
   appreciation, 35–6, 41, 60, 109, 122, 152
   judgment, 35–6, 41, 77, 86, 109, 122, 125, 128, 151, 153
   versus attitude or stance, 33–4

face, 76–8, 144; *see also* politeness; rapport management
   quality, 77, 78, 104
   relational, 77
   social identity, 77, 78
footing, 43, 161
French, 3

Gardner, Wendi, 30, 143
gender, 56, 58, 68, 69, 71, 114, 126
Gilman, Albert, 56, 79
Goffman, Erving, 29, 43–4, 118
gossip, 35, 51, 87, 91–5, 98, 109, 113–25, 135, 141
Gumperz, John J., 32

Haddington, Pentti, 34, 37, 38
Halliday, Michael A. K., 2, 33, 37
Haugh, Michael, 2, 14, 23, 29, 35, 76, 109
Hebrew, 3
Horn, Laurence R., 3, 15
Huang, Yan, 27, 57
Hungarian, 3, 4
Hunston, Susan, 23, 34, 36

identity, 15, 19, 21, 30–1, 34, 37, 40, 45, 46, 49, 50, 51, 53, 54, 55, 56, 58, 59, 61, 64, 68, 69, 77, 78, 81, 82, 86, 87, 104, 105, 111, 113, 114, 118, 119, 128, 133, 134, 135, 136, 137, 142, 143, 144, 145, 146, 147; *see also* context

collective, 30, 45, 143
group, 30, 45, 56, 58, 77, 82, 121, 123, 140, 142, 143, 154
individual, 30, 45, 56, 67, 77, 88, 104, 134, 139, 140, 143, 144
relational, 30, 45, 48, 49, 56, 77, 104, 114, 139, 143
interactional goals, 76, 77
   relational, 77
   transactional, 77
interpersonal pragmatic marker, 2, 14, 15, 23, 29, 32, 46, 55, 156
   evaluative, 2, 23, 156
   relational, 2, 23–4, 156
intersubjectivity, 35; *see also* subjectivity
Islam, 25, 29, 32, 97n, 126, 127, 135, 139

Kitagawa, Chisato, 113, 124, 128

Lampropoulou, Sofia, 125, 128
Langacker, Ronald W., 28, 37, 39–43, 44, 53
learnability, 15, 157
Leech, Geoffrey, 14, 33, 37
Lehrer, Adrienne, 113, 124, 128
Levinson, Stephen C., 30, 43, 44, 76, 144

Manderson, Lenore, 113, 114, 119, 124, 125, 126, 128
Martin J. R., 29, 35–6, 41, 87, 109, 118, 126, 130
membership, 2, 30, 81, 91–2, 100, 101, 109, 113, 114, 116, 118, 119, 121, 123, 130
Mey, Jacob L., 2, 14, 15
Moroccan Arabic, 16
Myers, Greg, 125, 128

Ochs, Elinor, 15, 29, 30, 32, 36, 40, 125, 157

Parker, Kelsey N., 31, 57
perspectivization, 38
perspectivizer, 1, 2, 23, 51, 55, 98, 104, 156
politeness, 76; *see also* face; rapport management
power, 23, 26, 37, 56–7, 74; *see also* authority

rapport management, 76–8; *see also* face; politeness

reverse-role vocative, 22n
rights and obligations, 23, 29, 31, 57, 59, 61, 76–8, 105, 133, 134, 136, 155; *see also* entitlement
  association rights, 31, 63, 104
  equity rights, 31, 63, 104, 105

Sadiqi, Fatima, 95
Schieffelin, Bambi, 15
Schiffrin, Deborah, 14
Searle, John R., 57, 85, 104, 109, 144
social acts, 32, 76; *see also* speech acts
  challenges, 153–4
  commissives, 100, 102–9, 124
  complaints, 85–95, 123
  criticisms, 35, 85, 92, 109, 113, 123–5, 128–9
  directives, 1, 19, 54, 57–85, 87, 102, 104, 105, 107, 108, 133, 144–7, 153
  offers, 32, 60, 148, 150
  representatives, 19, 85–96, 100, 108, 109–29, 132–44
  requests, 32, 40, 44, 57, 58, 60, 62, 63, 76, 80, 82–3, 133, 144–8
  suggestions, 44, 133, 144, 148–53
solidarity, 79–81
speech acts, 56, 85, 104, 109, 144, 157; *see also* social acts

Spencer-Oatey, Helen, 27, 29, 31, 76–8, 104
stancetaking, 33–7, 41, 43, 44; *see also* evaluation
  alignment, 37, 38, 41, 43, 45, 46, 47, 60, 62, 70, 84, 86, 89, 104, 110, 113, 119, 120, 122, 125, 136, 137, 145, 148, 152
  positioning, 35, 41
Stapleton, Karyn, 56–7
Stirling, Leslie, 113, 114, 119, 124, 125, 126, 128
subjectivity, 34, 36, 37; *see also* intersubjectivity

Thomas, Jenny A., 14
Thompson, Geoff, 23, 32, 34, 36
Traugott, Elizabeth Closs, 35
truisms, 109, 114, 125–9

Verhagen, Arie, 1, 23, 32, 35, 37, 38, 40, 42, 43, 45, 46, 156
Vohs, Kathleen D., 91

White, P. R. R., 29, 35–6, 41, 87, 109, 118, 126, 130
Wilson, John, 56–7

Zhang, Liqing, 91

EU representative:
Easy Access System Europe
Mustamäe tee 50, 10621 Tallinn, Estonia
Gpsr.requests@easproject.com